BLACK FACES
IN HIGH PLACES

BLACK FACES IN HIGH PLACES

Negroes in Government

by Helen G. Edmonds

*My people will never be satisfied until
they see black faces in high places.*
— MARY MCLEOD BETHUNE

HARCOURT BRACE JOVANOVICH, INC.

New York   Chicago   San Francisco   Atlanta   Dallas

To LuAnn, Harry, Jr., and John Edmonds, III

E
185
.96
E3

PRINTED IN THE UNITED STATES OF AMERICA

ISBN 0-15-371073-X

Preface and Acknowledgments

THIS book was occasioned by the basic need to examine several facets of American life at the close of the 1960's, inclusive of blacks in government. The 1960's were a decade of "Black Consciousness," filled with discordant voices, protests, and progress. The right to vote was becoming a reality for black Americans. Political officeholding, too, became a reality. An attempt to measure that officeholding is the purpose of this work.

In a large measure, the spirit of the time conditions what happens in history; hence, issues, movements, and programs form major parts of political success. It is for such a reason that the political successes herein written about are intertwined with the historical events and consequences of a spirited decade which landed Negro personalities into positions of responsibility.

A wish unfulfilled in a book of this kind is the desire to write in depth about hundreds of blacks who achieve the almost impossible in politics at the very grassroots of American life—cities, towns, and counties. No book of reasonable reading length, however, can describe all of their local political scenes, the hard work in getting out the vote, their training, vast community activities, local honors, successes, and failures.

They live and achieve in your community. I hope this book will be a challenge to high school boys and girls to pull together in their social studies classes the full activities of these unsung and unheralded men and women.

Thanks to the Southern Regional Council, Atlanta, Georgia, for its most accurate listing of, and work with, Southern black officeholders. Thanks to the hundreds of black officeholders across the nation who supplied me with source materials. Thanks to Mrs. Ethel Hill of Durham, North Carolina, for long hours of assistance.

HELEN G. EDMONDS
Dean, Graduate School of Arts and Sciences
North Carolina Central University
Durham, North Carolina

Contents

Introduction

FOR MANY years, one of the most respected spokesmen for the black people of America was Mary McLeod Bethune, who founded Florida's Bethune-Cookman College and who served as an adviser to President Franklin D. Roosevelt on racial questions during the New Deal. She often addressed large audiences, white as well as black, and she liked to finish a speech with this reminder: "My people will never be satisfied until they see black faces in high places."

What was almost a dream to Dr. Bethune had become, by 1970, an accomplished fact. By then, a good number of black faces were to be seen in a broad range of high places in government.

The trend began in the last half of the 1920's in the Northeast and in the Middle West, areas to which many Negroes had migrated from the South. In the industrial cities, where they were crowded into thickly populated neighborhoods, they began to run for, and win, offices in state and local government. One reached the United States House of Representatives.

Since the 1930's, in both these regions and also in California, they came to hold more and more offices. Many have been elected to state and local offices and to Congress. One has been elected to the United States Senate.

Large numbers of Federal, state, and municipal positions are filled by appointment, rather than by election. For a number of years, and especially since about 1945, the appointment of Negroes to important positions has become increasingly common. They have been made judges in all three levels of the Federal courts. They have been sent as ambassadors or ministers not only to a number of countries in Africa but also to European countries such as Sweden and Finland. They serve in all levels of the Cabinet structure. In the states and cities, they serve in appointive positions under governors and mayors.

They have also made marked political progress in the South. From the 1940's on, they have been elected to some city and county offices in that region. Between 1960 and 1970, they have won seats in the legislatures of all but one of the Southern states. In many instances, at least some white support has helped them to win. Indeed, some candidates for local office have been elected in places where most of the voters were white.

The increased black vote in the South, which has made possible most of their election victories in the region, has resulted from the unceasing efforts of civil rights leaders there, backed since the middle 1960's by the Federal voting rights acts and decisions of the Federal courts.

In spite of some early setbacks and some discouraging delays, the years since about 1930 have been a time of progress.

This book is the story of the black men and women who held office by election or appointment in those years before 1970 and also of some who won office in 1970. Their careers have demonstrated that people of their race can win governmental positions in a mixed society and do their job. Many of those who have been in office long enough have also proved that they can be reelected term after term.

Their increasing numbers show how much opportunity in government has widened for them during the past twenty-five or thirty years. There is every reason to expect that it will continue to widen in the years ahead.

You have often read and heard that the government of the United States is made up of three separate, coordinate branches—the executive, the legislative, and the judicial. So is the government of each one of the fifty states. So is the government of every city.

This book will use each of these three branches as a classification. If a man is a Congressman, he goes in the legislative branch. If he is an ambassador or a mayor, he goes in the executive branch. Each black in government described in this book, according to what he does, will be assigned to the appropriate branch.

People in the executive branch do more different things, a wider variety of things, than those in the other two branches. Their activities make more interesting reading.

This book will save the best for the last. The first large section will cover the legislative branch. The second large section will cover the judicial branch. Look forward to the third section.

THE
LEGISLATIVE
BRANCH

1

Congressmen Before 1950

IN THE South, the first thirty years of the twentieth century offered black people little or no opportunity to get ahead politically. Few of them were able to vote, and none were being elected to offices worth having. Something else, however, was happening. At the close of the Civil War, there had been some four million Negroes in the South, mostly in rural communities. By 1900, there were 8.8 million in the region, still living mostly in rural communities.

The rural economy of the South could not take care of that number of Negroes. There were not enough jobs or enough small farms to go around. By 1910, some of them had begun to believe that they could never earn a living in the South, and they began to move out.

Some went up the eastern coast to Washington, D.C., Philadelphia, New York, and other Eastern cities. Some went up the Mississippi Valley to St. Louis, Kansas City, Pittsburgh, and especially Chicago and Detroit. Others went west to Los Angeles and San Francisco. In the North and West, they settled in the big cities. Many found factory jobs. They no longer lived in the country, as they had in the South. By 1914, World War I had started, and Northern factories were working around the clock. Jobs were plentiful, and wages good.

In the early 1930's, the Great Depression and mechanized farming (with tractors instead of mules) in the South put more small farmers and farm workers out of work. Making a living there seemed hopeless. Many more black people left their homes in the South and went north or west as their older brothers had earlier. Once more, they settled in industrial cities and looked for factory work.

In the Northern cities and also in Los Angeles and San Francisco, because some neighborhoods were open to them and others were not, they tended to pack into tight districts, many of which soon became from 40 percent to 100 percent black.

In the North and West, no serious effort was made to keep black people from voting or from taking part in politics. Most of the experienced white politicians felt that they could be fitted into the existing party machinery and that their votes could be made useful at election time.

A black man who wanted to get ahead in politics recognized that the first step was to make himself known as a leader in his community. He worked with the NAACP and the Urban League, with interracial organizations such as the YMCA and the Boy Scouts, in one or two fraternal societies such as the Elks and Masons, and of course in a church. The church was a strong force, and a man prominent in his church soon had a following.

Once he was known as a community leader, he could work effectively in the local organization of a political party, at first at the precinct and ward level. In the 1920's, especially in the Chicago area, black politicians began to run for and win city and county offices. Two of them were able to build on their local success and popularity and win seats in the national House of Representatives about this time.

Before we go on to the careers of these two men, let us look at an important fact about the House of Representatives, one of the two branches of Congress. The House of Representatives has a fixed number of members, since 1912, usually 435. The number of members that represent each state depends on that state's population. One main reason why we have a national census every ten years is that the population figures determine the number of representatives each state is allowed in the House.

After each census, the whole country is divided into the proper number of Congressional districts, each one having about the same number of people as there are in each of the other districts.

In a region where there are no big cities and most families live at a distance from one another, a Congressional district may stretch for many miles in both directions in order to take in the proper number of people. In the vicinity of a big industrial city, exactly the reverse is true. A very small geographical area, sometimes only a single neighborhood in a big city, has plenty of population to fill a Congressional district. The crowded black neighborhoods in a number of Northern and Western cities form some Congressional districts of this type.

Only the voters who live within a Congressional district can elect a candidate to the House of Representatives. If he is well known to them and popular with them, it makes no difference if he is unknown in the rest of the state. In a thickly populated district, running for Congress is almost as local as running for the city council.

The First Illinois Congressional District, which included the crowded black neighborhoods of Chicago's South Side, was such a district. When the voters in it could agree on a single candidate, he was almost certain to be elected. The first two Negro members of the House of Representatives to be elected in a Northern state, one a Republican, the other a Democrat, were sent to Congress, one after the other, by the voters in this district.

Let us take a look at the careers of these two men, who started a trend.

OSCAR DE PRIEST

First Illinois District

Oscar De Priest was born in 1871, in Florence, Alabama. When he was only seven, his family, who left the South long before the big migration began, moved to Kansas. There he attended the public schools and then took business courses at the Salina Normal School. After completing his education, he set up a painting and decorating business in Chicago and also developed a real estate business. Soon he became active in politics. He was elected a county commissioner in Cook County, the county in which Chicago is located, and served two terms. He followed this success by being elected an alderman in the city government of Chicago. In 1928 he was chosen as a delegate to the Republican National Convention. In that same year, he ran for Congress in the First Illinois District and won. He was reelected twice, serving from 1929 to 1935.

ARTHUR W. MITCHELL

First Illinois District

Arthur W. Mitchell was born in rural Alabama, where he grew up. He graduated from Tuskegee Institute and went on to study law at Columbia University in New York City and at Harvard in Cambridge, Massachusetts. After getting his law degree, he spent many years teaching in rural Alabama, in the course of which he founded and headed the Armstrong Agricultural School in West Butler, Alabama. Then followed ten years in Washington, D.C., where he practiced law and dealt in real estate. Mitchell then moved to Chicago, where he practiced law from 1929 to 1939 and was also active in politics.

In 1934, he ran for Congress in the First Illinois District, as a Democrat, and won the seat which Oscar De Priest had occupied for the six years preceding. Reelected twice, he held his seat in the House of Representatives until 1941. He was thus active in all but the first two of the first eight years of Franklin D. Roosevelt's New Deal.

Congressmen De Priest and Mitchell showed the way to black people in the Northeast, North Central, and Western regions who were ambitious to win national office. Between 1941, when Mitchell's last term ended, and the close of 1970, when major research for this book had to be cut off, fourteen more Congressmen had been elected to the House.

Before you read about how they were elected and what they did after they reached the House, let's look at another important fact about the House itself.

A great deal of the work of the House is done by committees. There are three types of committees: standing (or permanent) committees, subcommittees of standing committees, and temporary committees. When a bill is presented to the House, it is sent to the appropriate committee for study. If the committee approves it, it goes back to the whole House for debate and passage or rejection. Many types of civil rights legislation are handled by the Judiciary Committee. Keep your eye on that one. Even more important for the poor and the deprived is the Education and Labor Committee, the committee headed for a number of years by Adam Clayton Powell. Some legislation of particular interest to black people is handled by the Veterans Affairs Committee. The two most powerful committees are the Rules Committee, which more or less manages the whole business of the House, and the Ways and Means Committee, which controls the necessary money for practically everything.

The chairman of a standing committee has great power. The chairman schedules meetings of his committee. He can also postpone calling a meeting if he has decided that he does not want a certain bill acted on. When his committee does meet, he can often make the decision as to what business it will take up. It is often possible for him to keep a bill he does not like bottled up in the committee, sometimes until it dies at the end of the session without ever being voted on by the House.

How does a man get to be a committee chairman? It is a question of the length of time he has been a member of the House. The man with a longer unbroken period of membership than those of his rivals gets the appointment. This is called seniority.

Since the term of office of a member of the House is only two years, the sole way in which he can build seniority is by being reelected term after term by the voters in his district back home.

Some of the fourteen Congressmen you are going to read about were elected time after time, and they became important committee chairmen. Others have not yet been long enough in the House to have accumulated much seniority. Three, elected in 1968, were just finishing their first terms in 1970. Five more, elected in 1970, will start as freshmen in 1971.

WILLIAM L. DAWSON

First Illinois District

Voters in the First Illinois District next elected **William L. Dawson,** a Chicago Democrat. Dawson was first elected in 1942, and he was reelected every two years up to his retirement in 1970. This long stay in the House of Representatives earned him a seniority far beyond that of any of the other Congressmen of his race elected later. He was often spoken of as the "dean" of that group.

Dawson was born in Albany, Georgia, in 1886. Though family funds were small, his father and mother kept urging their children to secure an education. Dawson worked his way through the Albany Normal School, graduating with honors in 1909. A little later, with fifty cents in his pocket, he joined the wave of migration to the North and arrived in Chicago in 1912. In 1915, at the age of twenty-nine, he entered Kent College of Law in Chicago.

In 1917, though he was some years above draft age, he volunteered to fight in World War I. Some Negro leaders of that day had persuaded President Woodrow Wilson to open an officers' training school for people of their race. Dawson was sent to that school, in Des Moines, Iowa, and came out of it as a second lieutenant. Later he was promoted to first lieutenant. In February, 1918, he was assigned to the 365th Illinois Infantry and sent to France. With his outfit, he took part in three battles and was wounded.

After his discharge from the Army in June, 1919, he again took up the study of law, this time at Northwestern University. He had the unusual experience of being admitted to the bar before he had finished law school.

A practicing lawyer is in a good position to go into politics. Dawson took the step. He had been a Republican, but he switched to the Democratic Party with the coming of Franklin D. Roosevelt's New Deal and began to move up the ladder in Chicago's politics. He rose from precinct captain to ward committeeman and then to vice chairman of the Cook County Democratic organization. He was elected alderman in the Chicago city government, and served from 1933 to 1939. His election to the Democratic State Central Committee gave him the opportunity to know and work with Democrats throughout Illinois. William L. Dawson had become the most powerful black politician in Chicago and in Illinois.

In 1942, he ran for Congress and won by a narrow margin, less than 3,000 votes. In subsequent elections his margins of victory grew much wider. In 1966, he received 91,119 votes to his opponent's 34,421. He was reelected regularly through 1968. In 1970, being eighty-four years old, he decided to retire. Congressman William L. Dawson died in November, 1970.

As a Congressman, he was soon a national figure in the Democratic Party. In 1944, he became Vice Chairman of the Democratic National Committee, the first Negro to hold that position. He was a moving force in policy-making decisions. In 1960, at the Democratic Convention, he seconded the nomination of Lyndon B. Johnson as Vice President. After the election, President John Kennedy announced that he had offered the Cabinet post of Postmaster General to Dawson. The Congressman decided, however, to remain in the House of Representatives. The President's offer was appropriate. Illinois was one of the key states for Kennedy, and he won in Illinois by less than 9,000 votes. Some of those votes came from Dawson's district.

DAWSON IN CONGRESS

After Dawson had accumulated the needed seniority, he was named as chairman of the important Committee on Government Operations, a position he held for many years.

This committee is often called the watchdog that keeps a steady eye on all the "housekeeping" expenses of running the government, and it is charged with inquiring into and judging the efficiency and economy of every operation. Practically no Federal expenditure is exempt from the committee's examination. For example, during the Eisenhower Administration, when the expenses of operating the White House reported over a period of time were twice those of the previous administration's over a similar period, it was the right and the duty of the committee to authorize a careful audit.

Congressman Dawson also served on many other committees. For instance, he was a member of the Committee for the

District of Columbia in 1954, when the Supreme Court handed down its decision declaring segregated schools in violation of the Constitution. Washington at that time had separate schools for black children and for white children. Educators there decided to be among the first to comply with the Court's decision and began at once to integrate the schools. Naturally enough, some small problems arose when children of both races first began to attend the same schools.

The House Committee for the District of Columbia had long been dominated by Southern members and by Southern influence. Some of this Southern group saw in this school situation an opportunity for striking a blow at integration. An investigation of the Washington school system was set in motion, and Southern educators were invited to appear before the committee, armed with reports and opinions aimed at establishing that integration could not work. At this time of open and bitter criticism of the Supreme Court's decision, the position in the committee of Dawson, a Northern Negro, was one that called for almost superhuman tact and diplomacy.

He was instrumental, however, in getting reports from educators and teachers in other parts of the country who had actually worked in integrated schools and other integrated settings. These helped to bring about a balance.

In matters of civil rights Dawson was a persistent and effective worker. During the 1940's and 1950's, Dawson repeatedly helped to kill bills which fostered or protected segregation.

Hospital accommodations for, and treatment of, veterans without regard to race or color owe much to his insistent efforts over a period of more than ten years.

Before 1949, the Inaugural Balls and other social affairs connected with the Presidency had invariably been segregated. For Negroes who had helped to elect the President, a hall in the black section of Washington had been provided, where they could hold their own party. Dawson used his position in the Democratic National Committee to change party policy, and the 1949 Inaugural Ball for President Truman was the first integrated Presidential affair ever, with over two hundred Negroes invited. Such affairs have been integrated ever since.

In 1957, Dawson urged that a clause banning discrimination be included in leases, licenses, and concession agreements for public use of Federal land and in all reservoir projects of the Department of Defense and the Department of the Interior. In 1958, the order took effect.

From 1943 on, he put pressure on each successive Congress for civil rights legislation. He did not make spectacular speeches, and he never bid for personal publicity; but in his quiet way he could exert very strong influence. In the whole area of race relations, Dawson has been one of the most productive Congressmen of this century. Negroes throughout the country who knew about his work came to think of him almost as their Congressman-at-large.

In Dawson's own mind, in spite of his genuine concern for civil rights, he always considered himself obligated to work not for black people only, but for people, regardless of race—the people of his Illinois district, the people of his state, and the people of his nation.

DAWSON'S VIEWS ON RACE RELATIONS AND PARTY POLITICS

Dawson never felt respect for blacks who hate whites or for whites who hate blacks. He did not work for civil rights only because he was a Negro. The principle which guided his work is that the ultimate political, social, and economic health of a democracy results from concern for all. Dawson never felt that Negroes can make political progress outside the ranks of a political party, because the country is structured by a party system. He tried to teach Negroes to make full use of the power of the ballot to reach their goals. He did it for Chicago's black neighborhoods, and the lesson is being applied in hundreds of towns and cities in the nation.

ADAM CLAYTON POWELL

Eighteenth New York District

New York City was the second big city to elect a black Congressman. Many Negroes had come up from the South to New York City in the 1920's and 1930's, and a very large number of them were concentrated in the Harlem section at

William L. Dawson

Adam Clayton Powell

the upper end of Manhattan. There they soon came to political maturity. It was their effective voting strength which won a seat in the House of Representatives for **Adam Clayton Powell** in the election of 1944.

Powell was born in New Haven, Connecticut, in 1908, the son of a prominent Baptist minister. The family moved shortly after his birth to New York City, where his father became pastor of Abyssinian Baptist Church in Harlem, a church said to have been in existence for 130 years.

Powell graduated from college at Colgate University. He then did graduate work at Columbia and served as business manager of his father's church. In 1936, he became assistant pastor, having completed his training for the ministry by that time. Later, he inherited the pastorate with its large membership of 15,000.

The young minister had great personal charm and a love for life. He liked the excitement and controversy of civic activities, and soon made a name for himself as a champion of justice and Negro rights. As early as 1930, he had organized a picketing campaign in Harlem for better hospital care. In 1938, he staged a similar campaign to get rents reduced in Harlem. In 1939, he turned his attention to securing more jobs for black workers. That year, the World's Fair was to open in New York City. Negroes felt that they were not being hired in suitable numbers. Again Powell organized a picketing campaign, which included delegates from more than 200 organizations. They paraded in front of the executive offices of the New York World's Fair in the Empire State Building. The result was that the number of Negroes working at the Fair went up from 300 to 700.

In 1940, Powell attacked on three fronts. He fought to have black pharmacists employed in Harlem drugstores. They were hired. He staged a bus strike in Harlem. The New York City bus system hired an additional 300 Negroes. He led a committee to the New York State Board of Regents, called attention to the fact that not one of over 2,000 faculty members at City College, Hunter College, Brooklyn College, and Queens College was a black scholar, and made the point that "class and color distinctions are the bygone luxuries of the 1920's."

In 1941, Powell decided to enter politics. The reputation he had built up and the active support of virtually every member of his huge congregation made him a sure winner at the local level. He was elected that year to the New York City Council. In 1944, he aimed for national office, a seat in the House of Representatives. The overwhelming black majority in his district proved its loyalty not only by electing him in 1944 but also by reelecting him time after time.

ADAM CLAYTON POWELL IN
THE HOUSE OF REPRESENTATIVES

After Powell reached the House in 1945, he continued to be outspoken, independent, and controversial. He always made good copy for the newspapers. In the 1950's and early 1960's, he had become the unofficial spokesman for civil rights groups all over the country. From 1955 on, he became noted for what the newspapers called the "Powell Amendment." To every health or education measure, he proposed adding: "provided these funds are not spent in school systems which have not desegregated." Though not in exactly the same words, this became Federal law in the Civil Rights Act of 1964.

By January, 1961, Powell's seniority made him chairman of the House's Committee on Education and Labor. His work as chairman of this important committee was extremely skillful and enormously productive. The Kennedy-Johnson years, 1961–1969, were memorable years for domestic legislation. The key acts designed to put into effect Kennedy's New Frontier and Johnson's Great Society all came through Adam Powell's committee. Details of the Economic Opportunity Act of 1964 were worked out in Powell's committee, and the Education Acts of 1965 were tailored there. By his skillful handling of antipoverty and welfare bills, Powell helped lift the economic status of deprived Americans. These and other laws stand as a monument to his chairmanship.

In 1966, Powell was caught in a sea of troubles. A libel suit brought against him by a Harlem woman came to its conclusion, and a New York court ordered him to pay a judgment. Aside from staying mostly outside the state, Powell paid no attention to repeated orders. He was widely blamed for showing no respect for the law.

His enemies in the House took advantage of this situation. They accused him of spending unauthorized sums of Federal money and asked for an investigation. When the new Congress met in January, 1967, they stampeded the House into a hasty decision. The House voted not to seat him, which meant also taking away his post as chairman of the Education and Labor Committee.

Powell brought suit in the Federal courts. While the case was pending, the House declared his seat vacant. In a special election, his Harlem supporters elected him again. He was still denied his seat. In November, 1968, he was elected once more. The following January, after hours of debate, the House voted to seat him, but two full years had been lost. Also another man had been made chairman of his committee.

In June, the Supreme Court ruled that Powell's constitutional rights had been violated when the House denied him his seat. It implied, however, that the House could have achieved the same result legally by first seating him and then expelling him.

It was a complicated affair, and people had many different opinions. Some thought that a lawmaker who showed disrepect for the courts, as Powell had, deserved to be punished. Others felt that he had been made to suffer *because* he was a Negro. Some had other opinions.

In the primary election in June, 1970, Powell was challenged by a black member of the State Assembly, Charles B. Rangel, and beaten by a small margin. A recount confirmed the result. Powell tried to get on the ballot as an independent, but did not succeed. Rangel, not Powell, would represent the Harlem voters beginning in 1971.

2

Four Congressmen Between 1950 and 1965

Two of the three Congressmen elected from Chicago left office well before 1950. This left one from Chicago, William L. Dawson, and one from New York City, Adam Clayton Powell. From 1950 to 1965, progress was steady but slow. Four new men joined the black delegation, two from Detroit, one from Philadelphia, and one from Los Angeles. Let us start with Detroit.

The Black Vote in Detroit

The third Northern metropolitan center to elect a black Congressman was Detroit. Since the early days of automobiles, Detroit has been the center of the car-making industry. Although factories are now located in various parts of the country, the big plants are concentrated in the vicinity of Detroit. During World War II, all sorts of war materials, including aircraft, were manufactured in the Detroit area.

Thousands of people migrating from the South came to Detroit for work and settled there. As in Chicago and in New York City, densely populated neighborhoods developed. The strong vote in these neighborhoods offered an opportunity to politically ambitious black men.

The first to take advantage of this opportunity to win national office was **Charles C. Diggs, Jr.**

CHARLES C. DIGGS, JR.

Thirteenth Michigan District

In 1954, Charles C. Diggs, Jr., ran for Congress in the Thirteenth District and won.

Up to a point, he was following in his father's footsteps, but in winning a seat in the House of Representatives, he went a step beyond his father. The elder Diggs had come to Detroit from Mississippi between 1910 and 1920. In Detroit, over the years, he had succeeded in building up an insurance business and an undertaking business which has been said to be the biggest black undertaking establishment in the world. A good part of a black undertaker's success comes from his being known and popular throughout his community. This means being active in church matters and in civic affairs. The elder Diggs's undertaking business was in the heart of Detroit's black belt, and he knew hundreds, probably thousands, of people on a first-name basis. In 1936, he took advantage of this popularity and won a seat in the Michigan State Senate. He was reelected several times.

His son, Charles, Jr., studied at the University of Michigan and Fisk University, then served in the Army in World War II, coming out a second lieutenant. Back home, he graduated from Wayne State University in 1946. He spent the next four years in both his father's businesses, not only as an executive but also as a licensed mortician. In 1950, at the age of twenty-seven, he, too, ran for a seat in the Michigan State Senate, won, and served two terms. In 1954, with four years of political education behind him, he ran for Congress in the Thirteenth District.

When young Diggs had run for the State Senate, his district had been both small and largely black. The Thirteenth Congressional District is larger and now about 75 percent black. In

1954 it was only 32 percent black. The black vote alone would not be enough to give him victory.

Labor unions in Detroit are well organized, strong, and interested in politics. For many years, the labor vote and the black vote have kept up an informal alliance, not completely stable but usually effective. Young Diggs campaigned hard to win a good part of this white labor vote. He won in 1954, was reelected in 1956, and every two years since then.

CHARLES C. DIGGS, JR., IN CONGRESS

The seniority which Congressman Diggs has built up has brought him to important and interesting committee posts.

He was a member of the Foreign Affairs Committee. The only way in which a single committee can handle expertly the great range of foreign affairs is to set up subcommittees, each one informed on, and concerned with, a single geographical area. Charles C. Diggs, Jr., became chairman of the subcommittee on Africa.

Rapid change in Africa, which has brought into being more than twenty new nations since 1957, has also presented a bewildering number of international problems and opportunities. From the racial and economic difficulties of South Africa to the intermittent warfare between the Arab states and Israel, all these affairs must be constantly studied by Diggs's subcommittee.

Diggs also served on the Committee for the District of Columbia. Since the District is exclusively Federal, it is controlled and supervised by Congress. Washington, D.C., fills the whole District. In recent years, Washington, like most big cities, has had serious problems. In poor neighborhoods, housing has been decaying badly. Crime is up. Unemployment of unskilled labor is high. New programs of handling transportation, traffic, and education are in process but uncompleted, with resultant difficulties. Meanwhile, the number of blacks in the city has grown from a little less than half to about three quarters of the total population. Most of Washington's difficulties therefore directly affect the lives of Negroes living there. All of these difficulties are the responsibility of the District Committee.

In the House, Diggs, a Democrat, voted for the Civil Rights Acts of 1957, 1960, 1964, and 1965. He supported the anti-

Charles C. Diggs, Jr.   Robert N. C. Nix

poverty programs and the huge education bills which allowed the Federal Government to provide training and help to many rank-and-file Americans. By his votes he has done his best to improve the position of his people throughout the nation.

The fourth Northern city to elect a black Congressman to the House of Representatives was Philadelphia. Philadelphia has a large and closely knit black community, many of whom are the sons and daughters of the Southern families who had come north a generation earlier. In a special election in 1958, the voters of the Second Pennsylvania Congressional District elected **Robert N. C. Nix.**

ROBERT N. C. NIX

Second Pennsylvania District

Born in Orangeburg, South Carolina, Robert N. C. Nix came north during World War I to get an education. He graduated from Lincoln University, took a law degree at the University of Pennsylvania, and began to practice law in Philadelphia in 1925.

He soon got into Democratic politics at the local level, and came to know "grassroots" politics more intimately than the majority of his Philadelphia contemporaries. He was leader of the 44th Ward for eight years, then switched to the 32nd, and was still leading it in 1970. He is a member of the Policy Committee of the Philadelphia Democratic Committee, and has been assistant treasurer of the Committee since 1953. He was a delegate to the National Democratic Convention from 1956 through 1968.

Nix was expert at getting out the Democratic vote in Philadelphia. Everybody knew him because he belonged to as many civic associations and city-wide public service groups as he could, and because he was prominent in his church. He was careful about keeping up his connections with all these organizations and especially about maintaining his position in his church.

All of these activities helped Nix when he came to run for office himself. The circumstances which led to his running were these: A white Democrat named Earl Chudoff had represented the Second District in the House of Representatives for four terms and part of a fifth. Early in 1958, he resigned to become a judge in Philadelphia. A special election had to be held to fill the empty seat. Nix became the Democratic candidate, and beat his Republican opponent in the election. Reelected regularly, he was still holding his seat in 1970.

ROBERT NIX IN CONGRESS

Robert Nix was put on the Post Office and Civil Service Committee, and later became chairman of one of its subcommittees, Postal Operations, Modernization and Facilities. He was also a member of the Foreign Affairs Committee, and chairman of its subcommittee on Foreign Economic Policy. Since 1961, he has served as Chairman of the Mexico-United States Interparliamentary Conference. He voted for the Civil Rights Acts passed since he came into the House.

The fifth big city to elect a black Congressman was Los Angeles. The migration of Southern Negroes to the Pacific Coast had brought large numbers to Los Angeles. Their vote, concentrated in certain sections of the city, set up opportunities for careers in either state or national politics. **Augustus F. Hawkins** took advantage of his opportunities in both areas. He had already had a long and distinguished career in the lower house of the California legislature before he was elected to Congress in 1962.

AUGUSTUS F. HAWKINS

Twenty-first California District

Originally from Shreveport, Louisiana, Hawkins went to college at the University of California at Los Angeles, graduated there, and then studied at the Institute of Government at the University of Southern California. He went into the real estate business, and also devoted considerable time to the fight against juvenile delinquency in Los Angeles County, where Mexican-American, American-Oriental, and Negro teen-agers had difficulty adjusting and were often in trouble. This social service soon made Hawkins well known.

In 1934, running as a Democrat, Hawkins was elected to the Assembly, the lower house of the California legislature. He was reelected every two years after that until 1962, serving fourteen terms.

In the course of his years in the legislature, Hawkins wrote over a hundred laws. Even a few examples will show the breadth of his activities: California's low-cost housing program, authorizations for the building and establishment of the Los Angeles Sports Arena and of California's child care centers; workmen's compensation for household servants; the 1961 Metropolitan Transit Authority Act; and the Fair Housing Act. He introduced the first Fair Employment Practices bill in California, and fought for it for 14 years, until it became law in 1959. He had a part in the establishment of law and medical schools at the University of California at Los Angeles, and of adult evening classes in the high schools. His leadership led to the appointment, for the first time in California, of blacks to judgeships, the Highway Patrol, the post office, and other positions.

Because of both his seniority and the respect paid to him, he was appointed chairman of several committees and subcom-

Augustus F. Hawkins

John Conyers, Jr.

mittees, including Labor and Capital, Unemployment, and the powerful Rules Committee. He was also elected chairman of the Joint Committee on Legislative Organization, the top committee of the California legislature.

Hawkins, strongly supported by the late President John F. Kennedy, ran for Congress in the Twenty-first District in 1962, and won by a tremendous margin. This is not surprising. Of the registered voters in his district, Democrats outnumbered Republicans five to one. About three quarters of the population was black. The proportion has since risen to about 84 percent.

AUGUSTUS HAWKINS IN CONGRESS

Hawkins is a member of the Education and Labor Committee and of the House Administration Committee, which oversees the expenditures and services of the House. He has been one of the authors of important laws, including the Economic Opportunity Act, the Vocational Education Act, the Old Americans Act, and the Equal Employment Opportunity section of the 1965 Civil Rights Act. He is an outstanding Congressman.

The second black Congressman from Michigan was, as might be expected, a man from Detroit. The man, **John Conyers, Jr.,** was also born in Detroit, part of a new generation which was Michigan-born.

JOHN CONYERS, JR.

First Michigan District

John Conyers went to school in the Detroit area until his education was interrupted by the Korean War. He spent a year in Korea as an officer in the Army Corps of Engineers. When he came back, he graduated from Wayne State University in Detroit, and also took his law degree there in 1958.

Like many black veterans, he worked in civil rights organizations and was interested in improving the status of the disadvantaged in the community. These activities led to his becoming, a little later, a board member of Detroit's NAACP and of the Civil Liberties Union of Michigan, perhaps also to his becoming Director of Education for a local of the United Automobile Workers. He made labor connections part of his political base.

After law school, he set out to build a law practice, meanwhile supporting himself with other jobs. For about two years he was field assistant to Congressman John Dingle, a position that taught him a lot about the work of a Congressman. In 1961, he was appointed a referee in the state's Worker's Compensation Department, a post which he held until he ran for Congress.

During all this period he was active in politics, working his way up in local committees of the Democratic Party organization. Until he ran for Congress, he had never tried to be elected to any office.

In 1964, Conyers ran for a seat in the House of Representatives, representing the First Michigan District. This district is made up of 14 Detroit wards with a population which was then more than half black. He won, and was reelected in 1966 and 1968.

In the House, he was the first, and is so far the only black member to be put on the Judiciary Committee, the committee which handles much civil rights legislation. He has worked and voted for all civil rights measures, including voting rights, as well as supporting a number of measures which affect the poor, such as Medicare and Truth in Lending. He also showed his devotion to civil rights by appearing with the late Martin Luther King, Jr., in demonstrations, and by organizing House fact-finding investigations of the degree to which civil rights were being protected in Mississippi and Alabama.

Conyers was thirty-five when elected, and is still comparatively young. In these days many people are concerned about the generation gap. It can be said of Conyers that he identifies more closely with college students and other people on the younger side of the gap than with the older generation. As one illustration of this, he made himself noticeable at the Democratic Convention of 1968 by being the only one of the black Congressmen to support the peace candidate, Sen. Eugene McCarthy, rather than the choice of the regulars, Hubert Humphrey. This took courage.

3

Congressmen Come Faster

S<small>T. LOUIS, MISSOURI</small>, has had a large black population for a long time. In 1960, it amounted to 214,377, and made up 28.6 percent of the city's total population. That percentage increased in the course of the 1960's. It is remarkable, therefore, that voters in St. Louis did not elect a black Congressman long before they did. In actuality, however, it was not until 1968 that they elected **William L. Clay.**

WILLIAM L. CLAY

First Missouri District

William L. Clay was born, grew up, and got his education in St. Louis. He graduated in 1953 from St. Louis University, where he had majored in political science and history, subjects that fascinated him.

After college, he managed an insurance company and became a real estate broker. In 1959, he went into city politics and was elected an alderman, holding office until 1964. After a report of his on the damage done to a community by unfair employment practices, entitled "The Anatomy of an Economic

William L. Clay   Louis Stokes

Murder," was published and made a stir, he wrote a Fair Employment Law which the city adopted.

Clay devoted much time and energy to opening more and better jobs to black people. At the same time that he was serving as an alderman, Clay was business representative of the State, County, and Municipal Employees Union. He put people into city jobs. In 1966, he was associated with the steamfitters' union, and opened up jobs in that trade. He also developed a series of workshops to train workers for more than half a dozen industries and businesses, from bakeries to banks. He had considerable success. One single result was the hiring of 800 blacks for white-collar jobs in St. Louis banks.

An activist, he sometimes used confrontation tactics to open new jobs for blacks. On one of these occasions, he disregarded an injunction and was declared in contempt of court. He served 112 days in jail as a result. To his supporters, a jail record earned in defense of economic democracy was a virtue, not a stain on his reputation.

In 1968, Clay decided to run for Congress in the First Missouri District. This district had a population about 57 percent black and 43 percent white. When he entered the Democratic primary, he found himself running against three other black candidates and four whites. He came out the winner.

In the November election, Clay beat his Republican opponent by a wide margin, 81,000 to 35,478. It is not possible to check which candidate got which votes, but it is estimated that 11,000 to 12,000 white votes went to Clay.

After William Clay took his seat in the House of Representatives in January, 1969, he was assigned to the Education and Labor Committee, the committee most concerned with legislation in his particular fields of interest.

At the same time that St. Louis was electing Missouri's first black Congressman, Cleveland was electing Ohio's first, **Louis Stokes.**

LOUIS STOKES

Twenty-first Ohio District

Louis Stokes was born in Cleveland and, except for three years of military service in World War II, grew up there. He graduated from Western Reserve University in Cleveland in 1948 and earned the degree of Doctor of Jurisprudence at the Cleveland Marshall Law School in 1953. He also did graduate work at Ohio State and in the Northwestern University law school.

He started practicing law in Cleveland in 1954. In his profession and in his many outside activities, he soon displayed the ability and leadership which led to his being put on the executive boards of all sorts of organizations and being made chairman or vice chairman of many committees. The organizations ranged from the YMCA and the Boy Scouts to the Ohio Bar Association and the Cleveland subcommittee of the United States Commission on Civil Rights. Some of these were black; others were interracial.

A decision of the Supreme Court ruled that every Congressional district should have as nearly as possible the same population as that of every other district. Many states having districts with unequal populations were required to redistrict, and usually had to get the new districting approved in the Federal courts.

A group of Ohio lawyers, including Louis Stokes, went before the Supreme Court seeking a court order requiring Ohio to redraw its Congressional districts promptly. They were successful, and these districts were redrawn before the elections of 1968.

As things worked out, the redistricting in Cuyahoga County not only encouraged Louis Stokes to run for Congress in the Twenty-first District, but also helped him to win.

A white Congressman, Charles Vanik, had been the Representative from the old Twenty-first District, elected every two years from 1954 through 1966.

After redistricting, the new boundaries cut off an area of the old Twenty-first District containing a very large block of white votes. This left the district with a fair-sized black majority. In 1968, Vanik therefore chose to abandon the Twenty-first District and run in the Twenty-second, which had gained a proportion of white voters through redistricting.

Stokes might not have chosen to run against a man as successful in getting elected as Vanik had proved himself to be. With Vanik out of the way, Stokes decided to enter the race in the Twenty-first District. In the Democratic primary, he found himself running against seven whites and six other black candidates. He got a little over 29,000 votes, which were enough to win him the nomination.

The November election brought up a situation which did not come up in connection with any of the black Congressmen you have read about thus far in this book.

The Republican candidate facing Stokes was another black Cleveland lawyer, Charles Lucas. Voting along racial lines was impossible. Voters black or white had to choose the man they liked. Lucas was able, experienced in politics, and well liked. Stokes was able and well liked. He was also perhaps helped by the fact that his brother, Carl Stokes, had been elected Mayor of Cleveland the year before, and in 1968 was making a very favorable impression. Whatever the cause, Stokes won.

In the House in 1969, Stokes was assigned to the Committee on Education and Labor and the Committee on Un-American Activities. He has fine qualifications. It is too early to tell what sort of record he will build.

New York City Again

In the same 1968 election which sent Stokes and William Clay to Congress from the Middle West, the voters in the Twelfth New York District were doing something no other Congressional district had ever done. By giving their vote to **Shirley A. Chisholm,** they were sending not only a black to represent them in Congress but the first black woman in America ever to be elected to such an office. Shirley Chisholm won not only an election but a place in American history.

SHIRLEY A. CHISHOLM

Twelfth New York District

Shirley A. Chisholm was born in Brooklyn, New York. She graduated with honors from Brooklyn College, and earned a Master's degree from Columbia. She was fitting herself for work in the fields of child care and the early education of children. She first put her training to work as a nursery school teacher. In 1953, she became director of the Hamilton-Madison Child Care Center of New York City, and in 1959, she was promoted to the position of educational consultant in the New York Division of Day Care.

Her first legislative experience was in the New York State Legislature, to which she was elected as a Democrat in 1964. Because her district was altered by redistricting, she had to run in an extra election in 1965 as well as in the regular election of 1966, and won both times. She was the second black woman to hold a seat in the Albany Assembly, the lower house of the New York Legislature. Bessie Buchanan was the first.

Mrs. Chisholm supported legislation extending unemployment insurance to maids and household servants, and she was in the front lines of the legislative battle for the SEEK program. This was a higher-education plan designed to give special training to disadvantaged young people whose school records do not meet college-entrance requirements but who give evidence of learning ability and intelligence.

Early in 1968, in compliance with a Federal court order to redraw certain Congressional districts so as to make their populations more equal, the New York State Legislature redrew the boundary lines in central Brooklyn. The newly shaped Twelfth District which resulted rested squarely on the Bedford-Stuyvesant neighborhood with its heavy black population. The district also took in parts of Crown Heights with Jewish voters, Bushwick with Italians, and Williamsburg with Puerto Ricans. Its population was 70 percent Negro, and its voters were 80 percent Democratic. As soon as Shirley Chisholm saw the map, she announced that she was running for Congress.

Two other black candidates entered the contest for the Democratic nomination, former State Senator William C. Thompson and Mrs. Dolly Robinson. Campaigning was hard and bitter. Since all the candidates were Negroes, race was neither an advantage nor a handicap to any one candidate. Personality, popularity, and the issues debated were the only considerations. In the primary, Shirley Chisholm scraped through with a plurality of only 788 votes.

Meanwhile, the Liberal Party chose the founder and former national director of CORE, James Farmer, as its candidate. In May, the Republicans also selected Farmer. Again, the race was between Negroes. Farmer was nationally known as a civil rights leader. Remember, however, that registered voters in the Twelfth District were 80 percent Democratic. Shirley Chisholm won by a proportion of about two and a half to one. It was estimated that more than nine tenths of the nonblack voters supported her. These made up about 30 percent of the total number of voters.

SHIRLEY CHISHOLM IN THE HOUSE

Most Congressmen coming into the House for the first time accept the committee assignments which are handed out to them. The selections are made, according to custom, by a party caucus, taking seniority into account. It is practically unheard of for a new Congressman to ask for a change.

Shirley Chisholm was appointed to an Agriculture Committee and put on the Subcommittee on Forestry and Rural Villages. Instead of making the best of this assignment, she broke the usual custom and asked to be reassigned to a committee which would relate to the urban affairs of New York City. She was transferred to the Committee on Veterans Affairs. This was not exactly what she wanted, but it was better than the Forestry and Rural Villages Subcommittee.

In 1969, Mrs. Chisholm supported bills to set up a study commission on Afro-American history and culture, to broaden the powers of the Department of Housing and Urban Affairs, to create a Cabinet-level Department of Consumer Affairs, and to repeal limiting provisions of the Social Security Act which relate number of children in a family to the amount of financial aid given. In her first speech to the House, in March, 1969, she declared that she would oppose every defense money bill "until the time when our values and priorities have been turned right side up again." The priorities which she had in mind were bills which would improve the lot of disadvantaged Americans in jobs, housing, and education.

The victories of three new black Congressmen in the 1968 election made 1968 a successful year. The 1970 election, in which five new Congressmen won seats, made 1970 the most successful year yet. These five will enter the new Congress when it meets in January, 1971.

Here are the five Congressmen elected in 1970.

When William L. Dawson announced in 1970 that he would not run for reelection that year, the seat in the House which he had occupied for twenty-seven years became open. **Ralph Metcalfe,** former Olympic track star and successful Chicago

Shirley A. Chisholm

Ralph H. Metcalfe

George Collins

Charles B. Rangel

businessman, decided to run for it in Dawson's old district. Voters in the district gave Metcalfe their loyal support, and he had very little trouble in winning both the primary and the general election.

While Ralph Metcalfe was winning the seat which had been Congressman Dawson's for many years, **George Collins** was working new political territory in the Chicago area. Collins, a Chicago alderman, defeated a Republican in a district that includes the heavily black West Side of Chicago and the blue-collar suburban cities of Cicero and Berwyn. Illinois will have two black Congressmen from Chicago in 1971.

In New York in 1970, **Charles B. Rangel,** a Harlem lawyer then in his fourth year in the Assembly, the lower House of New York's Legislature, decided that the loyalty of Harlem voters to Adam Clayton Powell was weakening. He believed that Powell could be defeated by a younger, more energetic man.

Rangel resolved to try. In the Democratic primary in June, he did beat Powell by a small but decisive margin. That was the hard part. In the general election he scored an overwhelming victory.

Parren J. Mitchell   Ronald V. Dellums

Parren J. Mitchell, a sociology professor at Morgan State College in Baltimore, defeated a Republican in 1970 in a district which includes parts of Baltimore city and county. The role of the black voter in Baltimore has been history-making. Hence, it was not unexpected that a black man would go to Congress. In addition to the strong black vote, Mitchell received considerable white support.

Ronald V. Dellums, a city councilman in Berkeley, California, defeated a Republican and a Peace and Freedom candidate in 1970 to win election to the United States House of Representatives. He was thirty-four years old. His district includes the cities of Berkeley and Oakland, the latter with a fast-growing black population.

Two women, though not Congresswomen, have been doing a great deal to help Congressmen by their services to two important House committees. They deserve mention. Let us give it to them here.

Mrs. Christine Ray Davis owed the position she achieved to Congressman William Dawson. He hired her to work as part of his personal staff and developed confidence in her ability. When he became chairman of the Committee on Government

Operations, he moved her over to the committee as staff director, under his supervision. This committee checks the expenditures and efficiency of every agency of the Federal Government, large or small. You can easily see that handling such a huge task would call for a very large staff. Actually, Mrs. Davis had eleven staffs under her direction, one for each of ten subcommittees, and a larger one for the full committee. She handled this big job well, but she would never have had it without Congressman Dawson and his seniority.

Mrs. Louise Maxienne Dargans Flemming owed her position to another Congressman with many years of service, Adam Clayton Powell. Mrs. Flemming, who grew up in New York City and graduated from Hunter College there, joined Adam Clayton Powell's staff in 1946. When Powell became chairman of the Education and Labor Committee in the House, he moved her up to the position of chief clerk of the committee.

In 1968, when Congressman Carl D. Perkins replaced Powell as chairman of the committee, he put in one of his own people as chief clerk of the committee; but he did not drop Mrs. Flemming, as he might have. He gave her a new assignment as director of research.

It will be some years before another black Congressman can accumulate the seniority which Dawson and Powell had when each gained possession of an important House committee. Until that time comes, Mrs. Davis and Mrs. Flemming need fear no rival.

BLACK REPRESENTATIVES IN THE HOUSE

You have now read about the sixteen blacks who have been elected to the House of Representatives since 1928. Nine of the first eleven, who were elected between 1942 and 1968, were still serving in the House in 1970.

In 1970, with a record number of victories, five new members were elected and will start serving in the House in 1971. Of these five, two, Metcalfe and Rangel, won the seats that were held for many years by Dawson and Powell, who will not be back in 1971. The other three winners are clear gain. In 1971, the group holding seats in the House at the same time will number twelve, a new high.

All sixteen were elected from large cities of the Northeast, North Central, and Western regions. Five came from Chicago (four of them from the famous First Illinois Congressional District). Three came from New York City. Detroit contributed two. Philadelphia, Los Angeles, St. Louis, Cleveland, and Baltimore each sent one. The sixteenth man, Dellums, was elected from a district which includes Oakland and Berkeley, across the Bay from San Francisco in California. Oakland and Berkeley have a common boundary where they touch, and their combined population is roughly half a million.

The twelve-member group which will be serving in the House in 1971 is big enough to establish the truth of a fact stated earlier in this book: Black people living in a concentrated big-city neighborhood can elect, and reelect, one of their own number to a seat in the House. Though they are in a minority in the nation, they have the voting power to win in a compact Congressional district.

It is worth noting that all nine men who were members of the House in 1970 and all five of those elected for the first time in 1970 had graduated from college. A large majority had earned degrees in graduate or professional schools, in addition. A large number were practicing lawyers. Others were successful businessmen. Still others were professors, educators, or social workers. Those who were so placed as to need some white support had the personalities to attract it. They make an able and distinguished group.

You have seen how the nine who had time to establish a record in the House before 1970 all worked to better the job opportunities, the economic position, the housing, and the rights of the disadvantaged, and have supported measures concerned with health, education, and welfare. These were given national priority by the Kennedy and Johnson Administrations and to some extent by the Nixon Administration. All have been members of civil rights organizations and have strongly supported civil rights. If we put aside an occasional offhand remark of Adam Clayton Powell's, it is fair to say that not one of them has advocated racial separatism, black nationalism, or any other "ism" except the American dream of freedom for all people, regardless of color.

4

In the United States Senate

FOR a good many years the Negro people of America have numbered roughly 11 percent of the country's total population. This is a sizable minority, but a minority, nevertheless.

In the large cities of the Northeastern, North Central, and Western regions, thickly populated black neighborhoods grew up, which, as you have seen, gave the black vote a majority in certain big-city Congressional districts. Within such districts, it is an effective instrument for electing candidates to office, and in recent years it has sometimes been able to elect black mayors in city-wide elections.

A state-wide election is another matter entirely. Every one of the states in which these big cities are located has a considerable white majority. So long as voters divide on the basis of race, the white majority can defeat the black minority.

As you already know, members of the House of Representatives are elected by compact, comparatively small districts. Members of the Senate, the upper house of Congress, are elected by a state-wide vote. These facts pretty well explain why sixteen blacks have been elected to the House in recent times, but only one black has been elected to the Senate.

The single black was **Edward W. Brooke.** The date was 1966. The state was Massachusetts.

EDWARD W. BROOKE

U.S. Senator from Massachusetts

Edward W. Brooke was born in 1919 in Washington, D.C. He graduated from Howard University there in 1941.

Also in 1941, he went into the Army and fought in World War II. He came out a captain, after about five years of service, mostly in Europe. For a time his assignment was to work with the Partisans, guerrilla bands of Italians who fought in the hills against Mussolini's Fascist troops and against the Germans. The Allies valued their help and tried to keep them supplied with arms and medicines. Brooke won two medals.

After he was released from the Army, he studied law at Boston University, and took law degrees in 1948 and 1950.

Brooke had decided to make Boston his home, and he began to practice law there. He also took part in a variety of civic and political activities, in which he soon distinguished himself. Two of the organizations for which he worked were the Boy Scouts of America and the Civil Rights under Law Organization. A little later he was made chairman of the Opera Company of Boston. He was an active veteran, and the Amvets elected him Massachusetts Commander for two years. During the next two years, he was judge advocate in the national Amvet organization.

Meanwhile, he had begun taking part in politics as a Republican. In 1950 and again in 1952, he ran for a seat in the state legislature. He lost both times, but he gained experience and found that he liked campaigning. In 1960, he ran for the office of Secretary of State, and lost once again.

In the following year, Governor John Volpe appointed him chairman of the Finance Commission for the City of Boston, a job which he kept for a year and a half. It was his first and last appointive office. Brooke wanted to win his positions by being elected to them, and he was soon to be successful.

The State Republican Convention met in Worcester to pick a slate for the election of 1962. There were two strong candidates for Attorney General, Brooke and Eliot Richardson, and there was a hot fight among the delegates over which man should be endorsed. By a close decision, Brooke got the nod. Richardson did not give up, and determined to run in the

Republican primary with or without an endorsement. He conducted a tough campaign. Brooke, however, won the primary by a margin of some 40,000 votes. In the November election, Brooke went on to beat his Democratic rival, and did it again in 1964, to win a second term as Commonwealth Attorney General. In those four successful years, he established himself as a powerful personality in state politics.

When Leverett Saltonstall, who had been a Republican Senator from Massachusetts for many years, let it be known that he would not run again in 1966, Brooke announced that he would run.

The Democratic Party picked a former governor of the state, Endicott Peabody, to oppose Brooke. Like Saltonstall, Peabody was a member of an old and prominent Massachusetts family.

In the November election, the vote for Brooke totaled 1,213,-714 to Peabody's 774,761. The black candidate had won by a majority of 438,953 out of not quite two million votes.

It was estimated that nine out of every ten Negro voters voted for Brooke, although many of them were Democrats who had to desert their party to do it. Even so, those votes did not come even close to the 1,213,714 votes which Brooke received. Fortunately for Brooke, many white liberals had liked his work as Attorney General and liked his ideas better than those of Peabody. Their votes supported the black vote. They did not vote for him because he was black. They voted for him because they thought he was the better man for the job.

Brooke had, of course, campaigned to win white votes as well as black votes. He knew that he needed both in order to be elected. In the election he had been able to get both. His victory in Massachusetts makes it reasonable to believe that a black candidate who can attract large numbers of both black and white votes has a good chance of winning a state-wide election in any Northern state.

EDWARD BROOKE IN THE U.S. SENATE

In the Senate in 1967, Brooke was assigned to two committees, Armed Services, and Banking and Currency. No doubt his work on the Finance Commission of the City of Boston and his knowledge of finance led to his assignment to the Banking and Currency Committee. These same factors, together with

Edward W. Brooke

his own military service and his activity with the Amvets, probably had a strong influence on the other assignment. One of the duties of the Armed Services Committee is to deal with the procurement and spending of the Defense Department's immense budget, in recent times over $80 billion a year. Much of his energy and time have had to go into the work of these two committees, and most of this work is not closely associated with problems of race or civil rights. He has backed civil rights with his vote, but, placed as he is, he has not usually been in a position to propose legislation in these areas. In the complex field of finance he has worked for both blacks and whites. His voting record has been that of a liberal Republican.

THE SENATE IN YEARS TO COME

It is not possible even to guess which state will follow the lead of Massachusetts and elect a second black senator. It will depend more on the man than on the voters of the state.

It is possible, however, to predict with confidence that other black candidates—with qualities equal to Brooke's—will come forward and will be elected to the Senate by the voters of their states.

FOUR POLITICAL MANAGERS

By the 1940's, in several states the black vote was big enough to work as the balance of power in a close election. Both major parties wanted it. Their national committees began making serious efforts to attract and hold it.

Each party found out one thing. To convince the voters that the effort was serious, it had to be managed by a Negro high in rank in the national headquarters of the party organization. Each party had two such men between 1944 and 1970.

The Democratic Party, then led by Franklin D. Roosevelt, got started on this program a little earlier than the Republicans. It named **Congressman William Dawson** of Chicago Deputy Chairman of the Democratic National Committee in 1944. He had already been vice chairman of the Cook County committee and a member of the Democratic State Central Committee in Illinois.

In 1960, the Democratic National Committee appointed **Louis E. Martin** to succeed Dawson as Deputy Chairman. Martin, born in Tennessee, graduated from the University of Michigan in 1934, then turned to newspaper work. By 1947, he was editor in chief of the *Chicago Defender*. In 1951, he was elected president of the National Newspaper Publishers Association and served two terms.

As Deputy Chairman, Martin toured the country in behalf of the Democratic Party during all of the Kennedy-Johnson years. There was seldom a national meeting of a Negro organization at which he was not present and making friends for his party. College audiences worshiped him. In 1960, he left to become vice president of the newspaper chain which includes the *Chicago Daily Defender*.

The Republican Party likewise had two eminent men between the early 1950's and 1970. The first was **Val Washington,** a native of Indiana, a graduate of Indiana University, and a Republican leader in the state. From there he moved into Republican politics in Chicago, and from there to Washington. He pioneered in forcing Republican Party leaders to recognize the absolute necessity of having a Negro at the top level of its party organization.

The second man to manage and coordinate the Republican effort was **Clarence Lee Townes, Jr.,** of Richmond, Virginia, a graduate of Virginia Union University. Townes took leave from his position as director of the training program for the Virginia Mutual Life Insurance Company in Richmond in order to work for the Republican Party. He was appointed special assistant to the Republican Advisory Committee in 1966. Townes was the first Negro to run for the Virginia House of Delegates on a Republican ticket. He was very active in state politics. His efforts to win black voters away from their previous Democratic allegiance paid off in 1968, when the state elected its first Republican governor in this century, Linwood Holton.

5

In
Northeastern State
Legislatures

Wᴇ ɢᴏ now from Congress, the "major league" of legislation, to the "minor leagues." Every state, county, and city has to collect taxes and spend money. It has to build and maintain roads or streets. It has to maintain services such as police, schools, colleges, perhaps a fire department, water system, hospitals, sanitation, and many more. It must have courts and jails. It may have to operate a transportation system. These and many other activities have to be authorized by legislative acts, or laws, and money has to be appropriated to pay for them.

Like the national government, every level of government has to have some sort of legislative body to do the authorizing, the taxing, and the appropriating. Every state has a legislature. A city has a council or a board of aldermen—and so on.

In the thirty years between 1940 and 1970, the number of Negroes elected to legislative posts at the state, county, or local level has grown large, and is growing larger.

After a short description of state legislatures, you can read about the blacks who were occupying seats in state legislatures in 1970.

Portrait of a State Legislature

There are fifty state legislatures. Forty-nine have both an upper and a lower house, just as Congress does. The fiftieth, Nebraska's, once had two houses, but it abolished one some years ago. The technical description of a legislature such as Nebraska's is *unicameral*—a fancy Latin word meaning "having only one room."

The names of the fifty legislative bodies vary from state to state. *Legislature* is the most common name, but twenty-one states call their legislatures the *General Assembly*. The official name in Montana, North Dakota, and Oregon is the *Legislative Assembly*. The strangest name, the *General Court*, was given long ago to the legislatures in Massachusetts and New Hampshire.

The upper house in forty-nine state legislatures and the only house in Nebraska's are all called the *Senate*. In most states the lower house is called the *House of Representatives*, but there are some exceptions. In Maryland, Virginia, and West Virginia, the lower house is called the *House of Delegates*. In California, Nevada, New York, and Wisconsin, it is the *Assembly*. New Jersey calls its lower house the *General Assembly*, in spite of the fact that in twenty-one states this is the name of the whole legislature.

The size of the legislatures varies from state to state. The upper house is always smaller than the lower house, with an average membership between 40 and 45. This number is small enough to allow thoughtful discussion of issues and bills, but rivalry between leaders and party politics often interferes. The lower house averages about 120, ranging all the way from 35 to 399 members. With this large number, each locality is represented, and its problems, needs, and wishes can be made known to the whole house.

Terms of office for state legislators also vary from state to state. In most states, Senators are elected for longer terms than members of the House. Two thirds of the states give Senators four-year terms. Forty-six states give members of the House two-year terms. Four states elect them for four years.

States with two-house legislatures are divided into two sets of election districts—one set for the election of Senators, and one set for the election of House members. One Senator is elected from each senatorial district, and usually one House member is elected from each representative district. A few states have larger and fewer representative districts, and more than one member is elected from a single district.

When more than two candidates are running in one district, a plurality rather than a majority is usually acceptable, that is, the candidate receiving the most votes is declared elected even though his total is less than half of the whole vote.

In most states, there is a requirement that the election districts be redrawn at fixed intervals, on the basis of the most recent census. In the past, however, this was not always done. A majority in the state's legislature sometimes voted to postpone redistricting. This delay and the normal movements of people often got the populations of districts all out of balance.

In the middle 1960's, when the Supreme Court ruled that each election district should have as nearly as possible the same number of people as every other comparable district, many states were required to redistrict at once and get their new plan approved by the courts.

The number of bills and resolutions placed before a legislature is too great for the total membership of either house to study them all in detail. As in the United States Congress, both houses of a state legislature are therefore organized on a committee system. Bills and resolutions are channeled off to the appropriate committees and are studied by them. Bills that receive support are brought back to the floor of the House or Senate according to a legislative calendar, debated there, and passed or rejected.

As in Congress, the position and power of a member of a state legislature depend to a large degree on the committees to which he belongs and his rank within a committee. Ordinarily, seniority is the main factor in a member's advancement, but in some legislatures merit also plays a part. Again as in Congress, the chairman or vice chairman of an important committee is in a position of great power and influence, not only within his committee but in the whole legislature.

There you have a quick picture of a typical state legislature.

Before we stopped to sketch out a picture of a state legislature, you were promised that you could read about the blacks

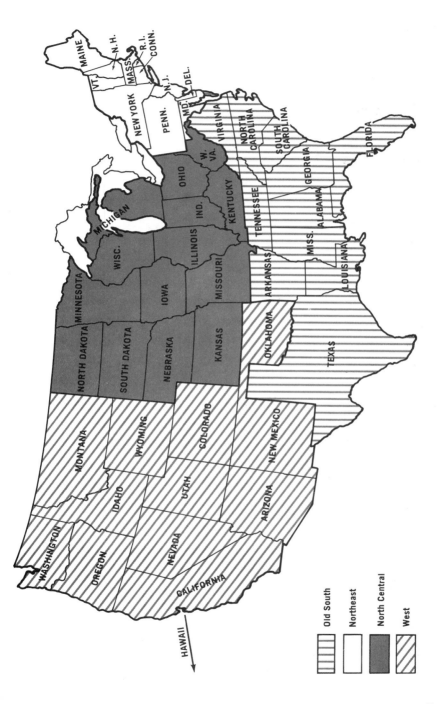

MAINE

VT. N.H. MASS. R.I. CONN.

NEW YORK PENN. N.J. DEL. MD.

VIRGINIA

NORTH CAROLINA

SOUTH CAROLINA

FLORIDA

W. VA.

OHIO

KENTUCKY

MICHIGAN

IND.

ILLINOIS

TENNESSEE

GEORGIA

ALABAMA

WISC.

IOWA

MISSOURI

MISS.

LOUISIANA

ARKANSAS

MINNESOTA

NORTH DAKOTA

SOUTH DAKOTA

NEBRASKA

KANSAS

OKLAHOMA

TEXAS

MONTANA

WYOMING

COLORADO

NEW MEXICO

IDAHO

UTAH

ARIZONA

WASHINGTON

OREGON

NEVADA

CALIFORNIA

HAWAII

Old South

Northeast

North Central

West

49

who were in 1970, or just before 1970, members of state legislatures.

They will be grouped in four regions. Three of these are the areas to which large numbers of blacks have migrated—the Northeast, the North Central, and the West. The fourth is the Old South (the eleven states which made up the Confederacy back in the time of the Civil War).

Using the Old South as a region pushes some states which people may think of as Southern into other regions. Maryland and Delaware (which were border states in the Civil War) go in the Northeast region. Kentucky (also a border state) goes in the North Central group, and West Virginia would if it had any black legislators. Oklahoma (which did not become a state until 1907, more than forty years after the Civil War ended) is put in the Western group.

The reason that we have taken only the eleven states of the Old South as a region is that many records—population figures, voting figures, and percentages of this and that—are based on those eleven states as a region. If we added four or five additional states to the region, we could not give any of those figures because they would no longer be true.

The Northeast comes first. The states are in alphabetical order.

Connecticut

Five blacks held seats in the Connecticut Legislature—one Senator and four members of the House. One was first elected in 1964, the other four in 1966.

Boce W. Barlow, Jr., a Democrat and State Senator, was born in Americus, Georgia. When he was only a year old, his family moved to Hartford, Connecticut. He graduated from Howard University and earned a law degree at Harvard Law School. He was a veteran of World War II. In the 1950's he was made a hearing examiner for the State Civil Rights Commission. He then became prosecutor in the Hartford Municipal Court for two years and judge in the same court for three years. He was well known and served on the boards of some fifteen civic organizations, some black, some interracial.

He was elected to the Senate in 1966, and reelected in 1968.

Voting was interracial, not strictly on racial lines. For example, in 1968, he was given some 17,000 votes and beat a white opponent by a good 2,000. Two thirds of the white voters in his district supported him. The voters chose him because he was an able man.

Otha N. Brown, Jr., a Democrat, like Barlow, first won his seat in the House and has since held it partly because of strong support from white voters.

Brown graduated from Central State College in Ohio, earned a Master's degree from the University of Connecticut, and a certificate in educational administration from the University of Bridgeport. He served for three years in the Armed Forces.

His first political job came when he was appointed to fill an unexpired term on the Norwalk Common Council, and was reelected. In 1964, he was elected to the Connecticut House of Representatives, the only Negro ever sent there from his district, which has a white majority. In 1968, he became notable as the only Democratic survivor in a Republican sweep. Over four fifths of the white voters supported him. While he has been in the Legislature, he has continued to serve on the Norwalk Common Council, of which he is majority leader. Young Negroes remember him because he sponsored the bill which made the teaching of black history a requirement.

Boce W. Barlow, Jr.	Herman M. Holloway, Sr.

Leonard G. Frazier was born in South Carolina. Later, he studied at Temple University in Philadelphia and at the University of Hawaii. He was a Marine in World War II. He was elected to the Connecticut House in 1966 and reelected in 1968. He is a sales representative handling communications appliances.

Lorenzo D. Morgan was born in Connecticut, and graduated from Rockville High School. He is a Navy veteran. He owns and operates a dry cleaning business. He was elected to the Connecticut House in 1966 and reelected in 1968.

Bruce L. Morris was born in New Haven. After attending two colleges, he specialized in engineering at the Connecticut State Technical College and the Colonial School of Tool Design. He is an engineering design consultant.

Morris is an Army veteran. He got his first political experience when he was elected a New Haven alderman in 1962. He was elected to the Connecticut House in 1966 and reelected in 1968.

It would appear that in at least some parts of Connecticut voters attach less importance to race than to the personal popularity and ability of a candidate.

Delaware

There were three blacks in the Delaware Legislature in 1970, **Senator Herman M. Holloway, Sr.,** and two representatives, **Charles E. Butcher** and **Oliver S. Fonville.** All three were elected from legislative districts that include black neighborhoods in Wilmington, a city with a substantial black population. The ratio of blacks to whites there is higher than anywhere else in the state.

The year before Herman Holloway was elected to the Senate, he was elected to the House to fill out an unexpired term. In 1964, he was elected to the Senate, the first black man to become a member of that body.

In the Senate, Holloway worked for the passage of Delaware's public accommodations law and for important acts dealing with educational TV, reorganization of the state mental health program, correctional reforms, and the retraining program for people on welfare.

Holloway has an unusual interest outside of state politics. He is on the board of governors of an organization called the "Preach Corps," with headquarters in Indiana. Every summer it sends a number of ministers, black and white, to foreign countries, where they talk to many people, laymen as well as ministers. In addition to establishing good human relationships, a major purpose is to try to make foreign attitudes toward American democracy more favorable.

Charles E. Butcher was born in Delaware and went to high school there. He is self-employed. He was elected to the House for the 1969–1970 term. His committee assignments were Elections and Revised Statutes.

Oliver S. Fonville was born in North Carolina but was brought to Delaware as a boy, and he went to high school in Wilmington. His regular work is as a bridge operator for the Delaware State Highway Department. He has served in the Legislature since 1965. His committee assignments were Health and Welfare, and Revenue and Taxation.

Maryland

The number of black members serving in the Maryland Legislature increased considerably between 1960 and 1970, and in 1970 it stood at eleven—two in the Senate and nine in the House of Delegates, the lower house. It is worth noting that both Senators and seven of the nine members of the House came from the Baltimore City–Baltimore County area. The black vote in Maryland's big city was using the ballot box to make its wishes unmistakably clear.

The two senators were **Mrs. Verda Welcome** and **Clarence M. Mitchell, III.**

Mrs. Welcome was born in North Carolina. After graduating from Morgan State College and studying at New York University and also at Columbia University, she became a teacher.

In 1953, when a member of the House of Delegates resigned, she was appointed to serve out the rest of his term. She returned to the House after being elected in 1959, and served there until 1963, the year she became a member of the Senate. She has been in the Senate ever since. When she was reelected

Mrs. Verda Welcome   **Clarence M. Mitchell, III**

in 1966, she got 20,338 votes, over 70 percent of the total, against only 8,099 for her opponent.

Mrs. Welcome was a delegate to the Democratic National Convention in 1964. She is on the board of Provident Hospital, the noted Baltimore hospital founded and built by blacks. She was appointed by the Mayor to his advisory council on urban renewal. She was a member of the Governor's Commission on Human Relations. President Johnson made her a member of the National Citizens Committee for Community Relations. Women of her race interested in holding political office in Maryland look at her career as a pioneering venture that shows them the way.

Clarence M. Mitchell, III, is the third generation of his family to be notable for work in behalf of civil rights. His maternal grandmother, Dr. Lillie Jackson, well known in NAACP circles, was always ready to fight discrimination at the drop of a hat. His father and mother were a notable husband-and-wife team of NAACP lawyers. Born in St. Paul, Minnesota, he chose to live in Baltimore, the home of his grandparents on his mother's side. He graduated from Morgan State College and earned a law degree at the University of Maryland. In private life, he is president of a real estate company.

In 1962, he was elected to the House of Delegates, getting more votes in his district than any other candidate on the ticket. In 1966, still only twenty-six years old, he was elected to the Senate, the youngest member ever to be seated there. In the Senate, he took the initiative in pushing through a Fair Employment Practices bill, a Fair Housing bill, and an Anti-cross Burning bill. (The third bill is a bill to ban any racist, nightriding organization such as the Ku Klux Klan. Its name comes from the Klan's practice of burning a large wooden cross as a warning to frighten victims into submission.) Some sixty other measures which he had supported in one house or the other were enacted into law in 1965, 1966, and 1967. Like Mrs. Welcome, he is a Democrat.

Floyd B. Adams was born in Meherrin, Virginia. He attended public schools in that area and later in Baltimore. Since 1967, he has been a steelworker, active in labor organizations and in civic organizations. He was elected to the House from Baltimore.

Aris T. Allen was born in San Antonio, Texas. He studied medicine at Howard University and is a physician. In 1951, he was a Flight Surgeon in the Air Force, with the rank of captain. He was elected to the House in 1966 and 1968 from the Annapolis–Anne Arundel County area, one of the two black members not from Baltimore. In 1966, he was the only black Republican to be elected. His district is predominantly white, but four white candidates running for the seat along with him so divided the vote that he won. In the House of Delegates he was chosen as minority whip (second to the party leader) by the Republicans. In the Annapolis area, he is a member of the County Board of Education, the County Planning Advisory Board, and other organizations.

Troy Brailey, a native of Virginia, got into politics in Maryland by means of his prominence in the labor movement. Earlier, Brailey had been associated with A. Philip Randolph and the Brotherhood of Sleeping Car Porters. Sleeping cars on trains have almost dropped out of use. They had double-deck beds that folded away by day. A black porter was in charge of each car. A. Philip Randolph organized the porters into a large union which was one of the strongest labor unions for blacks until airlines replaced long-distance train travel. At one time Brailey was a national vice president of the Negro American

Labor Council. For more than ten years he was a member of the Mayor's Task Force on Employment in Baltimore. He has been a member of the House of Delegates since 1967.

Joseph A. Chester, Sr., was born in Wilson, North Carolina, and served in the Navy during World War II. He was one of the first to bring blacks and whites together on an integrated ticket in the Baltimore area. Voters in his district were about 48 percent white. When he was elected to the House of Delegates in 1966, white votes helped him win. He was the first black put on the Ways and Means Committee.

Isaiah Dixon, Jr., was born in Baltimore. He went to Howard University, served in the Army during World War II, and is an insurance and real estate broker. He was elected to the House from a black district in 1966 and 1968.

Calvin A. Douglass graduated from Shaw University and studied law at the University of Maryland. From 1949 to 1959 he was assistant solicitor for the city of Baltimore, and from 1959 to 1961 magistrate of the Western Police Station. He was elected to the House in a district where 52 percent of the voters were white. About two fifths of the white voters supported him.

Arthur A. King is the second of the two House members not elected from the Baltimore area. He was elected from the Mt. Ranier–Beltsville area in Prince Georges County. He went to Maryland State College. In 1970, he was associated with a company which serves hospitals, doctors, and laboratories engaged in medical research. He was for a time chairman of the Prince Georges County Council on Human Relations. In 1966, and again in 1968, a large number of white votes helped to elect him to the House.

Mrs. Lena Lee is another woman in the Maryland Legislature. She was born in Pennsylvania, graduated from Morgan State College, and studied law at the University of Maryland. She is a lawyer and business woman. She was elected to the House in 1966 and again in 1968.

Lloyal Randolph was born in West Virginia but taken to Baltimore as a child, and went to school there. He served as chief clerk of the board of supervisors of elections in the city of Baltimore, and as chairman of the Democratic National Committee for Maryland Minorities. He was elected to the House of Delegates in 1968.

Massachusetts

Two members of the House in the Massachusetts legislature are black. Both were born in Roxbury, and both were elected from Roxbury districts. Roxbury was once a separate municipality, but more than one hundred and fifty years ago, it was made part of Boston. It has become a section where much of Boston's black population is concentrated.

Michael E. Haynes is a minister, pastor of the 12th Baptist Church, which is descended from the first African Baptist Church, established about one hundred and seventy years ago on Beacon Hill. The original church was once a principal station on the Underground Railroad. When Martin Luther King was working for his Ph.D. degree at Boston University, he sometimes preached at the 12th Baptist Church as a substitute minister.

Haynes was elected to the House in 1964 and has been re-elected ever since, leading his ticket with a huge majority each time. In the House, Haynes is Assistant Chaplain, and he serves on the Social Welfare and Urban Affairs committees.

Franklin W. Holgate graduated from the Boston School of Business Administration. Aside from his political activities, he is a sales manager and investment counselor.

Holgate was elected to the House in 1964 and has been re-elected since then. In 1968, three other black candidates ran against him but were defeated. In the House, he is a member of the Rules Committee and of the committees on Cities and Municipal Finance and on Federal Financial Assistance. He also holds the post of assistant majority leader.

New Jersey

In the late 1960's, there were four black members of the General Assembly, the lower house of New Jersey's legislature.

Addison M. McLeon was born in North Carolina but brought to Jersey City in 1923. After graduating from Lincoln University in Pennsylvania, he held two consecutive jobs in public housing, one in Washington, D.C., and the second, beginning in 1954, in Jersey City. He then became a real estate broker.

Michael E. Haynes   S. Howard Woodson

He was elected to the legislature in 1965 and 1967. In the 1967 primary, he beat out two white and two black opponents, and in the general election, won by a wide margin, 26,000 for him to only 16,000 for his rival. He has also been a member of the Jersey City Board of Education.

Ronald Owens is a native of Newark. He was educated in New Jersey—college at Rutgers, law school at Seton Hall. Shortly after, he was given a job as assistant corporation counsel for the city of Newark. He was elected to the Assembly in 1965, 1967, and 1969 from a Newark district which was about 60 percent black.

George C. Richardson has been an in-and-out officeholder. He was elected to the Assembly in 1961, but his party did not nominate him in 1963. He ran anyway, with only the support of a small splinter group, and failed. With weak support from another splinter group, he failed again in 1965. In 1967, however, he was sent back to the Assembly, representing Newark's South and East Wards. In 1970, Richardson ran for mayor in Newark, but lost in the primary to Kenneth Gibson.

S. Howard Woodson is pastor of the Shiloh Baptist Church in Trenton, a leader as well as a scholar. He studied at Cheyney State College in Pennsylvania and at Morehouse College in Atlanta, and did graduate work at Atlanta University. He made Trenton his home in 1946. In the next sixteen years or so, he held several positions not previously held by a black man in that city. In 1953, he was president of the Trenton Council of Churches. A little later he was appointed to the city's planning commission. In 1962, he was elected to the Trenton city council as a councilman-at-large, a first for his race.

In 1964, he entered the Assembly, and he has been reelected regularly since then. A sizable share of the large white vote in his district has helped keep him in office. In 1966, he was made chairman of the County and Municipal Government Committee, which processes a large number of bills and has great power. In the next year, Democrats in the House selected him as minority leader. Instead of choosing a new leader in 1969, they broke a long-standing custom and asked him to keep the job and lead them for another term.

New York

Negroes began to take part in politics in New York State before this century began. They worked within the framework of the regular party structure and soon became politically mature. By 1930, they had become a power to be considered in all state politics, and they could and did exert real force in New York City politics.

Even if all other factors are put aside, their numbers have made them politically important. By 1960, there were just over a million of them in the state. By 1970, there were considerably more than a million.

In 1960, they made up 23 percent of the whole population of the five boroughs of New York City, and 13 percent of the whole population of Buffalo. By 1965, those two percentages had gone up to 28 percent and 17 percent. They constituted more than a quarter of all the people living in Manhattan, the principal borough of New York City. There are more black people in New York City than in any other city in the world.

In the light of these figures, it is not surprising that in the late years of the 1960's, there were three black Senators and nine black representatives in New York's legislature, a total of twelve members. One came from Buffalo; ten from New York City; and the twelfth from the Greater New York City area, though not from the city proper.

Senator Joseph A. Galiber was born in New York City, went to college there, and studied law there. For fifteen years, he was attached to the district attorney's office in the Bronx, from 1950 to 1964. In 1967, he was a member of the New York State Constitutional Convention. In the next year, he ran for, and won, a seat in the Senate. Republicans there made him assistant majority leader.

Senator Basil A. Paterson is also a native of New York City, born in Manhattan. He went to college and studied law at St. John's University in the Borough of Queens. He is senior partner in a law firm and has sometimes taught political science at the State University's college at New Paltz. He has given time to the legislative committee of the Harlem Lawyers Association and the American Arbitration Association, as well as to the Harlem Voter Registration Association.

Paterson was elected to the Senate in 1965, and reelected in 1966 and 1968. He has had a distinguished record.

In the primary election of June, 1970, the team of former Supreme Court Justice Arthur Goldberg and Senator Paterson won the Democratic nominations for Governor and Lieutenant Governor.

Senator Waldaba Stewart graduated from Pace College and earned a Master's degree from Hunter, both in New York City. Stewart won election to the Senate in 1968, defeating two other black candidates. He was one of the group which designed and organized the Central Brooklyn Model Cities Program.

Bertram L. Baker is said to be the first black man ever elected to public office in Brooklyn. It happened in 1948. Running as a Democrat in a Brooklyn district about 85 percent black, Baker won a seat in the Assembly. Since then, he has been reelected to ten additional terms. The tenth time in 1968, no one ran against him.

The Baker-Metcalf Act, prohibiting discrimination in housing and real estate transactions, bears his name. Before many areas had set up human relations commissions, he worked to

Basil A. Paterson   **Hulan Jack**

have one established in New York. He also fought for the right of blacks to join volunteer fire departments. A law passed in 1967 now protects this right.

Guy R. Brewer, a graduate of Morehouse College, served as an assistant to the Borough President of Queens from 1960 on. He is also a newspaperman and consumer consultant. After serving in the New York State Constitutional Convention in 1967, he ran for a seat in the Assembly in 1968, with, as it turned out, nobody running against him. The fact that about 40 percent of the voters in his district are white might affect some elections, but not his.

Buffalo voters sent **Arthur O. Eve** to the Assembly. Buffalo is the second largest city in the state, with over half a million people, of whom 90,000 to 100,000 are black. Eve is an engineer who has been employed by the city. He also publishes the *Buffalo Challenger News Weekly,* which he owns and edits. He was elected in 1966 and 1968 from a district that is about 75 percent black. He got fair support also from white voters. The 1968 election, however, was a cliffhanger, finally coming out with 7,100 votes for him and 7,000 for his opponent.

Thomas R. Fortune, although born in Virginia, has lived in Brooklyn for many years. In 1946, after he returned from service in World War II, he organized and started Gateway Stores, Inc., in Brooklyn, which hires blacks from the Bedford-Stuyvesant neighborhood, where unemployment runs high. He worked for many years at the precinct and ward level for the Democratic organization in the black Brooklyn community. He was elected to the Assembly in 1968.

Hulan Jack is widely known in Democratic politics in New York and is a personality in Harlem. As a young man, he graduated from New York University. Aside from politics, he is vice president of the Upper Manhattan Small Business Development and Opportunities Corporation. Jack was first elected to the Assembly in 1941, and served until 1953, when he became Borough President of Manhattan, a post he held for eight years. Jack was once more elected to the Assembly in 1967, and was a delegate to the New York Constitutional Convention that same year. His district is largely black.

Charles B. Rangel was born in New York City. His education was interrupted by the Korean War, in which he won four decorations. Home again, he went to New York University, and studied law at St. John's. In 1961, he was appointed assistant U.S. attorney in the Southern District of New York. For a time he was an associate counsel to Anthony Travia, then Speaker of the House in Albany, and law assistant to Judge James L. Watson, who later became a Federal judge.

Rangel was elected to the Assembly in 1966, and served on the Joint Legislative Committee on Migrant Labor, and also on the Commission for the Revision of the Penal and Criminal Codes of Law.

Mark T. Southall was born in Virginia but educated in New York City, at the Henry George School of Social Science and Poh's Institute of Insurance. He is a real estate and insurance broker. Southall was elected to the Assembly in 1962, and has been reelected ever since. In 1968, nobody ran against him in the primary, and he won the November election with 14,000 to only 2,000. It is said that he got practically all of the white vote, which was about 2 percent of the total.

Edward A. Stevenson, Sr., a native of Jamaica, took a program of executive-training courses in New York, and then went to work in the city's Department of Correction in 1931. He slowly worked his way up until, in 1954, he became food service director, a position he still holds. He was elected to the Assembly in 1965.

Samuel D. Wright, Brooklyn-born, went to college at Suffolk University in Boston and studied law at Brooklyn Law School. After over ten years in the Air Force, he went to work in New York City's law department, becoming an assistant corporation counsel in 1963. He is now chairman of Legal Service Corporation A, an organization which provides lawyers for people too poor to pay for one in the Brownsville, East New York, Bushwick, and Williamsburg areas of Brooklyn.

Wright was elected to the Assembly in 1965, and is a member of the Joint Committee on Corporation Laws.

New York's long list of twelve legislators has made a lot of reading for you. On the other hand, it shows the growing number of black politicians who have been able to win office and hold it, term after term. It indicates the growing power of the black vote.

Pennsylvania, which comes next, has a long list, too, though not quite so long as New York's. We will try not to say too much about each person, so as to save you a little reading.

Pennsylvania

Like New York State, Pennsylvania has two of the thirty largest cities in the country, Philadelphia, with over two million people, and Pittsburgh, with over 600,000. Both have large black populations, concentrated in certain neighborhoods and consequently in certain election districts.

Of the Negroes serving in the legislature between 1968 and 1970, two Senators and seven members of the House were elected in Philadelphia districts, and two members of the House were elected in Pittsburgh. No blacks were elected to the legislature from any other parts of the state. This is the pattern of voting which you read about earlier in this book, the pattern that sent black Congressmen to Washington from Chicago, New York City, Detroit, Los Angeles, and Philadelphia.

You will now meet the eleven black members of the Pennsylvania Legislature.

Freeman P. Hankins   Peter J. Coehlo

Senator Herbert Arlene is a businessman in Philadelphia. He started in politics by running for a seat in the House in the strongly black 3rd District of Philadelphia. He won in 1959 and was reelected, holding his House seat until 1966, the year when he won a seat in the Senate.

Senator Freeman P. Hankins was born in Georgia. He went to Temple University in Philadelphia, and graduated from a college of embalming, prepared to become an undertaker. Like Senator Arlene, he began by running for a seat in the House. He was first elected in 1960, and reelected thereafter. In 1967, a Senate seat became vacant, and an election was held to fill it for the remainder of the unexpired term. Hankins entered the contest, beat out another black candidate in the primary, and took advantage of the large black majority in the district to win the vacant Senate seat.

Mrs. Sarah A. Anderson, Florida-born, graduated from the Philadelphia Normal School and taught school in Philadelphia. She soon became active in the city's Democratic organization and worked in politics at the ward level. In 1954, she was elected to a seat in the House and has been reelected ever since. She co-sponsored legislation for fair employment practices, fair housing, rehabilitation centers for job training, the community college act, and for the first state appropriation to help support the Mercy Douglass Hospital in Philadelphia.

James D. Barber, born in South Carolina, was educated at the Overbrook School and lives in Philadelphia. In 1968, he beat two black opponents in the primary, and, with the help of a large share of the white vote in his district, won his House seat in the general election.

K. Leroy Irvis is a Pittsburgh lawyer. Born in New York, he has a Master's degree from New York University and a law degree from the University of Pittsburgh. From 1957 to 1963, he was assistant district attorney. Irvis was elected to the House in 1958, and has been reelected ever since. In the House, he has been a rapidly rising leader of his party. He was minority whip in 1967–1968, and majority leader in 1969–1970.

Joel J. Johnson grew up in Philadelphia and, as a man, became active in local politics. In 1968, he was elected to the House in a district with a large black majority, after beating two other black candidates in the primary.

Theodore Johnson, like Irvis, came to the House from Pittsburgh. He was elected from a Pittsburgh-Allegheny County district in 1964, and has been reelected since then.

Paul M. Lawson, Pennsylvania-born, studied at Hampton Institute, Rutgers, and Penn State. He became associated with the United Automobile Workers–CIO and was chairman of one of the union's important boards. He was elected to the House from a black Philadelphia district in 1960. With both black and labor support, he has been reelected since then. With his labor experience, he has become chairman of the Committee on Labor Relations in the House.

Mitchell W. Melton is a Philadelphia insurance broker and Democratic committeeman from the 32nd Ward, the noted ward headed by Congressman Robert Nix. He was well known for a man so young, and a member of the Philadelphia Junior Chamber of Commerce. In a district 99 percent black, he ran for a seat in the House in 1968, beat another black candidate in the primary, and went on to win. Then aged only twenty-six, he became the youngest member of the House.

Ulysses Shelton was a Democratic committeeman in Philadelphia for twenty-five years. In 1960, he ran for a House seat in a district about 98 percent black, beat another black man in the primary, and won the election. He has been reelected ever since. In the House, he co-sponsored acts dealing with equal opportunity, integration of schools and playgrounds and play areas, as well as an antipoverty act. He is vice chairman of the Railroad Committee and a member of several other House committees.

Earl Vann came to Philadelphia from North Carolina, and went part way through the University of Pennsylvania. He held several semi-political jobs, such as building inspector and tax examiner. In 1964, he entered a special election and won a seat in the House. He was reelected in 1966 and 1968.

Rhode Island

Rhode Island has one black member in its House of Representatives. **Peter J. Coehlo** is a real estate broker and a special agent of the New York Life Insurance Company, living in East Providence. He studied at the Institute of Applied Sciences in Chicago, and spent over three years in the Air Force. After coming to Rhode Island, he took extension courses given by the University of Rhode Island. Beginning as early as 1948, he became active and effective in Democratic politics. In 1966, he won a seat in the House and was reelected in 1968. These victories were something of an achievement, since his district, which included East Providence, was 92 percent white. He got about three quarters of the white votes. This is the same sort of interracial voting pattern which we saw earlier in Connecticut. In the House, Coehlo was assigned to the Public Welfare and Corporations committees. He was also appointed to a commission to study the structure and programs of the Social Welfare Department.

We have now looked at the careers of forty-nine Senators and representatives serving at the same time in eight state legislatures in the Northeast.

Three states in the region—Maine, New Hampshire, and Vermont—offer no examples. This is natural. The population in all three is small. There are no large industrial cities to attract much of a black population.

There is nothing new about the election of Negroes to state

legislatures in the Northeast. What is new, a new high and a sign of black political progress, is the figure of forty-nine black Senators and representatives serving at one time in eight state legislatures in the Northeast. And there is reason to expect that the number will grow larger in the near future.

It is also worth noting that in Connecticut and Rhode Island and in a few instances elsewhere, the pattern of voting appears to be pretty much interracial—voting for the best man regardless of race. This is an encouraging sign to those who look forward hopefully to a closer and better relation between blacks and whites.

It would be hard to exaggerate the importance of education as a factor in political success. Of these forty-nine legislators, a very large majority are college graduates. Fifteen are lawyers, and others hold graduate degrees in other fields of study.

6

In North Central Legislatures

IN THE North Central region, the same development of voting power which you have just been reading about in the Northeastern cities also took place in cities such as Detroit, Chicago, Cleveland, and St. Louis. As a matter of fact, in the North Central region this voting power outdid the Northeast in electing black state Senators and representatives.

Illinois voters, who began this modern trend by electing Congressmen De Priest, Mitchell, and Dawson between the late 1920's and the early 1940's, chose other members of their race to hold seats in the state legislature. In 1970, the Illinois Legislature had no fewer than eighteen such members. In the same year, New York, the state in the Northeast which had the largest number in its legislature, had twelve, only two thirds of the Illinois total. Missouri, Michigan, and Ohio were also ahead of New York, with fourteen, thirteen, and thirteen.

Illinois

When people migrated from the South to Illinois, some settled in smaller cities, but the great bulk crowded into the South Side of Chicago and then spilled over into the West Side. Chicago and Cook County, in which Chicago is located, had a good many legislative districts with a racial mixture much like that of the famous First Illinois Congressional District. Chicago and Cook County were also strongly Democratic, at least from the 1932 election on. Once in a while the Republicans broke through and won an election, but not often. Cook County is usually a Democratic stronghold.

If you guessed from these two facts that most of the eighteen black members of the Illinois Legislature came from the Chicago area and that the majority of them are Democrats, you would be right. Seventeen out of the eighteen were elected from Cook County districts—four Senators and thirteen members of the House. Democrats at least five to one.

The eighteenth member of the group, also the fourteenth House member, **Kenneth Hall,** is a real exception. Hall lives down-state in East St. Louis, which is practically straight across the Mississippi River from St. Louis and might be called part of the St. Louis metropolitan area. He was not elected from a black district. His district includes Belleville, which is about 90 percent white. He is very well known in Democratic politics, a committeeman for almost twenty years, and the first Negro ever to be chairman of the state's Central Democratic Committee. Voters, regardless of color, support him.

Charles Chew, Jr., was elected to the Senate in 1962. In 1966, he beat two blacks and two whites who opposed him in the primary, and in the general election won his second term. His committees were Agriculture, Conservation, Highways and Traffic Regulation, and Industrial Affairs.

In 1966, **Senator Richard H. Newhouse** won about half the white votes in his district. He was thus able to beat a white opponent in the primary and win the office in the general election. Some of his committees were Education, Judiciary, and Public Welfare.

Senator Cecil A. Partee was born in Arkansas and graduated from Tennessee A. and I. University. He came to the Chicago area after college to study law at Northwestern. He became an assistant state's attorney in Cook County and a member of Chicago's Zoning Board of Appeals. In 1956, he ran for a seat in the Illinois House and served five terms. In 1966, he was elected to the Senate. His committees were Education, Elections, and Financial Institutions.

Senator Fred J. Smith has been in the Illinois Senate far longer than the three Senators whose stories you just read. Like Corneal Davis in the House, Fred J. Smith was first elected many years ago. In 1970, partly because of his seniority, he was president pro tem of the Senate. He has served on many committees.

Now we come to the House of Representatives.

Lewis A. H. Caldwell earned two degrees, B.A. and M.A., at Northwestern. He has been a social worker and probation officer in Chicago, and in 1970 was a sales representative with a large dairy company. Ever since 1955, he has been active in the Democratic Party organization, mostly at the ward level in the city. This and his work with many economic and cultural organizations gave him political prominence even before he reached the Legislature. He was first elected in 1966 and re-elected in 1968 and 1970.

James Young Carter was born in North Carolina. He graduated from Hampton Institute and Bates College in Maine, and studied law at Boston University. Later, he was a law professor at North Carolina Central University. In Chicago he became a commissioner in the Public Vehicle License Commission, a position he still held in 1970. He won a seat in the House in 1954 in a district only about 10 percent white, and has been reelected regularly. He took his seat in 1955, just sixty years after his notable grandfather, James Young, had become the first Negro to serve in the North Carolina Legislature.

Otis G. Collins is in the real estate and insurance business. He was elected to the House in 1968. Two of his committees were Public Welfare and Insurance.

Corneal A. Davis, after studying at Tougaloo College, earned a law degree at the John Marshall Law School in Chicago. He is a Democrat and a staunch one. He was always a great campaigner, and would go five hundred miles to help a Democrat get elected even to the smallest office. He has been a member of the Illinois House for a very long time—since 1941. By 1970, his seniority had made him chairman of four committees: Public Aid, Public Health, Public Welfare, and Public Safety.

Raymond W. Ewell is a Chicago lawyer. In a largely black district, he beat five other members of his race in the 1966 primary and went on to win a House seat. He was reelected in

The Illinois Group. Front 6: Graham, Ewell, Smith, Davis, Partee, Carter. Middle 6: Gardner, Sims, Chew, G. S. Washington, McLendon, Collins. Back 6: Taylor, Caldwell, Hall, Newhouse, H. Washington, Thompson.

1968. Two of his committees were Agriculture and County and Township Affairs.

J. Horace Gardner, born in Cairo, Illinois, has lived in Chicago since 1916. He entered politics in 1936 as a Republican, and won minor office in the late 1940's. Although his district was three quarters white, he was elected to the House in 1956, and he has been reelected at least up to 1970. The year 1956 was the year in which President Eisenhower led his party to a landslide victory, and carried many Republican candidates to victory with him.

Elwood Graham is another Chicago Republican first elected to the House in 1956, the Eisenhower victory year. He has been reelected at least up to 1970. His district was about a third white, and he probably got about a third of those white votes. In 1970, he was vice chairman of the Committee on Banks and Savings and Loan Associations, and a member of committees on Water Resources and Elections.

James A. McLendon, born in Georgia, graduated from Fisk University and studied law at Northwestern. In World War II, he was on the staff of the Army's Judge Advocate General, and came out with the rank of lieutenant colonel. He is an attorney for the Chicago Transit Authority. He was elected to the House in 1962 and reelected at least three times. In the House, his committees were Judiciary and Appropriations.

Isaac D. Sims is in the insurance business. He was elected to the House from the Twenty-seventh Ward in Chicago in 1966, 1968, and 1970. His committees were Insurance, Municipalities, and Public Welfare.

James C. Taylor, Arkansas-born, studied at the University of Illinois, and fought in the Korean War. He is a supervisor of highway maintenance and also superintendent of the Sixteenth Ward Bureau of Sanitation. A member of the Teamsters Union, he is knowledgeable on labor problems. After going through his primary unopposed, he was elected to the House in 1968. His committees were Municipalities and Revenue.

Robert L. Thompson was born in Louisiana and went to college in Arkansas. In Chicago, he was an inspector in the Fire Prevention Bureau for eight years, and deputy fire marshal for the state. He served on the city's Human Relations Commission, and in many civic organizations. Like Taylor, he went through his primary unopposed, and was elected in 1968.

Genoa S. Washington was active in Republican politics in Chicago for more than twenty years. He was elected to the House in the 1960's. Two of his committees were Revenue, and Industry and Labor Relations. In 1957 and 1958, Genoa Washington had the honor of serving as a member of the U.S. delegation to the United Nations.

Harold Washington, a Chicago native, studied law at Northwestern. For five years he was an assistant corporation counsel for the city. Service as an arbitrator for the State Industrial Commission gave him a thorough knowledge of labor relations. He was elected to the House in 1964, and has been reelected since, in 1968 after a victory over two black opponents.

Indiana

The Indiana House of Representatives had four black members in 1970, three from Indianapolis, the state's largest city, and one from South Bend, a manufacturing city in the northern part of the state. All three from Indianapolis were Republicans. The one from South Bend was a Democrat.

The two major parties are fairly even in Indiana; and in state-wide politics success swings from one to the other every few years. Indianapolis, however, tends to vote Republican; and the northern industrial cities close to Chicago—Hammond, East Chicago, Gary, and South Bend—tend to vote Democratic. Gary elected a black Democratic mayor in 1967.

Let's start in Indianapolis and with a lady, **Mrs. Harriette Bailey Conn.** After graduating from Talladega College in Alabama, she studied law at Indiana University. From 1955 to 1964, she was Deputy Attorney General in the state government, and after that became an assistant city attorney in Indianapolis. She was elected to the House in 1966, and reelected in 1968. She started with four committee assignments: Welfare and Social Security, Organization of Courts, Criminal Code, and Benevolent and Penal Institutions. In 1969, she also served on the Judiciary Committee.

Ray P. Crowe, born in Franklin, Indiana, was a schoolteacher for twenty-eight years, and is a vice president of Summit Laboratories, a company which manufactures cosmetics for the hair. He ran for a House seat in a district in which about three

Mrs. Harriette B. Conn   Clarence C. Love

quarters of the voters are white, and got about three quarters of the white votes to be elected in 1964. He was reelected in 1966 and 1968. He was assigned to committees on Education and on Corporations.

Choice Edwards is an assistant commercial manager in the Indiana Bell Telephone Company. He studied previously at Central State University in Ohio and at Indiana University. When he ran for a House seat in 1968, he had been politically active for only three years, but he was a co-founder of an organization called GOP Black Activists. In a district in which white voters made up not quite half of the total, he won election.

Bernard L. White, Jr., has always lived in South Bend. After graduating from Ball State University in Muncie, Indiana, he taught for a couple of years, then became a salesman for an electric company in South Bend. In 1970, he had a connection with IBM. Through business and his civic activities, he had become known and liked by many white voters.

He ran for a House seat in 1968, at the age of thirty-one, in a district about four fifths white. In the Democratic primary he had to run against ten candidates, eight of whom were white, but white support carried him to victory both in the primary and in the general election.

Iowa

Mrs. June A. Franklin of Des Moines is the representative from Polk County. First elected in 1966, she has since been reelected twice. In the House, Democratic members have chosen her as assistant minority leader, or whip.

Nationally, Mrs. Franklin is a member of the blue-ribbon committee to revise the rules of the Democratic Party and of the National Society of State Legislators. She is also secretary of the National Conference of Black Elected Officials. Her further interests are witnessed by her roles in the State Commission of the Aging, the NAACP, and the Des Moines Mayor's Task Force on Housing. Mrs. Franklin attended Drake University.

Kansas

Negroes in the Kansas Legislature are not a new thing. **Dr. William M. Blount,** the first of his race to serve there, was elected in 1924. In the 1960's, not one man, but three were members of the House.

James P. Davis was born in Memphis and went to college there. He studied law in Kansas, at Washburn University, and settled in Kansas City. There he practiced law and spent fifteen years as assistant county attorney. He was elected to the Legislature in 1960, from a largely black district, and has been reelected four times.

Clarence C. Love also comes from Kansas City, where he has a dry cleaning business. He studied at Kansas State College in Pittsburg. He ran for a House seat in 1966. The white vote in his district amounted to only about 35 percent, and six white candidates running against him in the primary split it into small pieces. He probably got a tenth of it himself. He was reelected in 1968.

Billy Q. McCray was elected to the Legislature from Wichita. He had studied journalism at two universities, then switched to accounting courses at the Wichita Business School. He spent four years in the Air Force at the time of the Korean War, coming out a master sergeant. He worked as an industrial photographer in the Boeing Aircraft plant for eighteen years altogether. He is now owner of a flower and record shop in Wichita. He was elected to the House in 1966 and 1968, aided by a substantial number of white votes.

Kentucky

The Kentucky Legislature had three black members in 1970, one Senator and two representatives. The Senator and one House member were women. All three Democrats were elected from the metropolitan area of Louisville, Kentucky's largest industrial city.

Mrs. Georgia M. Davis was a former assistant hospital administrator. She began her political career in 1962 as chairman of volunteers in behalf of a candidate for the U.S. Senate. She was equally active in backing a candidate for mayor in 1965. Meanwhile, she had run, herself, for a seat in the Kentucky Senate. She got between two fifths and half of the white vote in her district, which amounted to 40 percent of the total vote. She was elected in 1964 and reelected in 1966 and 1968.

Mrs. Georgia M. Davis

Basil Brown

Mrs. Mae Street Kidd is a native of Kentucky. In World War II, she worked overseas for the Red Cross. In business, she handles insurance and is a specialist in public relations. When she ran for a House seat, she got about half of the white vote, the whole of which amounted to a shade over half of the total vote. Because of the vigor and initiative she showed in helping to secure House passage of the open housing law known as the Kentucky Civil Rights Act of 1968, she was given the Martin Luther King–Robert F. Kennedy Award. Kentucky was the first state south of the Ohio River to enact such a law.

Hughes E. McGill, South Carolina–born, grew up in New York City. Except for military service on the famous Burma Road to China in World War II, he lived and worked in New York City until he moved to Louisville in 1957. There he was active in local politics for ten years. He then ran for, and won, a House seat. Like Mrs. Kidd, he worked vigorously for the fair housing bill of 1968.

Michigan

From the mid-1960's to 1970, the Michigan Legislature has contained thirteen black members—three in the Senate and ten in the House. Three were women. All thirteen were elected from districts in the metropolitan area of Detroit–Highland Park. Their large number points to the power of Detroit's Negro vote, just as Michigan's Congressmen show it at the national level.

Senator Basil Brown, born in Michigan, graduated from the college now named Western Michigan University, and studied law at the University of Michigan. He was at one time vice president of Diggs Enterprises, Inc. He was first elected in 1956, defeating a black woman lawyer, Cora Brown. He has been reelected ever since. In the Senate he has been Democratic majority floor leader, and he is chairman of the Judiciary Committee.

After **Senator Arthur Cartwright** came to Detroit from Alabama, he worked as a Wayne County constable and as a bailiff in the court of common pleas, jobs which made him widely known in political circles. He served one term in the lower house of the Legislature, from 1963 to 1965. In 1966, he was elected to the Senate. His committees included Health, Social Service, and Retirement.

Senator Coleman A. Young, like Cartwright, was born in Alabama, but he has lived in Detroit over forty years. Young's connection with the Wayne County CIO Council and his position as executive secretary of the National Negro Labor Council have made him well known to Michigan labor leaders, and have brought him strong union support. He was elected to the Senate in 1965. In the Senate he was a sponsor of Michigan's open housing law, and of another law providing more generous aid to dependent children, payable even though the parents are employed up to thirty-two hours per week. Like Senator Basil Brown, he has served as Democratic floor leader.

There you have the Senators. Now for the ten representatives in the Michigan Legislature:

James Bradley was first elected to the House in 1954, from a district which had few white voters. He has served at least eight consecutive terms.

George E. Edwards believes in education. He graduated from Morehouse College in Atlanta, and then studied at Atlanta University, New York University, Michigan State, and Indiana University. He was first elected in 1954, from a largely black district, and has held his seat for at least eight terms. His seniority has made him chairman of the Private Corporations Committee and vice chairman of the Committee on the Revision and Amendment of the Constitution.

Mrs. Daisy Elliott went to two Detroit colleges—Wayne State and the University of Detroit. She was first elected in 1962 and has been reelected at least three times. In connection with Negro History Week, she was honored by the House in 1969.

Mrs. Rosetta Ferguson, educated in Louisana and Michigan, has taken part in Democratic politics at every level from a Detroit ward to important office in the Wayne County committees of the Democratic Party organization. She was first elected in 1964, and has been reelected at least twice. She introduced the state's Fair Textbook Bill, requiring that social science textbooks used in both public and private schools include proper recognition of ethnic and racial minority groups and their achievements. It became law in 1966.

David S. Holmes graduated from college in Virginia and did graduate work at the University of Michigan. He was an official in the United Automobile Workers–CIO, and has labor support. He was elected to the House in 1959 to fill a vacancy, and reelected in 1960 and at least four more times.

Raymond W. Hood was born in Georgia. Later, he moved to Detroit and attended Highland Park Junior College. He was elected to the House in 1964, at the age of thirty-three, and reelected at least twice since then. In 1969, Democrats in the House selected him as majority whip.

Matthew McNeely was educated in the Detroit area. He was active in politics at the ward and district level, and was for a time educational director of Local 306 of UAW-CIO. He was first elected to the House in 1964, and has been reelected to at least two more terms. In 1969, the House elected him associate speaker—an honor but not usually a position of power.

James Del Rio is an older man, retired after a successful business career. At different times, the governor and the mayor have appointed him as an industrial adviser. He was first elected to the House in 1965, and reelected in 1966 and 1968. In his own way, he has been a crusader for civil rights.

Mrs. Nellis J. Saunders was elected to the House in 1966 and 1968, winning in 1968 by a proportion of four to one.

Mrs. Rosetta Ferguson   **Raymond Howard**

Jackie Vaughan, III, graduated with honors from Oberlin College, and then—helped financially by a Fulbright Scholarship for a very unusual three years in a row—earned a Bachelor of Literature degree at Oxford University in England. He is a professor, teaching Afro-American history and urban problems at two colleges in the Detroit area. He was elected to the House in 1966 and 1968, getting 92 percent of the vote in his district in 1966, and an amazing 97 percent in 1968.

Missouri

Missouri has two large industrial cities. St. Louis, on the Mississippi River, is the big one. At the western end of the state is Kansas City, smaller than St. Louis by about 300,000 people but roughly three times the size of Kansas City, Kansas, which is just across the Missouri River from it.

For a number of years, there have been enough black voters in each of these cities to elect candidates to state, county, and city offices, and possibly to Congress, but leaders have been a little slow to take full advantage of this vote. The first black State Senator was elected in 1960, but the second not until eight years later. A few members of the House have held seats for many years, but their number did not increase dramatically until the election of 1968. That was the year in which the vote was exploited to elect the first Congressman, the second State Senator, and several new members of the House.

This success in the 1968 elections raised the number of black members serving at the same time in the Missouri Legislature to fourteen, two in the Senate and an even dozen in the House. Ten were elected from St. Louis, and four from Kansas City. In the North Central states, Missouri's fourteen were topped only by the eighteen in the Illinois Legislature. Michigan and Ohio were tied for third place, each with thirteen.

Senator Raymond Howard graduated from the University of Wisconsin and studied law at St. Louis University. He served two terms in the House before running for the Senate. When he was elected to the Senate in 1968, he was thirty-four years old and the Senate's youngest member.

Senator Theodore D. McNeal has been an official in the Brotherhood of Sleeping Car Porters since 1937, and an international vice president since 1950. When he was elected to Missouri's Senate in 1960, he became the first black Senator in the state's history. Altogether, he has served on nine committees. In 1962, the *Globe-Democrat*, one of the two leading newspapers in St. Louis, cited him as the most effective first-term Senator.

Johnnie S. Aiken was born in Arkansas but lived in Missouri most of his life. He was general manager of the ABC Security Agency. He has been active in St. Louis politics for at least twenty years and a member of the regular Democratic organization in his ward.

J. B. Banks was born in Hermondale, Missouri. He attended St. Louis University and Washington University in St. Louis. After a period of teaching and coaching, he served an apprenticeship for three years in a certified public accountant's office. He became first a United States Claim Examiner, then an Adjudicator. Later, he turned to mortgage banking and is now Board Chairman of the Masonic Home Loan Association. He was elected to the House from a St. Louis district with a strong black vote.

Mrs. DeVerne Lee Calloway was the only woman among the fourteen members of the Legislature. She was born in Memphis, graduated from LeMoyne College there, and did graduate work at Atlanta University and Northwestern. In Missouri, she was elected to the House in 1962 and has been reelected at least three times. She has been vice chairman of two committees, Elections and Accounts, and chairman of the Federal-State Relations Committee. When the two parties were squabbling in the Legislature over redrawing Missouri's Congressional districts, she struggled to get a St. Louis district drawn in such a way that a black candidate would have a good chance of being elected in it. She succeeded in 1967. During World War II, she had served with the Red Cross in India, Burma, and China.

Harold L. Holliday is a lawyer, but he has worked for the state as a social worker and for the Federal Government in the Employment Service and the Veterans Administration. He was a second lieutenant in World War II. He was elected to the Missouri House from Kansas City in 1964, and has been reelected at least through 1970. He was made vice chairman of the Committee on Employment Security.

Herman Johnson is president of a real estate company and of an investment company in Kansas City, and also a member of the real estate board there and of the Home Builders Association. He was elected to the House in 1968. He had eliminated two black opponents in the primary, and defeated his rival in the general election by a proportion of over ten to one.

Leon M. Jordan, after graduating from Central State University in Ohio, became a detective in Kansas City. When he was made a lieutenant and found that there were no white policemen under his command, he resigned as a protest against discrimination. White lieutenants in Kansas City commonly commanded both races.

Jordan spent the years from 1947 to 1954 in Africa, reorganizing the constabulary in the Republic of Liberia. After his return to Kansas City, he started Freedom, Inc., a black organization which grew quickly from five members to 4,000, developed influence in five wards, and was instrumental in electing three candidates to the Legislature. His own election to the House came in 1964, and he was reelected in 1966 and 1968.

In the late summer of 1970, Leon Jordan was killed. His organization persuaded his widow, **Mrs. Orchid Jordan,** to run in his place in 1970, and she won handsomely.

Leroy Malcolm attended the public schools in St. Louis. As an athlete, he won the Golden Gloves Championship while still a teen-ager, and ended his boxing career in 1959. For five of those last years, he was a sparring partner for Charles "Sonny" Liston. Between 1960 and 1965, Malcolm was a project policeman in the Pruett-Igoe Housing Development. He left that position to join the sheriff's office. In 1968 he ran for a seat in the House in a predominantly black district and won.

Franklin Payne went through a technical school in St. Louis. At one time he was president of a local of the United Steelworkers of America, over in Illinois. In St. Louis, he worked for the city, supervising the maintenance of parking meters. He was elected to the House in 1966, and reelected in 1968 and 1970, from a district very largely black.

Nathaniel J. Rivers moved to St. Louis after college and after four years as a parole officer in Illinois. In St. Louis, he went into the insurance business and also became active in Democratic politics. He was elected to two terms as an alderman in the city government. In 1968, he was elected to the House, and reelected in 1970.

Henry Rose is a native of Kansas City. He worked for eighteen years in the motor vehicle unit of the State Department of Revenue. He was elected to the House in 1964 from a largely black district, and has been reelected to three additional terms.

James P. Troupe, Sr., has served in the House for a longer time than any of the other black members. Born in Georgia, he was brought to St. Louis as a child, and went to the city's public schools. Later, he became an official in the United Steelworkers of America. From 1951 to 1954, he was a commissioner in the St. Louis Housing Authority. He was first elected to the House in 1954, and he has been reelected every two years since then up to, and including, the election of 1970. In the House, he has been vice chairman of the Labor Committee.

Fred Williams, after attending a technical school and a business college, also studied at the University of Missouri. His regular work has been as a production planner in an aircraft factory of the McDonnell Douglas Corporation. In 1968, he beat one white and two blacks in the primary election, and went on to win a seat in the House. About two fifths of the voters in his district are white.

Nebraska

You will remember that Nebraska has a legislature not made up of an upper and a lower house. The Nebraska Legislature is a single house, called the Senate.

In 1970, Nebraska also had only one black Senator, **Edward R. Danner.** He came to Nebraska when he was seventeen, in 1917, and worked for many years in the wholesale meat business, which is an important industry in the state and especially in Omaha. Then he spent seven years as an organizer and field representative for the union that represents the workers in this industry, the United Packing House Workers.

Danner was elected to the Senate in 1962, from a district about nine tenths black, and has been reelected to serve at least through 1970. For two terms, starting in 1965 and 1967, he was chairman of the Committee on Labor. Looking back, Danner estimates that 79 percent of his bills have dealt with civil rights, employment, education, mentally retarded and handicapped children, and public welfare.

Mrs. Orchid Jordan   Edward R. Danner

Ohio

The black vote began to take on importance in Ohio politics as far back as 1932, the year in which Franklin D. Roosevelt, the man who started the New Deal, was elected President. In those early days, its impact was pretty much restricted to the state's three largest cities—Cleveland, Cincinnati, and Columbus. After World War II, it not only played a more powerful part in those bigger cities, but it also became effective in the smaller cities of Dayton and Toledo.

In 1970, thirteen blacks were members of Ohio's Legislature. The number was the same as the number in Michigan, but the distribution was very different. In Michigan, all thirteen came from the Detroit metropolitan area—one city. In Ohio, five came from Cleveland, three from Cincinnati, two from Columbus, two from Dayton, and one from Toledo—five cities, scattered all over the state.

Senator John W. E. Bowen is a lawyer in the capital city of Columbus. Before running for the Senate, he served several terms as a Republican member of the House. He was then elected to the Senate. His committees were Judiciary, Agriculture, and State Agencies.

Senator M. Morris Jackson, in private life, is in the real estate business. He was elected to the Senate from a Cleveland district, and has been reelected through several terms. He served on the Health and Welfare Committee and on the Education Committee, as well as on others of less importance.

Senator Calvin C. Johnson is a lawyer in Cincinnati, and was elected to the Senate from a district there. He served on the Judiciary Committee and the powerful Ways and Means Committee.

David D. Albritton was born in Alabama. He went to college at Ohio State, where he became a famous track star. He held the world record for the high jump in 1936. That same year he was one of the black members of the U.S. Olympic team in Berlin who infuriated Adolf Hitler by proving themselves superior to Germany's blond Nordics. He has long been honored by the Helms Foundation as an outstanding athlete. He is a teacher and coach, and is also in the insurance business.

Albritton ran as a Republican for a House seat in 1960. Although his Dayton district had a largely white vote, he was elected, and has been reelected at least four times. Albritton's continuing success in a mainly white district is probably at least partly due to personal factors—his reputation as a former world champion athlete, his popularity as a coach and teacher in Dayton, and the good job he has done as a legislator.

William F. Bowen runs his own insurance agency in Cincinnati. He graduated from Xavier University in Cincinnati. He also gained political experience by working for a time as administrative assistant to a Congressman. He was elected to the House in 1968. His committees were Health and Welfare; Finance; and Appropriations. In 1969, Democrats in the House chose him as minority whip.

After two years at Kent State, **Phillip M. DeLaine** came back to Cleveland, his home town, and joined the police force. DeLaine received several awards for excellent police work, including a citation from the Cleveland City Council in 1963. Some years later, in 1966, he was elected to the House, and reelected in 1968. His committees were Urban Affairs, Local Government, and Government Operation.

David D. Albritton   Phale D. Hale, Sr.

Phale D. Hale, Sr., graduated from Morehouse College in Atlanta and earned degrees from two theological seminaries. He
is a minister, and has been pastor of the Union Grove Baptist
Church in Columbus since very early in the 1950's. A Columbus
district elected him to the House in 1966 and again in 1968.
His committees were Health and Welfare, Local Government,
and Urban Affairs.

Thomas E. Hill attended college partly in West Virginia and
partly at Western Reserve University in Cleveland. He lives in
Cleveland. He was elected to the House in 1966 and reelected
in 1968 from a Cleveland district about 85 percent black. His
committees were Local Government, Urban Affairs, and State
Government.

Troy Lee James graduated from three colleges—Bethany in
West Virginia, and Western Reserve and Fenn in Cleveland.
In business, he is a distributor of food products. He was elected
to the House from a Cleveland district which is about 65 per-
cent black. His committees were Health and Welfare and State
Government.

Casey C. Jones went to Knoxville College in Tennessee and
to the University of Toledo in Ohio. He became personnel direc-

tor for Lucas County (the county in which Toledo is located) and, as an offshoot of that job, recording secretary for the Federation of State, County, and Municipal Employees. He also belongs to three other unions. His second job, directing public relations and recreation at the Miami Children's Home, he gave up when he ran for office in 1968. He was elected from a Lucas County district which is about half white. His committees were Education, and Health and Welfare.

William L. Mallory, a native and resident of Cincinnati, likes to call himself a high school dropout. He did drop out, but later worked his way through Central State College in Ohio and the University of Cincinnati. He became a teacher. Mallory was elected to the House in 1966 from a Cincinnati–Hamilton County district, and won again in 1968 and 1970, unopposed in the primary in 1970. His committees were Education, Local Government, and Urban Affairs.

After studying at a Virginia university, **C. J. McLin, Jr.,** graduated from the Cincinnati College of Embalming. He is an undertaker in Dayton. McLin was elected to the House from a Dayton district in 1968. His committees were Commerce, Government Operation, and Transportation.

Larry G. Smith attended Fenn College in Cleveland and also went to business college there. He operates his own real estate and insurance business in that city. He was elected to the House from a Cleveland district in 1966, and reelected in 1968. His committees were Commerce, State Government, and Transportation.

Oklahoma

Five blacks served in the Oklahoma Legislature in the late 1960's—one Senator and four members of the House. The Senator and three House members were elected from Oklahoma City districts. The fourth member of the House was elected from Tulsa.

Senator Melvin Porter was born in Oklahoma, but went to college at Tennessee A. and I. After college, he was one of the first two of his race to be admitted to Vanderbilt University, in Nashville, Tennessee, where he studied law. Later, in 1964, he was the first to win a seat in the Oklahoma Senate. He has been reelected. He was vice chairman of the Judiciary Committee, and served on two other committees.

Mrs. Hannah Diggs Atkins is a woman who has had a varied career. Born in North Carolina, she graduated from St. Augustine's College in that state. Much later, she studied library science at Oklahoma City University and the University of Oklahoma. In between, she worked as a reporter, a teacher of French, a librarian, and a research assistant in biochemistry at Meharry Medical College. She was elected to the House from Oklahoma City. In 1968, she had to go through two primary elections, the regular one and a run-off. In the regular one, she ran successfully against one black and seven whites. She was also successful in the run-off and the general election.

Archibald B. Hill, Jr., graduated from Morehouse College in Atlanta, and studied law at North Carolina College, now named North Carolina Central University. He was elected to the House from Oklahoma City.

Ben Hill was born in Sidney, Nova Scotia. He graduated from Wilberforce University in Ohio. In Tulsa, he is a minister and also editor of a newspaper, the *Oklahoma Eagle*. He was elected to the House from Tulsa in 1968. Two of his committees are Higher Education and Public Health.

Melvin Porter

Lloyd Augustus Barbee

Artis Visanio Johnson, Oklahoma-born, studied law at the University of Oklahoma and Lincoln University in Missouri. He was elected to the House from an Oklahoma City district in 1968.

Wisconsin

Wisconsin has only one large city, Milwaukee. Milwaukee is not only a port city on Lake Michigan but also a manufacturing center. Within the past twenty-five years, the black community there has grown to a substantial size. In the late 1960's, however, it had elected only one of its people to the Wisconsin Legislature.

Lloyd Augustus Barbee is a Milwaukee lawyer. He was born in Memphis, Tennessee, and graduated from LeMoyne College there. He went north to the University of Wisconsin to study law, and stayed on in that state. He was law examiner for the state's unemployment compensation department for five years, ending in 1962. In 1959, he was also made legal consultant to the Governor's Commission on Human Rights. In 1964, a largely black district in the Milwaukee area elected Barbee to the Wisconsin Assembly, and has reelected him to serve at least through 1970.

7

In
Western State
Legislatures

FROM San Diego to Seattle, the plants which built the aircraft and ships so badly needed in World War II had a constant need for manpower. Jobs were easy to get there; wages were high. Thousands of workers came—people of every sort. After the war ended, many stayed.

In the years following the war, additional numbers of Negroes migrated to the West. Some had gone through California on their way to and from the fighting in the Pacific, and had liked the looks of the country. From Denver, Colorado, west, cities which had had small black neighborhoods soon had bigger ones. Some, such as Los Angeles, or Oakland and Richmond, across the Bay from San Francisco, developed very large ones.

The votes of these newcomers to the Western cities were soon reflected in the make-up of the legislatures of the Western states.

Arizona

The comparatively small black population of Arizona is mainly centered in the rapidly growing cities of Phoenix and

Tucson. In the late 1960's, the Arizona Legislature had three black members—one Senator and two members of the House. One House member and the Senator were elected from the Phoenix metropolitan area. The other House member was from Tucson.

Senator Cloves C. Campbell was born in Louisiana but got to Arizona in time to graduate from Arizona State University in 1958. Four years later, he was elected to the House, and he was reelected in 1964. In 1965, he became the first man of his race to be elected to the Arizona Senate. His district included Glendale and Litchfield, which were once separate towns but are now part of metropolitan Phoenix. About three fifths of the voters in the district were white, but many of them voted for Campbell.

Leon Thompson is a retired policeman, originally from Albuquerque, New Mexico. He was elected to the House in 1960 from a district in much the same area as Senator Campbell's, but smaller. He has been reelected at least four times.

Mrs. Ethel Maynard, born in Connecticut, is a school health nurse in Tucson. She was elected to the House in 1966 and reelected in 1968. One of her committees, fittingly, is Public Health and Welfare.

California

California has been electing some Negroes to its Legislature for a long time, but not so many as you might expect. You may remember that Augustus Hawkins spent over twenty years in the California Assembly before he was elected to Congress in 1962. **W. Byrum Rumford,** of the Berkeley-Oakland area, served in the early 1960's, and his name was associated with equal opportunity and fair housing. There have been others, but not many.

In the late 1960's, however, six were members of the California Legislature—one Senator and five members of the Assembly. The Senator and three members of the Assembly were elected from Los Angeles districts. The fourth Assembly member was elected from San Francisco, and the fifth from a district in Oakland and Berkeley, across the Bay from San Francisco.

Senator Mervyn M. Dymally was born in Trinidad in the West Indies. He graduated from California State College at Los Angeles, and was at one time a teacher. In 1962 and again in 1964, he was elected to the Assembly, the lower house of the legislature. While in the Assembly, Dymally introduced the first bill to require the teaching of Negro history in California schools. In 1966, he was elected to the Senate, the first of his race to win a seat there. His district included parts of Watts and parts of downtown Los Angeles. The best guess is that about half the whites and about half the nonwhites other than blacks in his district voted for him.

In 1964–1965, the State Department in Washington sent Dymally on a lecture tour in Africa and the West Indies. In 1967, he was one of the organizers of the California Conference of Negro Elected Officials. In 1968, this group joined with similar groups in other states to sponsor a National Conference in Chicago. At the Chicago meetings, he and Percy Sutton, Borough President of Manhattan in New York City, were elected co-chairmen.

Mrs. Yvonne Brathwaite is a practicing lawer in Los Angeles. She attended college at the University of California at

Cloves C. Campbell   Mervyn M. Dymally

Los Angeles and studied law at the University of Southern California. She was elected to the Assembly in 1966 and re-elected in 1968. Measures for child care, humane treatment of juveniles, and disaster relief for qualified property owners, which she had sponsored or co-sponsored, all became laws. On the other hand, a bill of hers prohibiting the garnishment of wages without a court order was passed by both houses but vetoed by the governor.

Willis L. Brown, Jr., is a lawyer and the lone black Assemblyman elected from San Francisco. He graduated from law school at the University of California in 1958. After teaching law at Lincoln University in Missouri in 1959–1960, he returned to San Francisco. There, when he was ready, he ran for an Assembly seat. With the support of at least one railroad brotherhood, the Teamsters Union, and two powerful San Francisco newspapers, he was elected in 1964. Of nineteen bills which he wrote or helped to write, nine became law, and two others were passed but vetoed by the governor.

Bill Greene, born in Kansas City, Missouri, had accumulated varied experience in politics before he ran for office in California. He was devoted to civil rights, and had associated himself with CORE, Martin Luther King, Freedom Rides, and the Georgia Marches. As for his activities in California, you could say that Greene apprenticed himself to learn how to succeed in California politics. He served as legislative assistant to Senator Dymally. In 1963, he was the first black to work as a clerk in the California Assembly. That same year, he became a consultant to the state-wide Democratic leader and Assembly Speaker, Jesse Unruh. When Greene ran for an Assembly seat in 1966, the district in the Los Angeles area which elected him was one in which registered Democrats outnumbered Republicans seven to one.

After college at Talladega, **John J. Miller** earned a law degree at Howard University in 1957. The following year, Miller was appointed a graduate research fellow in law at the University of California at Berkeley. He is a member and former president of the Berkeley Board of Education. He is also a member of the Bay Area Conservation and Development Commission. He was elected to the Assembly from his Berkeley district and re-elected in 1968. He was vice chairman of the Committee on Criminal Procedures. In April, 1970, the Democrats in the

Assembly unanimously elected John J. Miller to succeed Jesse Unruh as majority leader and Speaker of the Assembly while Unruh was running for governor.

Leon Ralph graduated from the Air Force Academy and also studied political science at Los Angeles Valley College. Ralph, a member of the Watts-Compton Improvement Association, organized a black and Mexican-American club, which gave him a useful political base later on. He also served as administrative assistant to Assembly Speaker Jesse Unruh, an association which proved extremely helpful to him after he was in the Assembly.

Ralph was elected to the Assembly from a Los Angeles–Watts district in 1966 and again in 1968, in one election with 34,000 votes for him and only 10,000 for his Republican opponent. During Ralph's first term, he was able to steer through the Assembly a bill prohibiting discrimination in the apprentice training program. That same day Jesse Unruh made him a member of the powerful Ways and Means Committee. No other freshman member had been given such an appointment in a long time.

Colorado

In the late 1960's, three black men were members of the Colorado Legislature—one in the Senate and two in the House. All three were elected from the metropolitan area of Denver, which is the state's only large city.

George L. Brown served in the Air Force in World War II, then studied journalism at the University of Kansas, graduating in 1950. After college he went to work as a reporter on the *Denver Post.* In 1955, he was appointed to fill a vacancy in the Colorado Senate. In the following year, he ran for his seat and was elected. In 1970, he was in the midst of his third four-year term. A little over three quarters of the voters in his district are white, and they have consistently given him strong support. In 1962, he was one of four American journalists sent to Europe and Africa by the State Department to hold workshops and seminars in communications. He received an award for his reporting of the March on Washington in 1963 and the Selma-to-Montgomery March in 1965.

Paul L. Hamilton, born in Colorado, graduated from the University of Denver and became a teacher. In 1962, because of his work with boys, he was sent to attend the YMCA International Work Camp in Japan and the Philippines, and in 1963 to Kenya and Rhodesia in Africa, where he served with an organization started, managed, and financed by a black nonsectarian religious group. It was called Operation Crossroads-Africa, and it was a forerunner of the Peace Corps. He was elected to the House in 1968 from a Denver district in which about nine tenths of the voters are black or Spanish-American.

Jerome C. Rose was also born in Colorado. From 1955 on, he held various jobs in the state government, meanwhile continuing his education at the University of Denver. He had earned a Master's degree in Business Administration and was studying law. Among his state jobs, he was the first black Director of the Denver Motor Vehicles Division. He was elected to the House in 1968, from a district in which about a quarter of the voters were white. He got about half of the white vote.

Jerome C. Rose   **Woodrow Wilson**

Nevada

In the late 1960's, Nevada had one black member in its Assembly, **Woodrow Wilson,** elected from Las Vegas in 1966 and 1968. In Nevada, legislative districts are bigger than in most states, and a number of Assemblymen are elected from a single district. When Wilson ran in 1966, his district had nine seats to fill in the Assembly. Over fifteen candidates were running, all white except Wilson. The nine who got the most votes would all win. Wilson came out fifth. In Wilson's second term, he became chairman of the Health and Welfare Committee.

New Mexico

Lenton Malry has achieved a number of "firsts" in New Mexico. After graduating from Grambling College and earning a Master's degree from the University of Texas, he was the first of his race to get a Doctor's degree from the University of New Mexico. He was also the first to become a school principal in Albuquerque, where he lives. And, in 1968, he was the first of his race to be elected to the Legislature in New Mexico. Only 1 percent of the voters in his district were black. In a close race, however, he beat a white Republican by 600 votes.

Washington

In 1968, **George Fleming** was elected to the Washington State Legislature from the city of Seattle. He is a graduate of the University of Washington and majored in business administration. He was assigned to two important committees in the House: Educational and Local Government, and Appropriations. After one term, he ran for the Senate, was elected, and is serving a four-year term. He has reached the position in the Senate of Chairman of the Public Pensions and Social Security Committee. He is the state's first Negro Senator. The district from which he was elected has about 40 percent white voters.

Lenton Malry   George Fleming

You have just read about the fifteen who were members of the legislatures in six Western states in 1970.

Actually, the region consists of eleven states. Five—Idaho, Montana, Oregon, Utah, and Wyoming—had no blacks in their legislatures. The other six states had fifteen altogether. This number is three less than the number in the Illinois Legislature alone. As you can see, there is plenty of room for further progress in the Western states.

8

In
Southern State
Legislatures

WE COME now to the eleven states that once made up the Old South, the Confederacy of Civil War days. As you know, for many years the dominant spirit of Southern politics was white supremacy, and very few Negroes were allowed to do anything "important" in politics. For most of this century, not one was elected to any state legislature in this eleven-state region.

Pressure to break this barrier, however, was building up. Civil rights organizations fought to get rid of unfair restrictions which kept their people even from registering to vote. The movement from the country to the cities concentrated potential voters in neighborhoods in the larger cities. In some cities—notably Atlanta, where for many years the *Atlanta Constitution* and its internationally known editor, Ralph McGill, had championed fairness, justice, and progress for all Georgia's citizens, including black citizens—a few white liberals had begun to say that black people should be allowed and encouraged to take a greater part in politics.

The racial barrier was broken in 1962—in Atlanta. It was broken before the Federal Voting Rights Act was passed in 1965 and before reapportionment of legislative districts had resulted from the Supreme Court's one man—one vote decision.

It was broken while the black revolution of the 1960's was still in its early stages.

All of these later developments have helped to speed up the return of black faces to the legislatures of the Southern states. This return is going on. It is not complete. In 1970, one of the eleven states still had no Negro in its legislature. But before the end of 1970, the barrier had been broken in ten states, and by 1970, one state, Georgia, had no fewer than fourteen in its Legislature.

Alabama

Though Alabama comes first in this section, it did not make history with black state legislators until 1970. Macon, Barbour, and Bullock counties make up two legislative districts with heavy black voter registration. Macon County is the home of Tuskegee Institute, a black institution with its history going back to its founder, Booker T. Washington. After the civil rights crusade of the 1960's, the town of Tuskegee became virtually an all-black town. Its people are perhaps the best educated citizenry per square foot of any small town in the United States. The Tuskegee town and Macon County elected attorney **Fred D. Gray** to the Alabama State House in November, 1970. The other district sent **Thomas Reed.**

Florida

It was in Dade County, the county in which Miami is located, that Florida's color barrier was first broken. As a part of reapportionment, Dade County had been allotted an additional member in the House. No new district, however, had been created from which he was to be elected. A winning candidate had to be elected by a county-wide vote, which of course included Miami's. **Joe Lang Kershaw** won this seat in 1968, the first of his race to become a member of the Florida Legislature in this century, as well as the first ever from Dade County.

Kershaw had earned two degrees from Florida A. and M., and had become a teacher and coach. From time to time he had run for office, never with enough money to support a cam-

Joe Lang Kershaw   Julian Bond

paign and always, before 1968, losing. In 1968, his campaign slogan among Negroes was a play on the slogan of the young extremists, "Burn, Baby, Burn." He said the right three B's were "Bucks, Brains, and Ballots."

In the House, a bill of his to set up a Human Relations Commission designed to prevent racial or religious discrimination became law without the signature of Governor Claude Kirk. He wants to see a bill passed which will require an officeholder to resign from the position which he already has before he starts campaigning for a new one.

Georgia

Drives to register voters in Georgia had begun to bear fruit by 1970. By that date, fourteen black members held seats in the Legislature. Two were Senators. Twelve were members of the House. The cities of Augusta, Columbus, and Savannah had each elected one member to the House. The other eleven legislators—both of the Senators and nine members of the House—were all elected from districts in Fulton County and

De Kalb County. Atlanta proper is in Fulton County, but the Atlanta metropolitan area sprawls out over much of Fulton County and over at least half of De Kalb. It is fair to say that all these eleven were elected from Atlanta.

Atlanta is a special case among Southern cities. What has happened in Atlanta could hardly happen at the present time in any other city in the Deep South. There are many reasons for this. To name one, its complex of five black colleges and universities (Clark College, Morehouse College, Morris Brown College, Spelman College, and Atlanta University) makes it the center for the black leadership of the entire South and perhaps of the entire nation. Many leaders live in Atlanta. Many others, from all parts of the country, come there to study, to exchange ideas and experiences. Their different backgrounds, their diversity, give them a breadth of mind.

The white population of Atlanta is not typical of a Southern city, either. The *Atlanta Constitution* and its long-time editor, Ralph McGill, have already been spoken of. Another reason is the cosmopolitan background of the white business, social, and political leaders in the city. Large numbers of national corporations have Southern branch offices in Atlanta, and a great many whites have been sent from other regions of the country to manage and run these offices. They have brought with them a variety of traditions, many of which are not Southern. Along with the progress of business, they are interested in the city's progress in every field from sports to music and the arts. Many of them do not fear new ideas or social change. To repeat, Atlanta is a special case among Southern cities.

Leroy R. Johnson of Atlanta made history in 1962, when he was elected to the State Senate, the first of his race to sit in the Georgia General Assembly in ninety-two years. His Fulton County district was about 85 percent black, and he also received white support. His district has reelected him since then.

Johnson studied at Morehouse College and Atlanta University, and earned his law degree at North Carolina Central University, then called North Carolina College at Durham. From 1957 to 1962, he served as an investigator in the Fifth Judicial District on the staff of the U.S. Solicitor General, the first of his race to hold such a position in the Southeastern States.

Leroy R. Johnson

In addition to his Senate seat, other things have come to him. He was appointed to the State Democratic Committee. This position and his position in the Senate have made him a power in the state's politics. Another appointment, this time by President L. B. Johnson, gave him the unusual honor of representing the United States at the Independence Ceremony of the Republic of Zanzibar in Africa in 1963. That same year, the Atlanta Chamber of Commerce, practically an all-white organization, took the remarkable but well-justified step of naming him as one of the community's five outstanding young men.

Horace T. Ward is a practicing lawyer in Atlanta. He was elected to the State Senate by a Fulton County district in 1968, the second black Georgia Senator of modern times.

William H. Alexander graduated from Fort Valley College and earned law degrees at the University of Michigan and at Georgetown University. After working for the Social Security Administration for a time, he took up private law practice in 1963. In 1965, in a special election in a Fulton County district, he won a seat in the House, and he was reelected in 1968. He became vice-chairman of the Fulton County delegation to the General Assembly.

Julian Bond had been a top official in the Student Nonviolent Coordinating Committee (SNCC) until a disagreement on policy led to his withdrawal. He was nationally known as a civil rights leader. (See his picture on page 100.)

In 1965, Bond ran in an Atlanta district and won a seat in the House. In January, 1966, however, the House refused to seat him, alleging that certain statements of his implied treason against the United States.

The statements in question were part of a SNCC resolution, not, as it happened, written by Bond. The paragraph which the Georgia legislators thought clinched their case against him expressed sympathy for, and support of, young men who were unwilling to be drafted "to contribute their lives to the United States aggression in Vietnam in the name of the freedom we find false in this country."

Bond brought suit in the Federal courts to get the seat to which he had been elected. In December, 1966, the Supreme Court decided in his favor, ruling that he had fulfilled all the requirements (as they did later in respect to Adam Clayton Powell's seat in the United States House of Representatives), and ordered him seated. He was seated in the Georgia House in January, 1967, a year late. He still had his seat in 1970.

Fourteen white members who still held seats at the time when Bond was being denied his had voted to have Georgia resist the Supreme Court's desegregation decision by *interposition*. This can be defined as: opposition by a state to any act or decision of the United States Government which, in the eyes of that state, violates its sovereign rights. States have tried interposition, and the courts have always declared it illegal.

Some people believe that the vote of these fourteen white legislators came just as close to treason as the criticism of the Vietnam war and of the military draft alleged to have been made by Bond. Actually, neither interposition nor criticism such as that in the SNCC resolution fits the legal definition of treason. Both interposition and interference with the military draft are illegal. Which is worse is a matter of opinion. Since Bond had not written the SNCC resolution, neither one had any real bearing on the denial of his seat in the Georgia House.

Benjamin D. Brown was elected to the House just after the state had been reapportioned, in the special election held in 1965. He was successfully reelected in the regular elections of 1966 and 1968. In 1968, he was unopposed in his Atlanta district.

Like Benjamin Brown, **J. C. Daugherty** was first elected to the House in the special election of 1965, right after the state was reapportioned. His Atlanta district reelected him in the regular elections of 1966 and 1968. Daugherty graduated from Clark College and studied law at Howard University. He is a veteran of World War II and a practicing lawyer.

James E. Dean was elected to the House when he was a twenty-four-year-old social worker. He was a graduate of Clark College and had taken his training in social work at Atlanta University. He ran in a district which includes Kirkwood, an Atlanta suburb, and part of De Kalb County. In his campaign, he made one promise: The American system can work for Negroes, and their needs can be answered through the orderly process of the System. He defeated a civil rights leader in the Southern Christian Leadership Conference, Hosea Williams. Many blacks have been buying homes in Kirkwood, and whites have been leaving. Before Dean had been in office more than a few months, this population shift had reduced the number of whites in Kirkwood to less than half.

Richard A. Dent is one of the three House members not elected from the Atlanta area. He was elected in 1966 from the city of Augusta and has been reelected since then. Dent, a graduate of Paine College, operates his own business as a contractor selling and installing floor coverings.

Clarence G. Ezzard, Sr., was elected to the House in 1968 from an Atlanta district and was reelected in 1970. He is a retired mail carrier.

Mrs. Grace T. Hamilton has been active in civic affairs in Atlanta for many years. She was the dynamic executive director of the Urban League in Atlanta from 1943 to 1960, and a community relations consultant from 1961 to 1965. She had prepared herself at Atlanta University and at Ohio State, where she had earned a graduate degree. Like several others, she won her seat in the House in the special election of 1965, immediately after reapportionment of the state. She was re-elected in 1966, and twice more since then.

Bobby L. Hill comes from Savannah, the second member not from the Atlanta area. He went to Savannah State College and studied law at Howard University. When he ran for a House seat in 1968 in a district which had very few white voters, he beat an opponent of his own race by a proportion of better than four to one.

John Hood came to the House from a district in the Atlanta area. Hood was educated at Fort Valley State College. He was one of the group first elected in the special election of 1965, right after reapportionment, and he had to run again in 1966. He has been reelected.

E. J. Shepherd, after serving in the Marine Corps in World War II, has been a professional chef. He was elected from an Atlanta district in 1968 and again in 1970.

Albert W. Thompson is from Columbus, the third member not from the Atlanta area. He graduated from Savannah State College and studied law at Howard University. He, too, was one of the group first elected in the 1965 special election, following reapportionment. He was reelected in 1966 and won unopposed in 1968. In Columbus, he is on the USO Council, the Southern Area Council of the YMCA, and the Georgia State Economic Opportunity Committee. He was also invited to join the Chamber of Commerce in Columbus and did so.

Louisiana

Ernest N. Morial of New Orleans has had a career with a number of "firsts" in it. After going to Xavier University, he studied law at Louisiana State University's law school, finishing in 1954, the first of his race to graduate from this previously all-white school. Between 1965 and 1967, he served as Assistant U.S. Attorney. This job was also a first for his race. In 1967, Morial was elected to the state's House of Representatives. In the primary, he defeated three opponents, two of whom were white. In the general election, he was not opposed. He thus became the first Negro to be elected to the Louisiana Legislature in this century.

Ernest N. Morial   Robert G. Clark, Jr.

Mississippi

At the age of thirty-seven, **Robert G. Clark, Jr.,** performed a political miracle when he succeeded in getting elected to Mississippi's House of Representatives in 1967, from Holmes County.

Clark had earned degrees from Jackson State College in Mississippi and from Michigan State University. When not in the legislature, he is athletic director, business manager, and a teacher at All Saints Junior College in Holmes County. Holmes County is one of the ten poorest counties in the nation, and its population is about seven tenths black. What made Clark decide to run for a House seat was a decision by the County Board of Education. It refused to sponsor a work-experience program which would have aided 240 poor families. Clark was then heading a program to stamp out illiteracy in his area, which also needed support. He decided that poor people in the county needed a voice in the Legislature, which, as it was, would not spend state money for any such purpose, and did not look favorably on Federal or foundation grants to finance such programs, especially not in Holmes County.

Although Clark was a member of the Mississippi Freedom Party (a civil rights wing of the Democratic Party), he ran as an independent, thus steering neatly between opposing factions of voters. His opponent was a white planter and cattleman who had held the seat since 1956. Clark beat him by a thin margin—3,510 to 3,394. His victory made him the first Negro elected to either house of the Mississippi Legislature since Reconstruction.

North Carolina

The first Negro in modern times to be elected to the North Carolina Legislature was a lawyer, **Henry E. Frye.** After graduating from North Carolina A. and T. State University in 1953 and spending two years in Japan and Korea as an Air Force second lieutenant, he earned a Doctor's degree in law at the University of North Carolina's law school. For a time, he taught law at North Carolina Central University. Also for a time he was an Assistant U.S. Attorney, appointed during the Kennedy Administration. He then went into private law practice in the Greensboro area.

He ran for a House seat in a Guilford County district in 1968. In the primary, he won against eleven other candidates. In the general election, although the district had a very large proportion of white voters, he beat a white opponent.

In the House in 1969, he made a strong attempt to have the literacy test for voters cut out of the state constitution. This was a relic of the old laws which had kept blacks from voting. A person seeking to register as a voter had to show ability to read and write parts of the state constitution to the satisfaction of the registrar. This could make an unhappy situation in communities where prejudice might run high. The registrar's satisfaction was the joker in the old requirement. The House passed Frye's amendment with two readings, 85–25 and 81–21. It died for that session, however, in the Senate's Constitutional Amendments Committee.

Frye was reelected in 1970. Elected at the same time, **Joy J. Johnson** will join Frye in the House in 1971. Johnson comes from a multi-county district which includes his home town, Fairmont. He won the Democratic primary by means of the combined black and Indian vote, and he was unopposed in the general election. He is a graduate of Shaw University.

South Carolina

South Carolina broke the color barrier in 1970. Blacks make up more than 40 percent of the state's population but only 24 percent of the registered voters. The distribution of that 24 percent is heavier in certain counties than in others. In Richland County, in which Columbia, the state capital, is located, blacks represent 34 percent of the registered voters, and in Charleston County 35 percent. With the assistance of a fairly large number of white voters, Richland County elected two blacks in 1970 to serve in the next session of the Legislature: **James L. Felder** and **I. S. Leevy Johnson.** Charleston County elected **Herbert U. Fielding.** The three elected in South Carolina are all college-trained.

Tennessee

In the late 1960's, Tennessee's Legislature had eight black members—two in the Senate and six in the House. Four were elected from Memphis, three from Nashville, and one from Knoxville.

Memphis is the state's big city, with twice the population of Nashville and roughly three times that of Knoxville. The city is within walking distance of the state line between Tennessee and Mississippi, but there is little similarity between politics in Memphis and politics in Mississippi. As just one example, Memphis, with such people as Robert Church and George Lee, has had noticeable Republican Party strength for many years, while Mississippi has continued to be almost exclusively Democratic.

Senator J. O. Patterson is a Memphis lawyer. After he graduated from Fisk University in Nashville, he studied law at De Paul in Chicago. In his recent political career, he has been wearing two hats. He was elected to the Tennessee Senate in 1968. He was also elected a member of the Memphis City Council for a four-year term running from 1968 to 1972.

The other Senator, **Avon N. Williams, Jr.,** is also a lawyer, but he is from Nashville. After graduating from Johnson C. Smith University, he earned a Bachelor's and a Master's degree in

Henry E. Frye   M. G. Blakemore

law at Boston University. Since 1953, he has often practiced in association with another prominent lawyer, Z. Alexander Looby, and the two have handled over thirty civil rights cases which have been significant throughout the state and, in some instances, throughout the nation. Williams is general chairman of the Tennessee Voters Council and serves on Nashville's Council on Human Relations and also on the state-wide Council.

In 1966, **M. G. Blakemore** was elected to a House seat from Davidson County, the county in which Nashville is located. Blakemore prepared himself to work in any of three professions. He first became a teacher, then a dental technician, which he still is. He also studied law. He operates his own dental laboratory, and for twenty-five years, he has taught the construction of dental appliances at Meharry Medical College. When Blakemore started running for the Legislature, he had to run in the whole of Davidson County, and failed in 1960, 1962, and 1964. In 1965, the county was reapportioned, reducing the area he had to cover. In 1966, he was successful, running against three opponents, of whom two were white, and getting 60 percent of the total vote. In 1968, with only one black challenging him, he got 70 percent of the total vote.

Robert J. Booker is the lone black representative elected from Knoxville. After graduating from Knoxville College, he taught French in Chattanooga for a time, then returned to Knoxville to work for the city. In 1966, at the age of thirty-one, he won a seat in the House. When he was reelected in 1968, he beat a black opponent in the primary by a proportion of three to one. His district is about seven tenths black.

Alvin King, born in St. Louis, attended college in Memphis at LeMoyne and the local branch of the University of Tennessee. He was elected to the House from a largely black district in the Memphis area. At the age of thirty-three, operating a real estate and mortgage business and serving in the Legislature, King is typical of modern young black businessmen.

Harold M. Love is a Nashville agent for the Prudential Insurance Company. After attending Tennessee A. and I. University, he earned a Master's degree at Fisk University. In politics, before being elected to the Legislature, he won a two-year term on the Nashville City Council, from 1961 to 1963. Then, in 1964, he won a seat in the House from a district in the Nashville area.

I. H. Murphy is a Memphis lawyer. He studied at Oakwood College in Alabama and at Tennessee A. and I. University, and went to law school at New York University. He was elected to the House from a district in the Memphis area in 1968 and reelected in 1970.

James I. Taylor, after graduating from LeMoyne College in Memphis, taught in Memphis schools for fourteen years. Later he switched to the real estate business. In 1967, he tried for a place in the Memphis City Council but failed to be elected. The following year, he ran for the Legislature, in a Memphis district which has 17,000 black voters in it. This time he beat two black lawyers and won his seat in the House.

Texas

In the late 1960's, there were three black members in the Texas Legislature—one Senator and two members of the House. The Senator and one House member were elected from the Houston area, and the other House member from the Dallas area. Houston is, of course, by far the largest city in the entire

South. Both Houston and Dallas have considerable black populations.

Barbara Jordan, after graduating with honors from Texas Southern University, studied law at Boston University. She was elected to the Senate from District 11 in the Houston area in 1966, and reelected, unopposed, to a four-year term which began in January, 1969. She was the first and only woman member of the Senate.

In the Senate, she made a very rapid rise. She was one of five Senators appointed to the Texas Legislative Council (the research arm of the Legislature) for 1967–1968, and the only freshman Senator ever appointed to that body since it was set up in 1949. She has been made chairman of the Labor and Management Relations Committee and vice-chairman of the Committee on Privileges and Elections, in addition to being a member of eight other committees. Practically from the beginning, she has won the admiration and respect of both blacks and whites, especially of voters. There can be no doubt that United Press International was right in 1967 when it named her one of the ten most influential women in Texas.

Curtis M. Graves, who was elected to the House from Houston, has become a well-known personality in Houston and in the House. In the days of the civil rights crusades, he had been a student activist. Born in Louisiana, he started college at Xavier in New Orleans and finished it at Texas Southern University. After college, he managed a savings association for some years, up to 1966. He also worked as advertising manager of a black newspaper in Houston. His attitude gradually changed. By the time he reached the Legislature, he had adopted the principle that the condition of black people's lives could and should be improved within the American system.

Graves ran for a House seat in 1968, in a district which was only 42 percent black. He got 48,000 votes in the primary, more than enough. In the general election, his opponent was white, but Graves piled up 65,000 votes to only 6,000 for his opponent, winning in white precincts as easily as in black precincts.

In the House, Graves was not at first cordially received. When he put forward an innocent bill requiring that gas stations keep their rest rooms clean, it was defeated; and the vote was against Graves, not against the bill itself. One white

Barbara Jordan

William Ferguson Reid

legislator had shouted, "Vote against the Nigger!" Graves used this later as the title of the book he wrote about his experiences. Soon, however, his fellow members changed their attitude and came to treat him with genuine respect. In 1969, Graves, "fighting city hall," ran for mayor in Houston, made a strong campaign, but was defeated. He kept his seat in the House.

Zan Wesley Holmes, Jr., is a distinguished minister in Dallas. After college, he earned degrees in divinity and theology at Southern Methodist University. In Dallas he has served on the board of directors of many organizations, such as the Urban League, the United Fund, the United Nations Association, the Symphony Orchestra, and the Dallas War on Poverty. He was the first black minister to be elected president of the Dallas Pastors Association. When he ran for a House seat in 1968, he was not opposed in the primary, and in the general election he won with a total of 163,000 votes to his opponent's 148,000.

Virginia

From 1940 on, few elections went by without a Negro candidate or two campaigning for a place in the Virginia Legislature; but up to 1967, not one had succeeded in breaking the color barrier and winning election to either house of the Legislature.

In 1967, the first barrier gave way, and a Richmond doctor was elected to the House of Delegates. In 1969, the second barrier fell, and a Richmond lawyer was elected to the Senate. That same year, to top off this double success, a college professor at Norfolk State College was elected to the House of Delegates. Thus, in the late 1960's, two blacks gained seats in the House and one in the Senate.

Senator Lawrence Douglas Wilder is a Richmond lawyer. He attended college at Virginia Union University and studied law at Howard. Along the way, he had won a Bronze Star while serving with the Army in the Korean War. He developed a law practice in Richmond. His interest in civil rights also led him to work with the Urban League and as a cooperating lawyer with the NAACP Legal Defense Fund. In 1969, Wilder entered a special election in a Richmond-Henrico County district, and defeated the two white candidates opposing him. At the age of thirty-eight, he had crossed the color barrier and won a seat in the Virginia Senate.

William Ferguson Reid is a Richmond physician and surgeon. Like Senator Wilder, he had attended college at Virginia Union University and moved on to Howard—in his case, to study medicine. He became a Navy doctor with the rank of lieutenant, serving with the First Marine Division in Korea and later at Bethesda Naval Hospital near Washington, D.C. When he took up medical practice in Richmond, he was among the first black doctors to be admitted to the Richmond Medical Society, the Richmond Academy of Medicine, and the Medical Society of Virginia, and also among the first to be put on the staffs of three Richmond hospitals as a surgeon. When he ran for the House of Delegates in 1967, white voters made up about three quarters of the total in his district. In the primary, ten white candidates were in the race against him. He got a considerable share of the white vote, and the rest, divided among ten candidates, was not enough to help them.

In the general election, he won with 36,000 votes for him and 27,600 for his opponent. In winning a seat in the House, Reid had broken the color barrier two years before Senator Wilder had.

Dr. William P. Robinson, Sr., was born in Norfolk, and at the time when he ran for the Legislature, he was a professor and chairman of the Political Science Department at Norfolk State College. He had earned his Doctor's degree at New York University. Before coming back to Norfolk, he had spent twenty years as a professor and department head in at least three colleges and universities—Texas Southern University, Central State College in Ohio, and Alcorn State in Mississippi. Along with the scientific principles of political science, Robinson was also familiar with practical political campaigning at the local level. He was very well known, and well liked, in Norfolk.

When Dr. Robinson ran in November, 1969, it was in a big district where he and eight whites were competing for seven seats in the House. Population within the district was a little more than three to one white—310,000 to 98,000. According to the best guesses, more than 12,000 white votes came to Dr. Robinson, and these helped to make him one of the seven winners who were elected.

Professor Robinson ends the list of black people elected to Southern state legislatures between 1962 and 1970. In ten of the eleven states of the Old South, at least one black man had been elected. The Legislature in Tennessee had no fewer than eight black members, and the Georgia Legislature had the encouraging number of fourteen. As these successes indicate, recent black political progress in the South has been not only good but remarkable. Note that this progress is very *recent*. Except for the first beginnings in the Atlanta area of Georgia, practically none of this progress began before 1966, and by far the greater part of it came between 1968 and 1970. These dates are important.

The Voting Rights Act became Federal law in 1965. Before that, civil rights leaders had been struggling to register more Negro voters in the South, but against white obstruction it had been hard, uphill work. After 1965, strenuous drives to register voters were carried on in all the Southern states. In spite of continuing white resistance in some places, these were quite successful. By 1970, out of roughly 5,000,000 Negroes of voting age in the South, some 3,300,000 had been registered to vote.

Of these 3,300,000 voters, considerably more than half had never been registered to vote at all before 1965. It took time to get such large numbers through the necessary process. Some were timid and had to be persuaded. The campaign to get all these new voters registered had to be a continuing effort, carried on over a period of years. By 1970 it had not yet been completed, but in the five-year period after the Voting Rights Act went into effect, the number of registered black voters in the South had far more than doubled.

Most of the people about whom you have just been reading, those elected to Southern state legislatures between 1966 and 1970, were able to win partly because of this new, increased voting strength. In those five years, it helped elect candidates in places where none had been elected before. This strength is still growing. Look for even greater success in the years just ahead.

Earlier in this book, you read about the ability of the big cities in the Northeast, North Central, and Western regions, to elect black candidates to office. This ability will grow and increase. Probably, however, black voters and political leaders will take the biggest and most dramatic steps forward in these eleven states of the Old South.

Do you remember the principle which Texas State Representative Curtis Graves made up his mind to adopt? He believed that the condition of black people's lives can and should be improved within the American system. The new black voting strength in the South and the political success which has begun to result from it are exactly the agencies which may make that principle work in practice.

THE
JUDICIAL
BRANCH

9

Judges in the Federal District Courts

THE judicial branch of the Federal Government is the system of United States courts of law. In America, the judicial branch is on an equal footing with each of the other two branches, and the courts do not have to take orders from either the executive or the legislative branch.

The Constitution, which was completed in 1787 and put into operation in 1789, set up only the highest court, the Supreme Court, but it gave Congress the right to set up lower courts. Shortly after the new government started to operate in 1789, Congress did establish two sets of lower courts, the Circuit Courts, at the intermediate level, and the District Courts, at the bottom level. Since then, Congress has also set up a few special courts—one to hear appeals from military justice, one to try disputes over customs, or duty, on imported goods, and a few others.

There is only one Supreme Court. Originally, it was made up of a chief justice and five associate justices. The number of associate justices was later increased, and for a good many years there have been eight associate justices. Juries are never used in Supreme Court cases. With only a few extremely unusual exceptions, the Court takes on only cases appealed from lower courts. One of the Court's important functions is to decide whether a given law or court procedure violates the Constitution. If the Court decides that the law or the procedure does violate the Constitution, the law or procedure is in effect abolished. Such an examination of the constitutionality of a law is called *judicial review*. Many civil rights cases have been decided on the basis of judicial review.

The Circuit Courts of Appeals stand one step below the Supreme Court. There are eleven altogether. The District of Columbia forms one circuit. The rest of the country is divided into ten more circuits. Like the Supreme Court, the Circuit Courts try only cases appealed from lower courts. Juries are not used. Some cases are tried before a single judge; others, before a panel of judges. Some circuits have only three judges. Others have six, and some have as many as nine.

Federal courts at the bottom level are called District Courts. Originally, there were only thirteen districts. As the country grew bigger, with more people and more law cases, the districts were redrawn, and new ones were added. Now there are almost a hundred.

A District Court does not ordinarily handle appeals cases. A case brought to a District Court is usually coming before a court for the first time. In a District Court, both parties may agree, and often do agree, to put the decision in the hands of the judge alone. If, however, either party insists on a jury trial, the case is decided by a jury.

Judges in all the Federal courts, including the special courts, are always appointed. They are never elected, as judges in state, county, and city courts often are. When there is a vacancy in a Federal court, the President nominates a candidate for the position, and sends his name to the Senate. The Senate considers the President's choice, often questioning the man as to his past record and his views on subjects that might affect his work as a judge, and sometimes holding hearings so that other people may speak for or against his appointment. The Senate then votes to approve or reject the appointment. Senate approval completes the appointment.

The Constitution says that a Federal judge is to serve "during good behavior." In practice, this usually means that he can hold the position, if he wants to, for the rest of his working life.

A Federal judge at any level gets considerable honor because of his position. A justice of the Supreme Court naturally gets the most. There is only one Supreme Court, and it is the nation's highest court. There are only nine justices to share the honor. There are eleven Circuit Courts, some with only three judges, but some with nine. A Circuit Court judge has a highly honorable position, but he shares the honor with close to seventy other judges. The honor paid to a District Court judge is considerable, too, but it is even less exclusive. He has to share it with almost two hundred other District Court judges.

President Franklin D. Roosevelt started the practice of appointing black Federal judges in 1937, and each President since has continued it. William H. Hastie became the first black District judge when he was appointed in 1937. He later became the first black Circuit judge when he was appointed by President Harry S Truman in 1949. Thurgood Marshall, the noted civil rights lawyer, became the first Negro Supreme Court justice when he was appointed by President Lyndon B. Johnson in 1967. Three black judges have been appointed to the U.S. Court of Customs.

Let us start with the black judges in the District Courts and work up through the Circuit Courts of Appeals to the Supreme Court. Wherever we start, four judges have legitimate claims to come in twice, because they have served in two levels of the Federal courts. Two, Wade Hampton McCree, Jr., and Spottswood W. Robinson, III, after short periods as District Court judges, resigned because they had been appointed to Circuit Court positions, which they stepped into immediately. Two resigned from their first positions as Federal judges in order to go into other work, but were later appointed to higher courts. William H. Hastie was made a District judge in the Virgin Islands by President Roosevelt in 1937 but resigned after only two years. Later, he became governor of the Virgin Islands; and still later, President Truman made him the first black Circuit Court judge. After only about two years on the Circuit Court bench, Thurgood Marshall resigned when President Lyndon Johnson made him United States Solicitor General in 1965. He left that position in 1967, when President Johnson made him a Supreme Court justice. He was the first black lawyer to hold either of these positions.

BLACK DISTRICT JUDGES IN
THE VIRGIN ISLANDS

The first three black lawyers to be appointed District Court judges all served in the Virgin Islands. The Virgin Islands are a group of about a hundred islands a little to the southeast of Puerto Rico. Some are in plain sight from the eastern end of Puerto Rico. At one time they all belonged to Denmark, but in 1917, the United States bought over fifty of these islands and islets, paying $25 million. The three largest are St. Thomas, St. Croix, and St. John. Since these islands became part of the United States, they have been administered as a territory, as Alaska and Hawaii were before they became states. They are a responsibility of the U.S. Department of the Interior.

The people of the Virgin Islands have been full citizens of the United States since 1927. The pattern of the government of a territory, however, formerly called for the appointment of the top officials, such as the governor and the judge of the Federal court. A change was made, beginning in 1970, and the Virgin Islanders now elect their own governor for a four-year term. District Court judges serving there were appointed to eight-year terms, rather than for life as on the mainland.

About four fifths of the Virgin Islanders are of black descent. When President Franklin D. Roosevelt began the practice of appointing black District judges, appointing one in 1937 and one in 1939, each was to serve in the Virgin Islands. This location to some extent disarmed white-supremacy Senators, and the Senate confirmed his appointments.

Although Judge William H. Hastie was the first black District judge, he had two other "firsts" afterwards, and it would be a pity to break up the story of his career. Let us put him aside until we come to the Circuit Court judges.

Herman Emmons Moore was the second black District Court judge to serve in the Virgin Islands, taking Judge Hastie's place after Hastie resigned. Moore was born in Jackson, Mississippi, in 1893. He attended college at Howard University, graduating in 1914, and earned his law degree there in 1917. Two years later, he earned a Master's degree in law at Boston University.

He practiced law in Chicago and was a working Democrat there for twenty-five years, for the last five of which he was assistant commissioner on the Illinois Commerce Commission. He was an official in Chicago's Urban League and in the NAACP. He was nominated as District Court judge of the Virgin Islands by President Roosevelt and appointed in 1939. Although his original term was eight years, he was reappointed and served until 1958, when he was sixty-five years old. After he went into retirement, he continued to make his home in the Virgin Islands.

Walter Arthur Gordon followed Judge Moore as District Court judge in the Virgin Islands. Although Gordon was born in Atlanta, in 1894, the greater part of his life was spent in Berkeley, California. He earned a Bachelor's degree at the University of California there in 1918 and a Doctor's degree in law in 1923. He was an assistant football coach at the university for almost twenty-five years, starting in 1919. At one time he was a Berkeley policeman. He had a private law practice from 1923 to 1944, and for a time was attorney for a large insurance company. He was also active on the boards and commissions of a number of California civic organizations.

President Eisenhower appointed him governor of the Virgin Islands in 1955. In 1958, again named by President Eisenhower, he was appointed District judge to succeed Judge Moore.

Almeric Leander Christian was the next judge in the Virgin Islands District Court, following Judge Gordon. Christian was born in the Virgin Islands, on the island of St. Croix, in 1919. After a year at the University of Puerto Rico, he attended Columbia University, graduating in 1941. Law school, also at Columbia, was interrupted by four years in the Army as a first lieutenant in World War II. He earned his law degree in 1947, and returned to the Virgin Islands to practice law. On the civic side, he served on the Board of Education of the Virgin Islands, and put time into assisting the Episcopal Church and the Boy Scouts.

In 1962, Christian was appointed U.S. Attorney for the Virgin Islands District, a position which he held until President Richard Nixon appointed him judge of the District Court.

BLACK JUDGES IN THE MAINLAND DISTRICT COURTS

In the 1960's, Presidents John F. Kennedy, Lyndon B. Johnson, and Richard M. Nixon felt free to appoint black District judges to positions on the U.S. mainland. The color barrier had been broken by the judges appointed to the Virgin Islands District. Presidents Roosevelt and Truman had started a trend, and President Eisenhower had continued it. It is true that President Truman had been made to pay for his insistence on civil rights by the loss of several usually Democratic Southern states in the 1948 election, but he had won without them.

In the 1960's, the intense nation-wide interest in the civil rights struggle had changed many opinions and attitudes. The appointment of black Federal judges, if very carefully made, had become good politics. The three Presidents in office in the 1960's were in a position to appoint black District Court judges in the Northeast, North Central, and Western regions, and make political gains by doing so. With the single exception of Almeric Christian's appointment to the Virgin Islands District, all their appointments were made in Illinois, Michigan, Pennsylvania, New York, California, and the District of Columbia— places where the black vote was strong, and where white liberals were ready to applaud the appointments. They were not likely to cost many votes. They were far more likely to earn substantial numbers of votes from liberals.

For the reasons just mentioned, the three Presidents in office in the 1960's made many more appointments of black judges than the three Presidents serving from 1937 to 1960. In President Kennedy's Administration, shortened by his death, he appointed four judges to District Courts and one Circuit Court judge. President Johnson, who was in office a little more than five years, appointed one Supreme Court justice, two Circuit Court judges, five District Court judges, one judge to the Court of Customs, and completed one of President Kennedy's District Court appointments, which was hung up by delays in Senate confirmation. In the first year and a half of President Nixon's Administration, he appointed two judges to mainland District Courts and one to the Virgin Islands District.

James Benton Parsons was the first District Court judge appointed by President Kennedy. Parsons was born in 1911 in Kansas City, Missouri. After graduation from Millikin University, he earned a Master's degree in political science, studying at the University of Wisconsin and the University of Chicago. After four years in the Navy during World War II, he came back to the University of Chicago to earn a second Master's degree in 1946 and a law degree in 1949.

For a short time, he taught law at the John Marshall Law School in Chicago. He was then appointed Assistant Corporation Counsel for the City of Chicago. Later he spent nine years in the office of the U.S. Attorney in Chicago, handling cases especially in three areas: juvenile delinquency and rehabilitation, Selective Service (the military draft), and civil rights.

Meanwhile, he served as a board member or chairman of the city or state management of such organizations as the Boy Scouts, the National Conference of Christians and Jews, the Urban League, the Leukemia Research Foundation, and the Chicago Community Music Foundation.

In 1960, he was elected judge of the Superior Court of Cook County. About ten months later, in August, 1961, Presi-

James Benton Parsons   **Wade H. McCree, Jr.**

dent Kennedy appointed him a Federal judge in the Northern District of Illinois, which centers on Chicago.

In recognition of his many services, the governor of Illinois and the mayor of Chicago joined to declare February 17, 1967, "Judge James B. Parsons Day."

Judge Wade Hampton McCree, Jr., was also appointed by President Kennedy in 1961, in his case to the Eastern District of Michigan, which centers on Detroit. Five years later, President Johnson moved him up to the Circuit Court in the same general location.

Judge Spottswood W. Robinson, III, received an appointment from President Kennedy in 1963 to the District Court in the District of Columbia, and a second appointment to the same court from President Johnson in 1964. In 1966, however, after Robinson had served only about two years in the District Court, President Johnson moved him up to the Circuit Court in the District of Columbia.

Let us put off the stories of both these men until we come to the Circuit Court.

A. Leon Higginbotham, born in 1927 in Trenton, New Jersey, was only thirty-six when President Kennedy made him a District Court judge in 1963. He was the youngest black Federal judge ever appointed.

When he attended college, he started to study engineering at Purdue University, but soon switched to Antioch College in Ohio and a liberal arts course. He earned a law degree at Yale in 1952. His first job was as an assistant district attorney in Philadelphia. He was appointed to the state's Human Rights Commission, and in 1959 was elected president of the Philadelphia chapter of the NAACP.

In 1963, President Kennedy appointed him a judge in the Eastern District of Pennsylvania, which centers on Philadelphia. That same year, the national Junior Chamber of Commerce named him as one of the ten outstanding young men in the entire country.

William Benson Bryant was born in Alabama in 1911. He went to Washington, D.C., to attend college, graduating from Howard University in 1932 and earning a law degree in 1936. In the Depression years of the 1930's, he worked for a New Deal agency, the Work Projects Administration (WPA), and later for the Office of War Information. He was in the Army from 1943 to 1947, coming out a lieutenant colonel. Later, between 1951 and 1954, he was an Assistant U.S. Attorney for the District of Columbia, followed by a dozen years of private law practice in Washington, up to 1965.

In 1965, President Johnson appointed him a District judge in the District of Columbia.

Constance Baker Motley is the first black woman ever to serve as a judge in the Federal courts. Up to 1970, she was still the only one.

Constance Baker was born in New Haven, Connecticut, in 1921, and went through high school there. She did not go at once to college because her family did not have the necessary money. Before long, however, arrangements were made, and she graduated from New York University in 1943. Three years later, she earned a law degree at Columbia University.

While still a law student, she did some work for the NAACP Legal Defense and Educational Fund. After she became a member of the bar, she went on a full-time basis, and took part in the court battles for civil rights. By 1963, she had been on the winning side in nine civil rights cases before the Supreme Court.

In a special election in 1963, Mrs. Motley was elected to the New York State Senate, the third woman member in its history, the only one at the time she served, and the first black woman ever to be a member. In 1965, the New York City Council elected her Borough President of Manhattan. She was the first woman, as well as the first black woman, to hold the post of Borough President in New York City.

In 1966, President Johnson made her a Federal judge in the Southern District of New York. Two years later, her old college, New York University, made her one of its trustees.

Aubrey E. Robinson, Jr., born in Madison, New Jersey, attended college and law school at Cornell University. From 1948 on, he practiced law in Washington, D.C., associated with some notable law firms there.

In 1950, Robinson, together with other lawyers, argued and won the famous case of *Henderson vs. Southern Railway* before the Interstate Commerce Commission. Its decision was that the plaintiff Henderson had been discriminated against in the dining car of a Southern Railway train, as he had alleged. The case immediately became a landmark in public

Constance Baker Motley   Aubrey E. Robinson, Jr.

accommodations policy, as well as the basis of a Supreme Court warning in 1952. It finally resulted in the outlawing of segregation and discrimination in interstate travel accommodations.

Robinson was also well known in Washington because of his civic activities. He was a member of the board of directors of many organizations, such as the Family Service Association of America, the Barney Neighborhood Settlement House, Washington Action for Youth, and the Eugene and Agnes E. Meyer Foundation.

In 1965, he was made a judge in the District of Columbia juvenile court. In 1966, President Johnson appointed him a judge in the District Court for the District of Columbia.

Damon J. Keith was born in Detroit. He graduated from West Virginia State College in 1943, spent three years in the Army during World War II, and earned a law degree at Howard University in 1949. Seven years after being admitted to the bar, he also earned a Master's degree in law at Wayne State University in Detroit.

Keith practiced law in Detroit up to the time he became a Federal judge. In the latter part of this period, he was senior partner in a well-known law firm. He also did a great deal of public-service and civic work. For nine years he was president of Detroit's Housing Commission. He was appointed co-chairman of the Michigan Civil Rights Commission. He was first vice president of the Detroit chapter of the NAACP and a vice president of the United Negro College Fund. This list of his many activities could be made much longer.

In 1967, he became a District judge in the Eastern Michigan District, appointed by President Johnson.

Joseph Cornelius Waddy was born in Virginia in 1911. He graduated from London University in Pennsylvania in 1935, and earned a law degree from Howard University in 1938. From 1939 to 1962 Waddy practiced law in Washington, D.C., except for Army service between 1944 and 1946. Beginning in 1962, he spent five years as a judge in the Domestic Relations Branch of the Municipal Court in the District of Columbia. In 1967, President Johnson appointed him as a District judge in the District of Columbia. He was chairman of the board of trustees of Washington Action for Youth, 1962–1964; and before that he was chairman of the Citizens Advisory Council to the D.C. Commissioners.

David W. Williams was born in Atlanta in 1910, but was taken to Southern California as a child. He graduated from the University of California at Los Angeles and earned a law degree at the University of Southern California. Eighteen years of private law practice followed. Then from 1956 to 1962 he served as a judge in the Municipal Court in Los Angeles. In 1963, he moved up to the Superior Court, and was soon in positions of great responsibility. During 1965, he was presiding judge of a group of twenty-four criminal courts, and in charge of the Los Angeles County Grand Jury. The Los Angeles County Board of Supervisors praised him as "an outstanding judge and skilled administrator," because he had seen to it that almost 4,000 cases arising from the Los Angeles riots of 1965 were handled promptly, vetoed any group trials, and insisted that each defendant get an individual trial. Between 1966 and 1968, he was presiding judge of an eight-judge district court in Santa Monica. Judge Williams also gained recognition for his work with civic organizations.

In 1969, President Nixon, who grew up close to Los Angeles, appointed David Williams to the Federal bench, as a District Court judge in the Southern California District.

Barrington Parker was born in Rosslyn, Virginia; but while he was still a young child, his family moved to Washington, D.C., where his father practiced law. Barrington Parker attended college at Lincoln University in Pennsylvania, got a Master's degree in economics at the University of Pennsylvania, and studied law at the University of Chicago. In 1947, he came into his father's office and joined him in private law practice, working primarily in business matters, contracts, wills, and the like. His father died in 1965, but a third generation of Parkers, Barrington Parker, Jr., kept the father-son relation going in the office until Barrington Parker, Sr., became a Federal judge.

President Nixon appointed him a District Court judge in the District of Columbia early in 1970.

Judge Parker is an officer or member of a long list of organizations, for example, a co-chairman of the local organization of the United Negro College Fund and a board member of the local chapter of the American Civil Liberties Union.

Damon J. Keith   Barrington Parker

You have now read about all but three of the black lawyers appointed to be judges in the U.S. District Courts between 1937 and 1970. The stories of these three were put off until we came to the Circuit Courts of Appeals, because each one, after serving as a District Court judge, was later appointed a judge in a Circuit Court. It is time now to move up to the U.S. Circuit Courts of Appeals. In the account of the black judges serving in the Circuit Courts which follows, you will be able to read the stories of these three men.

10

Judges
in Other
Federal Courts

INDEPENDENCE of mind and remarkable talent carried **William H. Hastie** to one of the highest judicial positions in the nation, a position he still held with distinction in 1970. In the course of his career, without dramatics or confrontations, he kept moving into areas which no other black lawyer had previously entered. Racial barriers fell behind him, and other black lawyers have been able to follow where he showed the way.

Hastie was born in Knoxville, Tennessee, but grew up in Washington, D.C. He graduated from Amherst College in 1925, and earned both his law degree and a Doctor's degree in juridical science at Harvard. As a young lawyer, he became assistant solicitor for the Department of the Interior in the Federal Government. Harold Ickes, who was a power in President Franklin Roosevelt's Cabinet and Secretary of the Interior from 1933 to 1946, had a chance to observe Hastie's work. Although Ickes was a very hard man to impress, he was impressed with Hastie's talent. He urged President Roosevelt to move him up to higher positions.

In 1937, President Roosevelt appointed him to an eight-year term as the District judge in the Virgin Islands District. He thus became the first black District Court judge. After only two years, however, he resigned in order to become dean of the law school at Howard University, a position which he held until 1946. After World War II had begun, Hastie was asked also to serve as civilian aide to Secretary of War Henry Stimson. His advice in respect to the complaints of black troops in the then-segregated armed forces proved extremely valuable to both Stimson and President Roosevelt. He was also asked to join the Caribbean Commission and accepted.

In 1946, President Truman appointed him governor of the Virgin Islands. Hastie thus became the first black governor there, and served until 1949. At that time, President Truman appointed him a judge in the Third Circuit Court of Appeals in Philadelphia. A few years later, he became chief judge. It is fair to say that the relation of a chief judge of a Circuit Court to an ordinary Circuit Court judge is much the same as the relation of the Chief Justice of the Supreme Court to an associate justice. Short of the Supreme Court, Judge Hastie's position is the highest judicial position in the country. He was the first black judge to reach a Circuit Court, and also the first to become chief judge of that court.

Wade Hampton McCree, Jr., was born in Des Moines in 1920. He graduated from Fisk University in 1941, and started to study law at Harvard. Although he received a law degree from Harvard in 1944, his legal training was interrupted by four years of Army service in World War II, partly in Europe. He came out a captain. After a short stay in Massachusetts, he moved to Detroit, and was admitted to the Michigan bar in 1948. Following a short period of private law practice, he was appointed a commissioner in Michigan's Workmen's Compensation Commission, and held the position from 1952 to 1954. He was then elected a Wayne County circuit judge and served until 1961, when President Kennedy appointed him a Federal District judge in the Eastern District of Michigan.

In 1966, President Johnson raised him from the District Court to the Circuit Court, appointing him as a judge in the Sixth Circuit. The Sixth Circuit includes Michigan, Ohio, Kentucky, and Tennessee; but Judge McCree's headquarters continued to be in Detroit.

For a long time, Judge McCree has been a prominent civic leader in Detroit, serving on many boards and committees. In 1970, he was chairman of the Board of Trustees of Fisk University, his old college, vice moderator of the Unitarian-Uni-

William H. Hastie   Spottswood W. Robinson, III

versalist Association, and a trustee of the National Conference of Christians and Jews.

Spottswood W. Robinson, III, was born in 1916 in Richmond, Virginia. He graduated from Virginia Union University, and earned his law degree at Howard University in 1939, winning high honors at both institutions. Then, with the exception of a few years when he had to be in Richmond, Robinson taught law at Howard. He was dean of the law school for several years beginning in 1960. Meanwhile, beginning about 1943, and again with some exceptions when he had to be in Washington, Robinson practiced law in Richmond. In the years 1948–1950, he was the Virginia representative of the NAACP Legal Defense Fund.

In the 1940's, Robinson, Oliver Hill, and M. Martin had fought important civil rights cases attacking the "separate but equal" doctrine which had stood as the legal support of segregation. These cases, together with those handled by Thurgood Marshall and other NAACP staff members, were part of a campaign to weaken and undermine this doctrine. It prepared the way for the historic Supreme Court decision of 1954, which declared "separate but equal" schools in violation of the Constitution.

In 1963, President John F. Kennedy appointed Spottswood Robinson a District judge in the District of Columbia. The appointment was not completed by Senate action when President Kennedy was assassinated. President Johnson named him again early in 1964, and this time the appointment was confirmed. Robinson served in the District Court for about two years. Then, in 1966, President Johnson made him a Circuit judge in the District of Columbia Circuit.

The black judge who occupied the highest position in the Federal courts in 1970 is **Thurgood Marshall.** Marshall was born in Baltimore in 1908. His father was a country club steward, and his mother taught in the Baltimore City school system. Thurgood Marshall graduated with honors from Lincoln University in Pennsylvania in 1930, and earned a law degree from Howard University with highest honors in 1933, although he had to earn his tuition by working as a grocery clerk, dining car waiter, and baker.

In 1966, Marshall became an assistant to the late Charles Hamilton Houston, special counsel to the NAACP. When Houston retired to private practice in 1938, Marshall took his place in the New York City headquarters of the NAACP.

Between 1938 and 1958, Marshall proved himself a most able constitutional lawyer. He argued thirty-two cases before the Supreme Court and won twenty-nine, including the tradition-shattering *Brown vs. the Board of Education of Topeka.* The verdict in this case was the historic Supreme Court decision of 1954 declaring segregated schools in violation of the Constitution. Other cases leading to pivotal civil rights decisions were: *Smith vs. Allwright,* establishing the right of registered black voters to vote in the Democratic primary election in Texas; *Morgan vs. Virginia,* declaring unconstitutional the state's segregation law as applied to interstate bus passengers; and *Shelly vs. Kraemer,* declaring state enforcement of restrictive housing covenants a denial of rights guaranteed by the Fourteenth Amendment. In all these cases, Marshall took the position that segregation in any form is unconstitutional, and that the Fourteenth Amendment was intended to prohibit any form of racial distinction imposed or supported by law.

In 1961, after well over twenty years of struggle in behalf of racial justice, Marshall was named by President John F. Kennedy to serve as a judge in the Circuit Court for the Second Circuit, which includes New York. For more than a year the Senate Judiciary Committee stalled off a Senate vote on the appointment, twice postponing committee hearings for long periods. Black people throughout the country believed—naturally—that Southern members of the committee were dealing unjustly with Marshall, the man who had won so many civil rights victories in the Federal courts. Then speeches on the Senate floor by New York Senators Jacob Javits and Kenneth Keating, praising Marshall and urging immediate Senate action on his appointment, pressured the committee into allowing the matter to come to a vote. The Senate confirmed him.

Three years later, in 1965, President Johnson appointed Marshall U.S. Solicitor General. This is the second highest position in the Department of Justice, outranked only by the Attorney General. Marshall resigned from the Circuit Court bench in order to accept the new appointment. He was the first black lawyer ever to become Solicitor General.

In 1967, President Johnson named Marshall an associate justice of the Supreme Court. In announcing the nomination, the President said, "I believe it is the right thing to do, the right time to do it, the right man in the right place." The appointment was confirmed, and Thurgood Marshall, at the age of fifty-nine, became the first black associate justice of the nation's highest court.

BLACK JUDGES IN THE U.S. SPECIAL COURTS

You have been reading about the sixteen black judges who were appointed, between 1937 and 1970, to serve in one or more of the three levels of the regular Federal courts.

As you know, the United States also operates several special Federal courts. One of these special courts is the U.S. Court of Customs. Its function is to settle disputes over the valuation and classification of imported goods which arise between the government and importers.

Thurgood Marshall (top, left) in the Supreme Court

Up to 1970, three black lawyers have been appointed to be judges in the Court of Customs. Their stories follow.

Irvin Charles Mollison was born in 1898 in Vicksburg, Mississippi. His father was a lawyer, educated at Oberlin College in Ohio. The elder Mollison had held office in Mississippi during the Reconstruction era, but he moved to Chicago shortly after his son was born, and built up a law practice there. Mollison's mother, too, had attended college, at Fisk University.

Young Mollison decided to become a lawyer, as his father had. He went to the University of Chicago, where his work in history and political science was brilliant enough to earn him a job as a student assistant to a professor. He was hired, however, when the professor was away from the campus. When the professor returned and found that his new assistant was black, he fired him. Mollison graduated from the University of Chicago in 1920, and earned his law degree there in 1923.

Before many years passed, Mollison became active in Chicago politics. Although he began as a Republican, he switched in 1936 to the Democrats and President Roosevelt, as so many people did that year. Mollison's work for the Democratic Party in Chicago brought him some notice, which led to his being put on the city's Library Board and the School Board. In 1945, President Harry S Truman named him to serve as a judge in the U.S. Court of Customs, the first black judge in that court. Mollison died in 1962 after seventeen years as a Federal judge.

Scovel Richardson was born in 1912 in Nashville, Tennessee, but later moved to Chicago. He took a Bachelor's degree and a Master's degree at the University of Illinois, and his law degree at Howard in 1937. Except for one year during World War II, when he was senior attorney for the Office of Price Administration in Washington, D.C., Richardson taught law from 1939 to 1953 at Lincoln University in Missouri. He was made dean of the law school in 1944. In 1953, he was appointed to the U.S. Board of Parole, and he was chairman of this board from 1954 to 1957.

In 1957, President Eisenhower named him to be a judge in the U.S. Court of Customs in New York City. In 1966, he became Presiding Judge of the Third Division of this court.

Judge Richardson is a trustee of Howard University, a trustee of the National Council on Crime and Delinquency, and a member of the Permanent Judicial Commission of the United Presbyterian Church, as well as an elder in his local church.

James Lopez Watson was born in New York City in 1922. His college education was interrupted by Army service in World War II. He was wounded in Italy, and received several decorations. On his return, he graduated from New York University in 1947, and earned his law degree at the Brooklyn Law School in 1951.

In 1951, Watson started to practice law and take part in New York politics. As a lawyer, he gained valuable experience by his practice before the Board of Immigration Appeals. In 1954, he was elected to the New York State Senate and served two terms. In 1963, he was elected a judge in the Civil Court of the City of New York, and served in that court and briefly in other New York courts up to 1966. In 1966, President Johnson named him as a judge in the U.S. Court of Customs in New York City. He soon became Presiding Judge of this court.

SUMMARY

Of the nineteen black Federal judges, four served at two levels in the courts, and were therefore each appointed twice. If you prefer to take Spottswood Robinson's double appointment to the District Court as two, there were twenty-four appointments in all between 1937 and 1970.

If you go over the appointments and discover that nineteen of the twenty-four were made by Democratic Presidents against only five made by Republican Presidents, the totals may seem very lopsided. Democratic Presidents, however, had much more time in which to act. Within our period, Democratic Presidents were in the White House for twenty-three years, against a little short of ten years for the Republicans.

No President has thus far asked a black lawyer to take the position of judge of a Federal court located in the Old South. The time for that step is yet to come.

Meanwhile, the Senate, taken as a whole, has shown no unwillingness to approve the appointments of black Federal judges. It is widely believed that some Southern members of the Senate Judiciary Committee used deliberate delaying tactics to postpone a Senate vote on Thurgood Marshall's appointment to the Circuit Court in the Second Circuit. When the whole Senate did finally vote, however, he was promptly approved.

SUMMARY: BLACK FEDERAL JUDGES, 1937–1970

	Courts	Appointee	By President	Date	Term
1.	**U.S. Supreme Court**	Thurgood Marshall	Lyndon B. Johnson	1967	Life
2.	**U.S. Circuit Court**				
	Third Circuit (Chief Judge)	William H. Hastie	Harry S Truman	1949	Life
	Second Circuit	Thurgood Marshall	John F. Kennedy	1961	Life
	Sixth Circuit	Wade H. McCree, Jr.	Lyndon B. Johnson	1966	Life
	District of Columbia	Spottswood Robinson, III	Lyndon B. Johnson	1966	Life
3.	**U.S. District Court**				
	Virgin Islands	William H. Hastie	Franklin Roosevelt	1937	8 years
	Virgin Islands	Herman E. Moore	Franklin Roosevelt	1939	8 years
	Virgin Islands	Walter Gordon	Dwight D. Eisenhower	1958	8 years
	Northern Illinois	James B. Parsons	John F. Kennedy	1961	Life
	Eastern Michigan	Wade H. McCree, Jr.	John F. Kennedy	1961	Life
	District of Columbia	Spottswood Robinson, III	John F. Kennedy	1963	
			Lyndon B. Johnson	1964	Life
	Eastern Pennsylvania	A. Leon Higginbotham	John F. Kennedy	1963	Life
	District of Columbia	William B. Bryant	Lyndon B. Johnson	1965	Life
	Southern New York	Constance Baker Motley	Lyndon B. Johnson	1966	Life
	District of Columbia	Aubrey E. Robinson, Jr.	Lyndon B. Johnson	1966	Life
	District of Columbia	Joseph C. Waddy	Lyndon B. Johnson	1967	Life
	Eastern Michigan	Damon J. Keith	Lyndon B. Johnson	1967	Life
	Southern California	David W. Williams	Richard M. Nixon	1969	Life
	Virgin Islands	Almeric L. Christian	Richard M. Nixon	1969	8 years
	District of Columbia	Barrington Parker	Richard M. Nixon	1970	Life
4.	**U.S. Special Courts**				
	Court of Customs	Irvin C. Mollison	Harry S Truman	1945	Life
	Court of Customs	Scovel Richardson	Dwight D. Eisenhower	1957	Life
	Court of Customs	James L. Watson	Lyndon B. Johnson	1966	Life

11

Judges in Northeastern Courts

EACH one of the fifty states has its own system of courts. These courts often deal with large numbers and a great variety of cases. In the main, however, they have three basic functions: to enforce the law; to settle disputes between individual people, companies, or organizations, or any combination of these; and to protect the rights guaranteed to a person by the state and Federal constitutions.

ORGANIZATION OF THE COURTS

Courts making up a state system are arranged in steps similar to those you read about in the Federal system of courts, except that there are usually more steps.

At the very bottom, a small town or rural community usually has a justice of the peace. A city usually has one or more police courts or magistrate courts, as they are sometimes called. It may also have a municipal court, which can take on a wider variety of cases than a police court. None of these courts ever uses a jury. A judge in any of these courts relies more on common sense than on knowledge of the law, and he may not be a lawyer at all. His authority is limited. He can impose small fines, or very short jail sentences, but never large ones. He can handle disputes which involve money only if the total amount is not over some fixed limit, such as $100. Cases can be appealed to a regular trial court.

Some cities, in the hope of handling certain classes of cases more intelligently and more humanely, have set up special courts. Only two of these need to be mentioned here: a juvenile court, to deal with children below a certain age who are in trouble, and a domestic relations court, to deal with family and marital problems, including legal separation of husband and wife, and sometimes divorce. No juries are used. Judges are expected to have special legal training and usually some sociological or psychological study to qualify them to deal wisely with the problems these special courts face. Judges in these special courts are often appointed, not elected.

Above the level of the courts already spoken of, there are state courts at three levels. The courts at the lowest of these three levels are where the great majority of cases first come to trial before a jury. In about a third of the states, these are county courts, each located in the courthouse in the county seat. Other states are divided into judicial districts, or circuits. Each district usually takes in more than one county, perhaps as many as three or four. In some places, the court is called a district court, because it is the trial court for a judicial district. In other places, it may be called a circuit court because it normally holds a session at regular intervals in each of the counties included in the district. The court remains the same, regardless of which name is given to it. Either a county court or a district court may sometimes be called a court of common pleas. A judge at this level presides over a trial, rules on questions of law or of procedure. The jury decides questions of fact. A judge in a trial court should be an experienced and well-trained lawyer.

On the step above these trial courts a majority of the states have a set of appeals courts (or *appellate courts*) midway between the trial courts and the state supreme court. Some states jump straight from the trial courts to the state supreme court, with no intervening step.

Cases tried in the appellate courts have all been brought up by appeal from lower courts, and are not being tried for the first time. No juries are used. A judge or a panel of judges makes all decisions. The state appellate courts are similar in function and position to the U.S. Circuit Courts of Appeals in the Federal court system.

One step above the appellate courts, on the top step, is a single state supreme court. With few exceptions, it tries only cases appealed from lower courts. No juries are used. A panel of judges makes all decisions. A decision of the state supreme court is final in almost all cases. The only exception is a case which raises a "Federal question." If the decision depends upon the precise meaning of some part of the U.S. Constitution, or of a Federal law or treaty, the case raises a Federal question, and may be appealed to the U.S. Supreme Court.

In some states, the names given to the courts at the three top levels are not the same as the names used for them in other states. In New York State, for example, several levels have peculiar and misleading names. The names, however, do not change the way these courts operate; and from one state to another, the pattern of the organization of the courts is not very different.

SELECTION OF JUDGES

Different states have different ways of choosing judges and putting them in office. In some states a judge is usually appointed to serve his first term, but after the first term, which is usually short, he must win any additional terms by election. In other states, practically all judges at all levels are elected. In one of these states, about the only judges who are appointed are those appointed to serve out the unexpired remainder of the term of an elected judge who has died or retired. In some states, judges of the supreme courts and sometimes also of the appellate courts must be named by the state's governor and confirmed by the State Senate, a method of appointment similar to that of Federal judges.

In courts at the lowest level of a state system, a judge's term of office is usually short, often only two years and almost never more than six. In courts at the middle level, terms of office are normally a little longer, usually six or eight years. For supreme court judges and, in some states, appellate judges, terms of office as long as fourteen years are common.

Up to retirement age, there is no limit to the number of terms a judge can serve, provided that he can get himself re-elected or reappointed to each new term.

A JUDGE'S POSITION IN THE COMMUNITY

Eminent and scholarly black men and women have served, and are serving, as judges at all levels of the state courts in many states.

In most fields of activity, a person's stature is likely to be pretty much determined by the rank he holds. In a university, a professor is more important and more respected than an instructor. An Army colonel easily outweighs a corporal.

Rank, however, is neither a reliable nor a true measuring stick for judges. Some black judges who serve in courts near the bottom of state systems of courts are known throughout their states or even throughout the nation, and are paid respect virtually equal to that given to a black Congressman.

The reputation which they enjoy does not depend upon the rank of the courts in which they serve. It comes from their high education, their scholarly attainments, their leadership in their churches and in organizations for social and cultural betterment, for civil rights and human relations. They are notable as speakers on important occasions and as unofficial advisers to governors of states and to Presidents of the United States. Their true measure is not the job but the man; and on this basis many black judges stand very tall.

In modern times, the first states to have numbers of Negro judges serving in their courts were states of the Northeast. New York probably took the lead in this, but Pennsylvania was a very close second, if behind New York at all.

New York

Let us start with New York. Before we go any farther, however, it is only fair to tell you a little more about the peculiar names used for some of the courts in New York. If you get mixed up about any of the New York courts later, turn back here and find out what it is equivalent to in an ordinary state court system.

In the first place, the New York State Supreme Court is not the state's highest court, as you would expect a supreme court to be. Mostly, but not entirely, it is equivalent to the district courts or circuit courts in most state systems. The Supreme Court has eleven districts, which cover the state. The majority of civil and criminal cases first come to trial in the Supreme Court, although every county has a county court, and there are other lower courts which handle some such cases for their first trial.

The New York State Supreme Court also has four appellate divisions. These are equivalent to the appellate courts in many states. They try cases appealed from the rest of the Supreme Court and from other lower courts. Justices in these appellate courts are selected by the governor from among the Supreme Court judges, each to serve five years in the appellate court. Supreme Court judges and also the judges in the Court of Appeals (which comes next) are practically always elected, and serve for terms of fourteen years.

The Court of Appeals is the highest court in New York State. There is only one. It has a chief judge and six associate judges. It tries only cases brought up from lower courts by appeal. Its decision is final, except in rare instances when a case is taken on to the U.S. Supreme Court. As you can see, this is the court which would be called the supreme court in most states.

In the state, and especially in New York City, there are a multitude of overlapping lower courts. For example, in New York City there are at least sixteen different lower courts in which a suit might have its first trial. This does not mean different buildings. It means separate and distinct courts, each with its own powers and jurisdiction. It would take you weeks to learn all their names and all the small differences between them.

No story of the Negro judges in the state of New York would be complete without a few words about three who finished their service in the courts before 1970: **Francis Ellis Rivers, Hubert Delaney,** and **Jane M. Bolin.**

Francis E. Rivers graduated from Yale with a record which gave him membership in the national honors fraternity Phi Beta Kappa, and earned his law degree at Columbia. From 1938 to 1943, Rivers was Assistant District Attorney in New

York County. This was at the time when Thomas E. Dewey, later governor of New York and a candidate for President, was District Attorney. In 1944, Rivers was elected a justice of the county court of New York County. In 1953, he was reelected to a ten-year term, and retired in 1963. The fact that the Republican, Democratic, and Liberal parties all endorsed him for reelection in 1953 is an indication of the high regard in which he was held by many elements of the people of the city.

After Rivers' retirement from his duties as a judge, he has continued to be active in civic affairs and as a Hearing Examiner of the Waterfront Commission. He is president of the board of directors of the NAACP Legal Defense and Education Fund, and serves on the boards of Freedom House, New York Association for the Blind, Brotherhood in Action, and other organizations. His activities and influence have touched virtually every segment of New York City's civil and cultural life.

Hubert Delaney was the son of a noted North Carolina church leader who became an Episcopal suffragan bishop in that state. Hubert Delaney chose not to follow in his father's footsteps and become a minister. He chose law and, like his brothers and sisters, marked out a career for himself in public service. He worked his way through City College in New York, and studied law at New York University.

Delaney's first political appointment came from New York City's famous reform mayor, Fiorello La Guardia, who made him a tax commissioner, and Delaney proved himself an honest commissioner, a rare thing in those days. In 1942, Mayor La Guardia gave him a new appointment, making him a judge in the Court of Domestic Relations. He held this position until 1956. At that time, Democratic Mayor Robert Wagner, busy opening up jobs for worthy Democrats, dropped him to make a place for Edward Dudley.

In 1939, three years before the appointment of Hubert Delaney, Mayor La Guardia had appointed another black judge to the Court of Domestic Relations in New York City. Mayor La Guardia was pioneering when he made that appointment, and with it he set an entirely new precedent—a milestone for black women. The judge whom he appointed was Jane M. Bolin, the first Negro woman ever made a judge of a regularly established court in the United States. He did it twenty-seven years before President Lyndon B. Johnson appointed Constance Baker Motley a District judge in the Southern District of New York, the first black woman ever made a Federal judge.

Jane M. Bolin had graduated from Vassar College, and had earned her law degree at Yale. She had engaged in private law practice in New York City from 1931 almost up to the time she was made a judge in 1939. Judge Bolin was also active in civic and educational affairs. She served on the boards of the NAACP, the Greater New York Urban League, Wiltwych School for Boys, the New Lincoln School, the Child Welfare League, Citizens Committee for Children, United Neighborhood Houses, and National Scholarship Service and Fund for Negro Students.

By 1950, at least eight black judges were serving in courts in New York City. Three of them you have just been reading about. Three others had begun as municipal judges as early as 1931: Myles Paige, Charles A. Toney (now dead), and James S. Watson.

The black judge who reached the highest position in New York's state courts in the 1960's was—and is—**Harold A. Stevens.** Harold Stevens came from South Carolina. His grandfather had graduated from the University of South Carolina during the Reconstruction era, and his mother had been a teacher in the public schools there. Stevens went through Benedict College and earned his law degree at Boston College. He practiced law for two years in Boston and for twelve years in New York City.

When Stevens entered politics in New York City, his reputation as an able, rising lawyer and his religion brought him both black and Catholic support. Two terms in the New York State Legislature, 1947–1950, broadened his interest in the judicial process. In 1950, he was elected a judge in the Court of General Sessions. Six years later, he was elected a judge in the State Supreme Court. The Supreme Court has four Appellate Divisions. These are midway between the regular Supreme Court and the state's highest court, the Court of Appeals. The governor staffs these Appellate Divisions by appointing elected Supreme Court judges as associate justices to serve for five years or as presiding justices to serve for the full term of fourteen years. Judge Harold Stevens was first appointed an associate justice, and in 1969 appointed Presiding Justice of the

First Appellate Division. Next to the seven judges in the Court of Appeals, Judge Stevens holds the highest position in the courts of the state.

Stevens' church and community activities in behalf of brotherhood have merited him board memberships and chairmanships in numerous cultural and charitable organizations, honorary degrees from nine universities, and a Papal award.

In 1969 and 1970, there were a number of other black Supreme Court judges. In the First Judicial District, which includes two boroughs of New York City, Manhattan and the Bronx, were **Amos Bowman, Thomas Dickens, Jawn Sandifer, Darwin Telesford, Andrew Tyler,** and **Ivan Warner,** the last-named serving in the Bronx.

In the Second Judicial District, which also includes two boroughs of New York City, Brooklyn and Richmond (Staten

Harold A. Stevens   **Raymond Pace Alexander**

Island), were **Thomas R. Jones, Franklin W. Norton,** and **Oliver D. Williams.**

In addition, **Edward Dudley,** who had spent five years beginning in 1949 as this nation's first black ambassador to Liberia, had become a Supreme Court judge in the 1960's but had the assignment of presiding over the Criminal Court as administrative judge. Also, **Thomas Weaver** and **James Yeargin** were both Supreme Court judges but assigned to serve with the Criminal Court of New York City.

A number of black judges were serving at the municipal level in the Greater New York area. **Henry Bramwell, George Fleary, James H. Shaw, Samuel Welcome,** and **Albert P. Williams** were in the Civil Court in Brooklyn. **Herbert B. Evans** and **Clifford A. Scott** were in Manhattan, and **Kenneth N. Browne** was in Queens. Out on Long Island, **Marquette Floyd** was a judge in Suffolk County, which is not a part of New York City proper but is definitely a part of the Greater New York City area.

Pennsylvania

The political power of the large black populations of Philadelphia and Pittsburgh developed in the 1940's to a point which practically guaranteed the appointment of judges within the next few years. The first actual appointment was made in Pittsburgh when **Homer Brown** was named a judge in the Allegheny Court of Common Pleas. Brown was still serving in 1970.

Philadelphia soon followed with a series of black municipal and superior court judges.

Raymond Pace Alexander, born in Philadelphia, graduated from the University of Pennsylvania and earned his law degree at Harvard. His law school record was so distinguished that he was recommended to a white law firm in Philadelphia, but this firm turned him down because he was black. He set up his own law business with his lawyer-wife and others as partners, and soon established himself as one of Philadelphia's most brilliant lawyers.

One of Raymond Alexander's most notable civil rights cases was concerned with Girard College in Philadelphia. A wealthy man had left his fortune to establish this college, and his will had stipulated that only white students were to be admitted.

Raymond Alexander and an associate, **William T. Coleman, Jr.,** brought suit to break the will, so that black students might be admitted. The city of Philadelphia was a trustee of the college, and there were other public trustees. Alexander argued that the city could not rightfully take part in maintaining a segregated institution. After a long and complex legal struggle, the United States Supreme Court ruled that the college must be desegregated.

Raymond Alexander was a member of the Philadelphia City Council for many years. In 1958, he was appointed a municipal judge.

Theodore Spaulding of the famous Spaulding clan of North Carolina was a judge of the superior court in the Philadelphia area in 1970.

In 1960, **Juanita Kidd Stout** scored a "first" similar to, but not the same as, Jane M. Bolin's in 1939. Juanita Kidd Stout came from Oklahoma. She had earned a Bachelor's and Master's degree in law at Indiana University. For a time thereafter she had taught law, at Florida A. & M. University and at Texas Southern University. Later, while she was working for U.S. Circuit Court Judge William Hastie in Philadelphia, she received a short appointment as judge of the county court in Philadelphia. In 1960, she was elected to a ten-year term as judge in the same court. This made her the first black woman elected to be a judge anywhere in the United States. (Jane M. Bolin, as you may remember, had been appointed, not elected, to her position.) Juanita Kidd Stout's achievement led magazines and newspapers such as *Time,* the *Wall Street Journal, Life,* the *Reader's Digest,* and *Sepia* to publish feature articles about her.

Several other black judges were serving in Pennsylvania about 1970. **Herbert R. Cain, Jr.,** was judge of the court of common pleas, and **Paul Dandridge** was serving in the municipal court, both in the Philadelphia area. **Henry Smith** and **Warren Watson** were also judges in the court of common pleas.

Maryland

In Maryland, as in New York State, the Court of Appeals is the state's highest court, and the Supreme Court is not supreme. Three black judges were serving in the Supreme Court of Baltimore City about 1970: **Harry Cole, Joseph Harward,** and **Robert Watts.**

John Hargrove was a municipal court judge in Baltimore.

James Taylor was a judge in the county court of Prince George's County, the Maryland county which borders two sides of the District of Columbia.

Connecticut

Connecticut has a number of medium-sized industrial cities —Hartford, Bridgeport, New Haven, and, although smaller, Waterbury and Stamford. None of the state's three black judges serving in 1970, however, was connected with the three largest of the cities just mentioned. **Robert L. Levister** was a circuit court judge in Stamford. **Robert D. Glass** was a juvenile court judge in the Waterbury area. **Arthur G. Williams** was a judge in the court of common pleas in Madison, a small city on the shore of Long Island Sound with about 5,000 people.

12

Judges in Other State Courts

THE rise of black judges in other regions of the country was not very different from what you have already seen in the Northeast. In the North Central region, as in the Northeast, some reached the higher courts in their states. In the South, although a number of black judges came into office, none reached the higher courts by 1970.

The only surprising feature was the late coming of black judges in California. Cities such as Los Angeles had been electing blacks to the state legislature as early as the 1930's, but it was many years before the first judge appeared in a California court.

Augustus Hawkins, for example, was first elected to the California legislature in 1934, and was reelected until 1962, when he was elected to the U.S. House of Representatives. While he was in the state legislature, he noted that the state had not one black judge. There was evidently some sort of barrier which kept black lawyers from becoming judges in California.

He went to work to remove that barrier. It took him several years. Finally he succeeded, and judges of his race began to appear in the courts. In the 1960's, their number increased, but because of the late start in California, there were fewer of them than in New York, Pennsylvania, Ohio, or Illinois.

IN NORTH CENTRAL COURTS

Illinois

Many years ago, two of the black judges in Illinois became nationally known, **Archibald Carey** and **Mrs. Edith Spurlock Sampson.**

Archibald Carey was pastor of a Methodist Episcopal church in Chicago from 1930 to 1949. During this time, he kept up other interests, including the study of law. After he earned a law degree at the John Marshall School of Law in Chicago, he became very active in politics. As one result of this activity, he was an elected alderman for eight years in Chicago's city government.

In 1953, President Eisenhower appointed him an alternate U.S. delegate to the United Nations, and later made him vice chairman of the President's Committee on Defense Contracts Compliance, the forerunner of the agencies later set up to advance the Federal policy of equal employment opportunity. After his Federal service, he was appointed as a judge in the Cook County circuit court in Chicago.

Mrs. Edith Sampson, who came from Pittsburgh, earned her first law degree at the John Marshall Law School and a Master's degree in law at Loyola University, both in Chicago. Along with her private law practice, she also served as a referee in the Cook County juvenile court. In 1950, President Truman made her an alternate delegate to the United Nations, the first black woman ever given such a post, and she served two terms, until 1953. Later, in 1962, she was elected an associate judge in Chicago's municipal court, and in 1966, she was elected judge of the Cook County circuit court.

Three other black judges in the Cook County circuit court were **James Crosson, Richard Harewood,** and **George N. Leighton. Mark E. Jones** and **William S. White** were judges in the state circuit court, and **Glenn T. Johnson** and **Sidney Jones** were associate judges there.

Michigan

Nearly all the black judges serving in Michigan in 1970 were on the benches of courts within the city of Detroit or in the Detroit metropolitan area. The single exception was **Judge John T. Letts** in the circuit court in Grand Rapids.

Five black judges were serving in the recorder's court in Detroit: **George W. Crockett, Jr., Elvin Davenport, Robert L. Evans, William C. Hague,** and **Henry Heading.** Judge Crockett made headlines across the country in 1969 when he released some black youths charged with firing back at police who had burst into a Detroit church shooting, when they were raiding it without having taken the preliminary steps required by law.

Julian P. Rodgers was a judge in the Wayne County court of common pleas. **Edward F. Bell** and **Charles S. Farmer** were Wayne County circuit court judges. **Ollie Bivens** was a judge in the district court in Flint, a city in the Detroit metropolitan area.

At one time, **Otis Smith** reached the State Supreme Court. Also in the past, Wade Hampton McCree was a Wayne County circuit court judge, before he was made a Federal judge in 1961.

Ohio

The state's highest court is the Supreme Court of Ohio. It has seven justices. Late in 1968, **Robert Duncan** was appointed by Governor James Rhodes to be one of these seven justices, and he began his service in January, 1969. Justice Duncan was the first of his race to reach the Supreme Court bench in Ohio.

Cleveland has had black judges in its courts since the early 1940's, though none with a rank as high as Robert Duncan's. The first one to be elected to the state court of appeals was **Charles White.** He has served for many years, and he has been active in civic and cultural affairs.

It was in 1942 that **Perry B. Jackson** first became a Cleveland judge. Jackson graduated from Western Reserve University and also studied law there. He then had various legal jobs, and at different times was elected to the Ohio Legislature and the city council in Cleveland. In 1942, Jackson was appointed a Cleveland municipal judge, and elected for additional terms lasting up to 1960. He was then elected judge in the division of domestic relations of the court of common pleas. In 1964,

Robert Duncan   Perry B. Jackson

he was appointed judge in the court of common pleas, and elected to a new term in 1966.

In the late 1960's, he was a director on the boards of at least twenty civic, welfare, and cultural organizations, and held national office in the Elks and Masons. He had received honorary degrees from a college and a university in Cleveland and one from Monrovia College in Liberia.

Cincinnati, more conservative than Cleveland, did not get its first black judge until 1965. The man was **William N. Lovelace.** He had graduated from Knoxville College in Tennessee, and had earned a law degree at Chase College of Law in Cincinnati. After a period of YMCA work, he became probation officer for the county court, then prosecutor. He was the first lawyer of his race to serve on the grievance committee of the Cincinnati Bar Association.

In January, 1965, he was appointed a municipal judge. In the following November, when he ran for a new term, the number of votes he received was a remarkable tribute to him. He got more than the winning candidate for mayor did, 66,262 for him compared to 66,192 for the new mayor.

William A. McClain   William Lovelace and His Wife

Other black judges were beginning to hold office about this time. **George W. White** became a judge in the court of common pleas in the Cleveland area. Four judges, **Lloyd W. Brown, Lillian W. Burke** (the first black woman to be a judge in Ohio), **Fred G. Coleman,** and **Theodore W. Williams,** were all serving in Cleveland's municipal court. Also **Augustus Parker,** a city councilman for many years, was appointed a chief judge of Cleveland's municipal court. He died in office.

There were black judges in the municipal courts of several other cities: **Joseph Rhoulac** in Akron, **Arthur Fisher** in Dayton, and **Robert V. Franklin** in Toledo.

Two years before Cincinnati got its first black judge, a black lawyer, **William A. McClain,** was promoted to the important position of City Solicitor. A city solicitor is the chief law officer in a city government. He has charge of all lawsuits or other law cases in which the city is a party, and he gives legal advice to other city officials. In a city as big as Cincinnati, the post commands great respect.

William McClain graduated from Wittenberg University in Ohio, and earned a law degree at the University of Michigan. He started as Assistant City Solicitor in Cincinnati as early as

1942, and after his second promotion became City Solicitor in 1963. McClain is known as a specialist in the legal aspects of city government and has written scholarly articles on various problems of modern cities.

Missouri, Indiana, Iowa, and Colorado

In Missouri, St. Louis had two black judges, **Bruce R. Watkins** in the circuit court and **Frank Bledsoe.** A few miles northwest of St. Louis, in the all-black town of Kinloch, **Robert Smith** was municipal judge.

In Jackson County, the county in which Kansas City is located, a new circuit court judge, **Lewis H. Clymer,** was appointed in February, 1970. He was the first black lawyer to serve as a judge in that court. Judge Clymer attended college and earned his law degree at Howard University. During World War II, he was a minorities specialist with the War Manpower Commission. In 1960, he was appointed a municipal judge in Kansas City, and elected thereafter, winning a new four-year term in 1967, which was not completed when he was made a circuit court judge. The National Urban League recently honored him with a twenty-five-year pin.

In Indiana, two black judges were on the bench of the superior court in Indianapolis: **Wilbur Grant** and **Rufus C. Kuykendall.** Each had more than ten years' experience as a judge by 1970.

Iowa, which had only one black member in its state legislature in 1970, had two black judges. **Luther Glanton** was a municipal court judge in Des Moines, and **William Parker** served in the same position in Waterloo.

Colorado had only one black judge. **James Flannigan** was a city and county judge in Denver.

IN WESTERN COURTS

Black political power in California is greater and more effective than in any other Western state. There was a time, however, when there were no black police on the highway patrol, no black judges in the courts, and no blacks in some other state jobs. An unmentioned barrier kept black people from being seriously considered for any of these positions. This exclusion disturbed Augustus Hawkins during the many years he served in the California Assembly, before he became a notable Congressman. As his power in the Assembly grew, he kept increasing pressure to open all these fields to black people, and especially to open the courts to black judges. After years of constant effort, he succeeded. By 1970, a gratifying number of black judges were serving in California courts, especially in the southern half of the state.

Three black municipal judges were serving in Los Angeles: **Edwin L. Jefferson, Xenophan Lang,** and **Mrs. Vaino Spencer.**

When Mrs. Vaino Spencer was appointed in 1961, she became the first black woman judge not only in California but in all the West. She had graduated, with highest honors, from Los Angeles City College, and earned her law degree at Southwestern School of Law. Because of her civil rights activities and her political and legal career, she has fully deserved the many awards and tributes she has received from organizations and newspapers.

Sherman W. Smith   Mrs. Elreta Alexander

Four black judges were serving as judges of the superior court in the Los Angeles area in 1970: **Earl C. Broady, Thomas L. Griffith, Jr., Bernard Jefferson,** and **Sherman W. Smith.** Sherman W. Smith was part of a younger group which campaigned hard for John F. Kennedy in 1960 and was active in Democratic politics. Smith graduated from West Virginia State College and earned a law degree with honors from Howard University in 1948. After fourteen years of private law practice in Southern California, he gave it up in 1963 to accept an appointment as a municipal judge in Los Angeles. Three years later, in 1966, he was appointed to serve in the superior court. In 1970 he was presiding judge over the Adult Criminal Court.

Before becoming a judge, Smith had also been active in business and civic affairs. He had been the builder and owner of a motel, a director of a savings and loan association, and one of the founders of the San Diego branch of the Urban League and of Men of Tomorrow, a state-wide organization of the black leaders in California communities.

Also in Southern California, but not in Los Angeles, **Albert Matthews** and **William Ross** were municipal court judges in Compton, and **Earl B. Gilliam** was a municipal judge in San Diego.

In the San Francisco Bay area, **Joseph Kennedy** and **Raymond J. Reynolds** were municipal court judges in San Francisco, **Alan Broussard** a municipal court judge in Alameda, and **Lionel Wilson** a judge of the superior court in Oakland.

In 1970, the state of Washington had four black judges, all serving in Seattle. Three were at the superior court level: **Charles M. Stokes, Charles L. Smith,** and **Jerome Farris.** The fourth, **Charles V. Johnson,** was a judge in the Traffic Court.

In Nevada, **Robert E. Mullen** was a judge in the municipal court in Las Vegas.

IN SOUTHERN STATE COURTS

Only three Southern states, North Carolina, South Carolina, and Tennessee, had black judges serving in any of their courts in 1970.

North Carolina had two, both appointed near the end of the 1960's. The first was a woman, **Mrs. Elreta Alexander,** a native

North Carolinian who had studied law at Columbia University. She was appointed in 1968 as a district court judge in the Guilford County–Greensboro District. In the following year, 1969, she was elected to a full term in the same court.

The second was **Clifton Johnson.** Johnson was born in North Carolina and had earned his law degree at North Carolina College at Durham. In 1969, he was appointed a district court judge in the Mecklenburg County–Charlotte District.

Before South Carolina elected three black legislators in 1970, a black judge was already on the bench. **Richard Fields** was a district court judge in Charleston.

In Tennessee, **Caulwell Biggers** was a county court judge.

IN DISTRICT OF COLUMBIA COURTS

Franklin D. Roosevelt, who was the first President to appoint a black Federal judge to serve in the U.S. District Court in the Virgin Islands, was also the first to appoint a Negro judge to serve in the municipal court in the District of Columbia.

The man whom President Roosevelt chose as the first black appointee for the post was **Armond Scott.** Scott was born in Wilmington, North Carolina, and made his home there until the Wilmington Race Riot of 1898. In the course of that riot, he was chased by howling white mobs, and only the unexpected help of a white conductor on a train allowed him to escape with his life. Scott was active in Washington, D.C., throughout those bleak years from 1900 to 1933, when blacks appeared to be making no progress. President Roosevelt's New Deal began to change things in 1933. In 1935, the President named him to a four-year term as a municipal judge in the District of Columbia, and reappointed him in 1939 and 1943, giving him three consecutive terms.

The next three Presidents kept up the custom President Roosevelt had established by appointing Scott. President Truman appointed two black judges to the municipal bench, **Andrew Howard** and **J. Emory Smith.** The term had been increased from four years to ten years. In 1956, President Eisenhower appointed **Austin Ficklin,** also for a ten-year term.

President Kennedy made three such appointments: one in 1961 to Andrew Howard for a second term, and two in 1962.

By 1962, the law governing these appointments had been changed. Thereafter, Senate approval was needed to complete the appointment. One appointment, made in this way, went to **Joseph Waddy,** later made a judge in the U.S. District Court. President Kennedy's other 1962 appointment went to **Marjorie M. Lawson,** the first black woman to be nominated to this position and approved. Marjorie Lawson graduated from the University of Michigan, studied law at the Terrell Law School in Washington, and earned a second law degree at Columbia University. She was a member of her husband's law firm. During the Truman Administration she was a member of the Committee on Fair Employment Practices. In 1958, she became race-relations adviser to John F. Kennedy, then still a Senator, and in 1960 was director of civil rights during his campaign for the presidency. In 1962, President Kennedy not only made her a member of the Committee on Equal Employment Opportunity but also appointed her a judge of the municipal court in the District of Columbia.

Aubrey E. Robinson, Jr., whom President Johnson made a U.S. District Court judge in 1966, had started a term as a juvenile court judge in the District of Columbia in 1965, but gave it up to take on the new assignment.

A FINAL WORD ON BLACK STATE JUDGES

Now you have had the stories of the black judges serving in state courts about 1970.

You probably noticed that the largest number of black judges were to be found in the large industrial cities of the Northeast, North Central, and Western regions, the same cities which had the voting power to elect black Congressmen and members of state legislatures. The presence of black judges in the courts located in these cities is the result, direct or indirect, of that black voting power.

When a black judge is elected, he is usually, although not always, elected by the black vote concentrated within his judicial district. This is clearly the direct result of black voting power.

When a black judge is appointed, rather than elected, the

influence of black voting power is not so easy to see, but it is there. Suppose that one of the two major parties has just scored a victory in an election in a large city. Suppose, too, that black wards in the city provided much of its majority. The winning candidates cannot forget their friends the minute they get into office. They must do something promptly for the political leaders who got out the vote for them. They owe a political debt to these leaders.

One way a political party pays off a debt is to pass out a few appointments. If these black leaders would like to see a certain black lawyer made a judge, the party can see to it that he is appointed.

If the black lawyer whom these leaders select is already well known and highly regarded, his appointment as a judge reflects credit on the party and costs it nothing. If he is not yet well known, his appointment is still worthwhile because it helps to ensure continuing black support in future elections.

The pattern just described does not always hold good. Sometimes voting power is not the decisive factor. For example, Newark in New Jersey, Gary in Indiana, and Wichita in Kansas had enough black voters to elect black mayors, but none of the three cities had a black judge.

On the other hand, some places with comparatively small black populations did have black judges. For example, in the 1960 census, the state of Connecticut had only about 110,000 black people, including children too young to vote, out of a total population of about two and a half million. It is hard to believe that the black vote came near being decisive in any Connecticut city, yet Connecticut had three black judges. It is worth noting that the black members of Connecticut's legislature were also exceptions to the common pattern. A number of them were elected in districts with large white majorities.

THE
EXECUTIVE
BRANCH

INTRODUCTION

A GOVERNMENT, large or small, has to have an executive branch. In the national government, the chief executive is the President. In a state, the chief executive is the governor. In a city, the chief executive is usually the mayor.

A chief executive's job is to put in operation and keep in operation the various laws, programs, and services which his government is supposed to maintain and provide. For example, the mayor of a city must collect municipal taxes, revenue, grants, and other moneys so as to be able to pay the costs of government. He must maintain police and fire departments, the city's schools, one or more courts, one or more jails, a sewage system, the city's streets, bridges, and parks, often also a water system, the collection of trash and garbage, snow removal, and bus lines, sometimes one or more colleges, as well as hundreds of other things. He must also stand ready to deal with emergencies such as outbreaks of disease, riots, floods, or great storms.

Of course, the mayor does not run all these activities personally. He has department heads and many other officials under him, but he is responsible for what all of them do or fail to do.

The governor of a state has a bigger geographical area and a list of activities to supervise and manage that is slightly different from a mayor's but at least as long. Like a mayor, he has department heads and many officials to run things, but he is responsible for what they do or fail to do.

The President's job is even more complex. He is required to administer Federal laws, programs, and services in all fifty states, handle international relations throughout the world, and manage the activities of quite a number of millions of employees—counting in the Armed Forces.

The entire executive branch of the Federal Government is there to help him perform these duties. It has twelve major executive departments: State, Treasury, Defense, Post Office, Justice, Interior, Commerce, Labor, Agriculture, Transportation, Housing and Urban Development, and Health, Education and Welfare. The Department of Health, Education and Welfare was established by President Eisenhower in 1957. Two other departments are even newer. The Department of Housing and Urban Development and the Department of Transportation were set up for the first time in President Johnson's Administration. There were only ten major departments while John F. Kennedy was President.

Below the level of the Cabinet members are hundreds of positions ranging downward from Under Secretary through assistant secretaries, deputy secretaries, assistants to assistants, directors and assistant directors, commissioners and assistant commissioners. There are also ambassadors, envoys, consuls, governors of territories, and a hundred or more other types of officials.

There are also a number of agencies and commissions which are not connected with any of the regular departments. They are often spoken of as independent because they are not part of a regular department.

In the United States, no Negro has as yet been elected President or Vice President, though black candidates' names have been put in nomination by a major political party. In modern times, no Negro has been elected governor of a state, though there have been black governors of a territory. There have been, and are now, a number of black mayors, some of them mayors of very large cities.

For a good many years now, increasing numbers of black men and women have been serving in the executive branch of the Federal Government, at every level up to, and including, Cabinet rank.

Starting with the next chapter, you can read the stories of the black men and women who have risen to high places in the executive branch of the national government. The stories of the black mayors will come a little later.

13

Officials in the Department of State

THE Department of State works primarily with foreign countries, and its main function is to maintain workable relations between the United States and those foreign countries. It works also with international organizations such as the United Nations with the same aim.

The State Department is a far-flung organization. In addition to the staff it keeps at home, large numbers of its people are stationed all over the world. It maintains ambassadors or other envoys in the capitals of most foreign nations. Members of the Foreign Service, which includes consuls, are stationed in major cities all over the world. In addition, it sends out many small groups with special missions in one or more foreign countries. Over all, these are aimed at furthering United States interests abroad or improving the nation's image in the countries visited.

Probably more black men and women have held important posts in the State Department than in any other department of the executive branch of the Government. To start with, let's turn to some of those who helped with the formation of the United Nations and of those who served a little later as American delegates to that organization.

AT THE UNITED NATIONS

Before World War II had come to an end, President Franklin D. Roosevelt dreamed of an international organization to keep peace throughout the world. When he and the British Prime Minister, Winston Churchill, met with Joseph Stalin, head of the Soviet Union, at Yalta in February, 1945, the three men discussed the advisability of starting such a body, and all three favored it at least to some extent. About two months later, President Roosevelt unfortunately died, but not before invitations had gone out to roughly fifty nations to come to San Francisco to draw up a charter for the proposed organization. The San Francisco conference began on April 25, 1945. During the next two months, ideas and wordings were suggested and debated and often modified. By June 26, the charter was written in its final form and adopted by the vote of the delegates.

The next step was ratification of the charter by the home governments. If enough nations ratified it, the United Nations would be born. The United States Senate formally ratified the charter on July 28. By October, 1945, the necessary number of nations had given their ratifications, and the United Nations came into being.

Among the American observers who had been accredited by the State Department to attend the San Francisco meeting were four black leaders. One was **Mary McLeod Bethune,** a trusted adviser on race relations to the late President Roosevelt and at San Francisco representing the National Council of Negro Women. Another was **Dr. Mordecai W. Johnson,** head of Howard University. The other two were the two top men in the NAACP, **Dr. W. E. B. DuBois** and **Walter White.** As observers, they could not vote along with the actual delegates; but there was nothing to prevent them from discussing with the delegates what ought to be said in the charter.

Also present in San Francisco and serving as a delegate was **Ralph Bunche,** then Acting Chief of the Division of Dependent Territories of the Department of State. His studies and his special experience in African and Asian affairs had made him an authority on identifying minority problems, whether racial, religious, ethnic, or other. Not only his work in shaping the United Nations Charter, but also his achievements in Israel and elsewhere entitled him to special treatment here.

Ralph J. Bunche was born in Detroit. His family was poor, and as a boy he sold newspapers and shined shoes. When he was twelve, his family moved to Los Angeles. There he did brilliantly in high school and graduated with high honors from the University of California at Los Angeles in 1927. He did graduate work at Harvard, earning a Master's degree and a Doctor's degree there. He is said to be the first black student to earn a Doctor's degree in political science.

In the early 1930's, he became head of the Political Science Department at Howard University. He also did field work with and for the Swedish sociologist Gunnar Myrdal, whose book *An American Dilemma* is perhaps the most scientific and authoritative study of American race relations ever published. Also during the 1930's, two fellowships took him to Africa for study and travel, and one of these also allowed him to become familiar with Southeast Asia and the islands of the East Indies.

During World War II, he worked for the Office of Strategic Services as a senior social analyst specializing in African and Far Eastern affairs. He helped to draft guidelines for territories and trusteeships, working out policies which eventually became a part of the United Nations Charter.

By this time, Bunche was engaged in a variety of governmental and international affairs. He was moved to a higher position in the Department of State, served on the Caribbean Commission, headed a couple of conferences, and held various posts in the young United Nations.

Bunche's most publicized achievement came out of his work with the United Nations. In 1947, a United Nations resolution proposed the withdrawal of Great Britain from Palestine and a partition of the area. In 1948, when Great Britain did actually withdraw, the new State of Israel proclaimed its independence. Almost at once, five Arab nations—Lebanon, Jordan, Syria and Egypt (then united as the United Arab Republic), and Iraq—joined their military forces "to restore order in Palestine." Heavy fighting was soon in progress.

The United Nations, in an attempt to stop the war, sent a team of mediators, headed by Count Folke Bernadotte, with Ralph Bunche in the second position. After securing two short

Ralph J. Bunche   James M. Nabrit

and often-broken truces, the Count was assassinated, and Ralph Bunche became the chief mediator. He was able to negotiate armistices between Israel and each one of the Arab states. This "Four Armistice Agreement" brought about an immediate end to the fighting.

Although the basic causes of conflict were not settled then and have not been settled since, even a few years' peace between Israel and the Arab states was a notable achievement. Ralph Bunche came back a hero. In recognition of his services, he was awarded the Nobel Peace Prize in 1950, the first American of his race to receive that honor. City College of New York asked him to become its president. Harvard offered him a full professorship. He declined both offers. The United Nations made him Under Secretary for Special Political Affairs, a very high and responsible position.

For a time he kept one foot in the U.S. Department of State and the other in the United Nations. Finally, he chose the United Nations as the more fruitful place for him to work. In 1970, he still held his post there as Under Secretary for Special Political Affairs.

James M. Nabrit has had a notable career as an educator and lawyer, in addition to his work in the State Department. He was born in 1900 into an Atlanta family practically every member of which has distinguished himself and contributed to the advancement of black people.

James Nabrit graduated from Morehouse College in Atlanta and earned his law degree at Northwestern University. He became a lawyer and a professor of law at Howard University, and later became Dean of the Law School. It was under his leadership that the Law School began to put very strong emphasis on the study of constitutional law, the field which is so vital to the successful handling of many civil rights cases. Most of the black lawyers trying civil rights cases after about 1930 had been trained intensively in this area at the Howard University School of Law. Nabrit sometimes teamed up with former students to try civil rights cases. In the early 1960's, James Nabrit was chosen to succeed Dr. Mordecai Johnson as president of Howard University.

Along the way, Nabrit had found time to do some work for the United States Government. During World War II, he was a member of the Selective Service and Price Control boards. In 1954, he was legal adviser to the governor of the Virgin Islands. Twice he went to Geneva, Switzerland, as a delegate to the International Labor Conference.

It was during the time when James Nabrit was president of Howard University that President Johnson selected him as Deputy Representative of the United States to the United Nations, with the personal rank of Ambassador. The appointment came in 1965.

U.S. DELEGATES AT THE UNITED NATIONS

Each member country in the United Nations has at least one delegate in the General Assembly, and may have up to five, although it has only one vote. Eleven nations are represented on the Security Council of the U.N. Six of these are elected for two-year terms. The other five are permanent members. The United States is one of the permanent members. There are also a number of agencies under the jurisdiction of the U.N., such as the United Nations Educational,

Scientific, and Cultural Organization (usually called UNESCO) and the United Nations Children's Fund (the name of this agency was shortened, but it is still called UNICEF).

In 1946, at the first general meeting of the U.N., one member of the U.S. Commission to UNESCO was black, **Charles S. Johnson.**

Since 1950, there has been an unbroken succession of black delegates or alternate delegates in the U.S. delegation to the General Assembly. Along with these, a good many black leaders have represented the U.S. in various agencies in the U.N. or in other capacities.

Both groups are listed below.

BLACK U.S. DELEGATES IN THE GENERAL ASSEMBLY

Edith Sampson	Alternate delegate, 1950–1953
Channing Tobias	Alternate delegate, 1951–1952
Archibald Carey	Member, U.S. delegation, 1953–1954
Charles Mahoney	Member, U.S. delegation, 1954–1955
Robert Brokenburr	Alternate delegate, 1955–1956
Richard Jones	Member, U.S. delegation, 1956–1957
Genoa Washington	Member, U.S. delegation, 1957–1958
Marian Anderson	Alternate delegate, 1958–1959
Clifton Wharton	Alternate delegate, 1959–1960
Zelma George	Alternate delegate, 1960–1961
James M. Nabrit	Member, U.S. delegation, 1965–1966
Patricia Roberts Harris	Member, U.S. delegation, 1966–1967
William T. Coleman	Alternate delegate, 1969–1970
Helen G. Edmonds	Alternate delegate, 1970–1971

BLACK U.S. LEADERS ELSEWHERE IN THE U.N.

Charles S. Johnson	U.S. Commission to UNESCO, 1946
John Howard Morrow	U.S. Permanent Representative to UNESCO, 1961–1963
Franklin Williams	U.S. Representative to Economic and Social Council, 1964–1965
James Nabrit, Jr.	Deputy Representative to Security Council, 1966–1967
Mrs. Marjorie Lawson	U.S. Representative to Commission for Social Development, 1965–1968
Mrs. Patricia Harris	Member of U.S. delegation, 1966–1967
Mrs. Elizabeth Koontz	U.S. Representative on the Commission on the Status of Women, 1969–
Mrs. Carmel Marr	Legal Adviser to the U.S. Mission to the United Nations, 1953–

OFFICIALS IN THE STATE DEPARTMENT IN WASHINGTON

W. Beverly Carter, Jr., was appointed Deputy Assistant Secretary of State for African Affairs by President Nixon in 1969. In this role, he helps to formulate U.S. foreign policy in respect to African nations, and sees that it is followed out in practice.

Beverly Carter was born in Coatesville, Pennsylvania, in 1921. He went to school in Philadelphia, and graduated from Lincoln University in Pennsylvania in 1944. For the next twenty years he was engaged in newspaper work. He started on the *Philadelphia Tribune*, one of the oldest black-owned newspapers in the country. Later, he was city editor of the *Afro-American*, also in Philadelphia. In 1955, he became publisher of a paper in the *Pittsburgh Courier* chain. In connection with his newspaper work, he traveled widely in Europe and Africa.

In 1965, he entered the Foreign Service of the U.S. Information Agency. That year he became Press Attaché in Kenya, and was later promoted to Public Affairs Officer there. In 1968, he became head of USIA in Nigeria, with the diplomatic rank of Counselor of Embassy for Public Affairs. (The USIA is not part of the State Department, but a USIA man may also be given diplomatic rank, as Carter was.) A year later, his appointment as Deputy Assistant Secretary of State for African Affairs brought him back to Washington and to his present post.

Barbara M. Watson became Administrator of the Bureau of Security and Consular Affairs in 1968, and was reappointed by President Nixon in 1969. She is the first woman to hold so high an administrative position in the State Department.

Barbara Watson was born in New York City, the daughter of the first Negro lawyer elected to be a judge there. She graduated from Barnard College and earned a law degree at New York University. Miss Watson then became Foreign Student Adviser at Hampton Institute; next, attorney on the New York City Board of Statutory Consolidation; and finally, Executive Director of the New York City Commission to the United Nations.

In the summer of 1966, she entered the State Department

as Special Assistant to the Under Secretary for Administration. Within a year she was appointed Deputy Administrator of the Bureau of Security and Consular Affairs. In 1967, she was promoted to Acting Administrator. In 1968, an appointment from President Johnson removed the word *Acting* from her title. The bureau is in charge of passport and visa matters and special consular activities.

Mrs. Charlotte Moton Hubbard was made Deputy Assistant Secretary of State for Public Affairs in 1964, appointed by President Johnson.

She was born at Hampton Institute, the daughter of a notable educator and second president of Tuskegee Institute, Robert Russa Moton. She studied at Tuskegee and at Boston University. After a brief period of teaching at Hampton Institute and soon after this country entered World War II, she joined the Federal Security Agency, in which she helped communities organize to provide welfare, recreation, and services for Armed Services personnel and war workers. After World War II, Mrs. Hubbard went into the Community Relations Division of the Girl Scouts. With these experiences behind her, it was a natural step for her to become Community Services Director for a Washington, D.C., TV station in 1952. In 1964 came her appointment as Deputy Assistant Secretary of State for Public Affairs.

Chester C. Carter moved up rapidly in the State Department between 1963 and 1967.

Carter was born in Kansas, but moved to California in time to get most of his education there. He graduated from the University of Southern California, and earned his law degree at Loyola University of Los Angeles.

For a time, Carter worked as a civil defense coordinator in the Veterans Administration and also in the administration of the Peace Corps. In 1963, President Kennedy appointed him Deputy Assistant Secretary of State for Congressional Relations. In the summer of 1964, President Johnson appointed him Deputy Chief of Protocol. (*Protocol* means the rules of diplomatic or governmental etiquette which apply to formal occasions or ceremonies. As an example, who should be placed nearest the head of the table at a formal banquet? If anyone is misplaced, either he or someone of higher rank but seated farther down the table is sure to be insulted.) Three years later, President Johnson gave him the personal rank of Ambassador, to go along with his protocol position.

OFFICIALS IN THE
STATE DEPARTMENT ABROAD

This country sends a diplomatic agent to represent it in the capital of each foreign nation with which it keeps up diplomatic relations. Normally, our agent has the rank of *ambassador;* in a few instances, the lower rank of *minister.* Either an ambassador or a minister is nominated by the President and must be confirmed by the Senate. Incidentally, the headquarters of an ambassador is called an *embassy.* The headquarters of a minister is called a *legation.*

An embassy or legation usually has a staff, sometimes one of considerable size. Some of the staff members are experts in various fields, such as economics and trade, mining, engineering, press relations, health and nutrition, and so on. Some are well acquainted with the country to which they are sent, and with its history, language, laws, customs, and culture, perhaps much better acquainted than the ambassador himself.

For the past twenty-five years or so, the practice of appointing black diplomats to represent this country in foreign capitals has been growing more and more common. President Harry S Truman had a hand in making it more common. His first step was the appointment of **Ralph O'Hara Lanier** as U.S. Minister to Liberia in 1945.

Both President Truman and President Roosevelt just before him believed that it was a President's responsibility to improve the position of Negro citizens in America. President Truman took a number of steps to open new opportunities to black people. The diplomatic service was one such opportunity.

Since a minister or ambassador had to be confirmed by the Senate, it was not practical to pick people and places which the Senate would not agree to. For his first appointment, Truman chose Lanier as the man and Liberia as the place.

The Republic of Liberia, as you know, was established by

freed slaves who returned to Africa from this country, beginning about 1847. Over the years, the United States had sent a number of Negro officials to work for it in Liberia. President Truman's appointment of a black minister to serve in a black republic with an American background seemed so natural and suitable that it did not stir up even the Southern Senators. With the successful appointment of Ralph O'Hara Lanier as Minister to Liberia, the President had taken his first step.

Lanier was an educator. When he returned to this country after his service in Liberia, he became president of Texas Southern University in Houston.

Within the next four years, the Republic of Liberia was reclassified and put on a higher diplomatic level in the eyes of the United States Government. Thereafter, our chief diplomatic representative in Liberia was to be a full ambassador, no longer a minister.

Accordingly, in 1949, President Truman named **Edward R. Dudley** of New York to be the first United States Ambassador to Liberia, the first black Ambassador Extraordinary and Plenipotentiary ever to represent the United States abroad. (That mouth-filling title used to have a somewhat different meaning before an ambassador could communicate daily with his home government by telephone, telegram, or cable. Now it just means an ambassador of the first rank.) President Truman and Edward R. Dudley had broken a barrier and set a precedent for future appointments.

Dudley was born near Roanoke, Virginia, in 1891. When he was ready to study law, he came to New York City and earned a law degree at St. John's University. In 1942, he was appointed assistant attorney general for New York State. In 1945 he joined the legal staff of the NAACP and also became legal aide to Governor William Hastie of the Virgin Islands. During the five years from 1949 to 1954 when he was Ambassador to Liberia, he increased the warm relationship between that country and the United States. After his return, he was appointed Justice in the Domestic Relations Court of New York City. He resigned that position in 1961 to become Borough President of Manhattan. In 1970, he was a judge in the State Supreme Court of New York.

Jesse D. Locker was born in the same year as Edward Dudley, 1891, but in Cincinnati. He earned a law degree from

Howard University, and practiced law for nearly thirty-five years before going into politics. Once he started, he was very active. He served several terms as a member of the Cincinnati City Council, and by 1953 had become its president pro-tem. In 1953, President Eisenhower appointed him to succeed Edward Dudley as Ambassador to Liberia. Locker took over in 1954, and died at his post in 1955.

Locker's post was filled by **Richard Lee Jones,** another Eisenhower appointee. Jones was born in the South in 1893. His college work, first at the University of Cincinnati, then at the University of Illinois, was interrupted by World War I, in which he served as a second lieutenant. In the early 1920's, he moved to Chicago. For a time he was business manager of the *Chicago Defender,* a very large weekly black newspaper. This and other work made him extremely prominent in Chicago. In World War II, he went back into military service, this time as a major. Later he was promoted to reserve brigadier general in the Illinois National Guard. In 1954, he was sent to Liberia to direct this country's Point Four Program there. When Ambassador Locker died, Richard Lee Jones was appointed to take his place. He served from 1955 to 1960.

We come now to a man with a different sort of career and a different sort of success. **Clifton R. Wharton** began a professional career in the Foreign Service of the State Department in 1925, when he was twenty-six. For most of the next thirty years he was working his way up in the consular service.

He started as a vice consul in Monrovia, the capital of Liberia. He became a full consul in 1927, and served as a consul in various African cities up to 1941, and on the island of Madagascar in 1942. He was then transferred to Portugal and served as consul in various Portuguese cities up to 1950. In that year, Wharton was promoted to consul general. He served as consul general for three years in Lisbon, the capital city of Portugal, and for several years at Marseilles, the big city of southern France. He was then moved from the consular service into the diplomatic corps.

In 1958, President Eisenhower appointed him Minister to Rumania. Three years later, in 1961, President Kennedy selected him as Ambassador to Norway. He thus served as a black Minister and as a black Ambassador in two predominantly white countries. The Senate, by this time, had evidently

Clifton R. Wharton   John Howard Morrow

been pretty well trained to accept black diplomats, and it had obediently confirmed both appointments. Wharton retired in 1964, after some forty years in the State Department.

The story of **John Howard Morrow** is the story of a college professor turned statesman. Born in New Jersey, Morrow graduated with highest honors and Phi Beta Kappa from New Jersey's Rutgers University, then went on to earn a Master's degree and a Doctor's degree in French at the University of Pennsylvania. He became a professor of French and head of the Modern Language Department successively at Talladega College in Alabama, Clark College in Atlanta, and North Carolina Central University.

In 1959, President Eisenhower named Morrow as the first United States Ambassador to the Republic of Guinea, an African state which had just left the French Community and declared its independence. (The official language of Guinea is French, and this fact may have played a small part in the President's choice of a French professor as our first Ambassador there.) Morrow served in Guinea for two years. When he discovered that Guinea's first President, Sekou Touré, was planning to make a state visit outside of Africa, Morrow was able to persuade him to make that visit to the United States. At a time when many of the established nations of the world were trying to outbid each other for the favor of the new African nations, President Sekou Touré's visit to the United States was a small feather in the cap of United States diplomacy.

Morrow left Guinea in 1961, but he continued to serve the State Department for some years. At first he was a member of the United States Delegation to the United Nations, with the personal rank of Ambassador. Also in 1961, he was vice chairman of an educational delegation to Ethiopia, in eastern Africa. From 1961 to 1963, he was in Paris as United States Permanent Representative to UNESCO, with the personal rank of Minister. When Morrow finally left the State Department, he was invited back to his old college, Rutgers University, and became chairman of the Foreign Language Department there. He has published a book about his experiences in Guinea.

Carl Thomas Rowan gave up government work after only five years, but in those five years he scored two "firsts" and one "second."

Rowan was born in Tennessee in 1925, and grew up there. He left college at Tennessee A. and I. University to join the Navy in World War II. At the age of nineteen he won a commission. After the war, he graduated from Oberlin College in 1947, and earned a Master's degree in journalism from the University of Minnesota in 1948. He then went to work for the *Minneapolis Tribune*, a large white newspaper. He stayed with the *Tribune* from 1948 to 1961, distinguishing himself as a reporter of great skill, talent, and initiative. He had his own column, after a time. He also wrote several books, the most popular of which was *South of Freedom*. He was well known to both black and white readers.

In 1961, he was appointed Deputy Assistant Secretary of State for Public Affairs. Two years later, President Kennedy made him Ambassador to Finland, the first black United States Ambassador to Finland and the second to any European nation. (Clifton Wharton was the first.)

When Edward R. Murrow, the noted TV commentator, became ill and retired in 1964, President Johnson appointed

Carl Rowan to take his place as Director of the United States Information Agency (USIA). Rowan thus became the first black Director of that agency, which includes the radio Voice of America. In 1965, Rowan resigned, to go back to newspaper work and his own writing.

Mercer Cook, like John Howard Morrow, was a French professor before he became a diplomat.

Cook was born in Washington, D.C., in 1903, and graduated from Amherst College in 1925. He earned his Master's degree and Doctor's degree in Romance languages at Brown University. From 1936 to 1943, he was Professor of French at Atlanta University. Between 1943 and 1945, he was in the Republic of Haiti in the West Indies, in charge of the teaching of English. For the next fourteen years he was Professor of Romance Languages at Howard University, and went back there as head of the department after he left diplomacy in 1966. In 1960, he went to Paris as Director of the African Affairs Program of the Congress of Cultural Freedom.

In 1961, President Kennedy made Dr. Mercer Cook our Ambassador to the Republic of Niger. In 1964, Cook was moved and made Ambassador to Senegal. Both these new countries had been French colonies in western Africa, so that his knowledge of French was helpful. In 1965, the diplomatic posts of Senegal and Gambia were merged into one, and Cook became Ambassador to both countries. Gambia had been a tiny British colony before becoming independent. In Gambia, he could use his English.

Clinton Everett Knox came from a distinguished and highly educated family in New Bedford, Massachusetts. He graduated from Williams College with Phi Beta Kappa in 1930, and earned a Master's degree in history at Brown University in 1931. He then began teaching history at Morgan State College in Baltimore, at the same time working toward his Doctor's degree in history. He received the degree from Harvard in 1939, but continued teaching at Morgan State until he joined the Army during World War II.

Dr. Knox entered the Department of State in 1945. For a dozen years, his main job was research into records dealing with northern and western Europe. From 1947 to 1963, he was mainly in Paris, with various duties, especially in connection with the United States Mission to the North Atlantic Treaty Organization (NATO).

Beginning in 1963, his life became more active. He was assigned to the American Embassy in Honduras, in Central America, with the title of Counselor of Embassy and Deputy Chief of Missions. In 1964, President Johnson appointed him Ambassador to Dahomey in western Africa, and in 1965 he was installed in the Embassy there. In 1969, President Nixon made him United States Ambassador to the Republic of Haiti in the West Indies.

Mrs. Patricia Roberts Harris is the first black woman ever to have served as the United States Ambassador to a foreign country. She was born in Illinois in 1924, graduated from Howard University in 1945, and, after graduate study in several places, earned the degree of Doctor of Laws at George Washington University in 1960. For a year or two, she worked as a trial lawyer for the Department of Justice. Then she divided her time between the Justice Department and teaching at Howard University, mostly in the law school. She was made dean of the law school. She was also extremely active in civic organizations, civil rights organizations, and a variety of commissions. President Kennedy appointed her co-director of the National Women's Commission on Civil Rights.

In 1965, President Johnson appointed her Ambassador to Luxembourg. Luxembourg is a constitutional grand duchy, entirely surrounded by Belgium, France, and Germany. One previous United States Ambassador there was a woman, but not a black woman. When Mrs. Harris returned to this country in 1967, she served as a member of the United States Delegation to the United Nations, with the personal rank of Ambassador.

Hugh H. Smythe is a sociologist and anthropologist. When at home, he has been a sociology professor at Brooklyn College in New York since 1953, though he is often away. He was born in Pittsburgh in 1914. He earned a Bachelor's degree at Virginia State University in 1936, a Master's degree at Atlanta University in 1937, and a Doctor's degree at Northwestern University in 1945. After 1937, Dr. Smythe taught and carried on research at several American colleges and universities, and also at Yamaguchi National University of Japan, Chulalongkorn University in Thailand, and the National Research Council of Thailand. Smythe was an enthusiastic supporter of the African-American Institute, served on the Human Rights Commission of UNICEF, lectured at the Foreign Service Institute, and trained Peace Corps volunteers. Because of his interest in Africa, he has done a great deal of research on the region, and in 1960 he and his wife published a study on Nigeria. He also made major contributions to the 1960 UNESCO Conference, held in Boston, which used the theme: "Africa—Images and Realities."

In 1965, President Johnson appointed Dr. Smythe United States Ambassador to the Syrian Arab Republic in the Middle East. Two years later, Smythe was shifted to Malta, again as Ambassador. Malta, a former British colony, was granted independence in 1964. It consists of three rather small islands in the Mediterranean.

Franklin H. Williams takes us back to western Africa. He was born in Flushing, New York, in 1917. He graduated from college at Lincoln University in Pennsylvania in 1941, and earned

Hugh H. Smythe in Malta

Elliott P. Skinner

a law degree at Fordham University in 1945. For a short time he became an assistant to Thurgood Marshall, then special counsel for the NAACP. Between 1950 and 1959, he was West Coast regional director of the NAACP, and helped to reorganize branch offices in nine Western states. His first Federal employment came when he worked as an assistant to Sargent Shriver, then director of the Peace Corps.

In 1964, Williams was appointed United States Representative to the Economic and Social Council of the United Nations, with the personal rank of Ambassador.

In 1965, President Johnson appointed him United States Ambassador to Ghana on the west coast of Africa. Soon after Williams was installed in Ghana, the country passed through a crisis. Kwama Nkrumah, the dictator, was suddenly stripped of all his powers, while he was out of the country on a brief trip. A group of leaders called the National Liberation Council took over. Everybody feared a bloody civil war, but it never started. The bloodless revolution was a success, and the government became more democratic. A happening such as this puts a great strain on a new Ambassador, but Williams came through it without making a mistake.

In 1966, **Elliott Percival Skinner,** an anthropology professor who had spent two or three years in western Africa when he was a graduate student, was appointed United States Ambassador to Upper Volta. Upper Volta is an inland African nation, lying just north of Ghana.

Skinner was born on the island of Trinidad in 1924, but became a naturalized United States citizen in 1944, while serving in the United States Army. He graduated from New York University. He earned a Master's degree in 1952 and a Doctor's degree in 1955, both in anthropology, at Columbia University. A grant of money allowed him to do research in western Africa from 1953 to 1955. Another grant took him to French Guiana in South America. Dr. Skinner was an anthropology professor at New York University and later at Columbia. He is the author of a number of studies of Africa and Upper Volta.

In 1968, **Samuel Clifford Adams, Jr.,** was appointed Ambassador to the Republic of Niger, an inland nation just north of Nigeria in western Africa. As Adams' term as Ambassador to Niger began to approach its end, President Nixon appointed him assistant administrator of the Agency for International Development (AID) and head of the Africa Bureau. These assignments marked new high points in Adams' advancement as a professional in the Foreign Service, one in the field abroad, the others in the offices of the State Department in Washington.

A native of Texas and a graduate of Fisk University, Adams had earned a Doctor's degree at the University of Chicago in 1947. He then studied at the London School of Economics and the Maxwell School of Public Administration in Syracuse, New York.

In 1952, he entered the Foreign Service. By 1954, Dr. Adams was engaged in the administration of foreign aid to underdeveloped countries—at first with the International Cooperation Administration (ICA), then with its successor, the Agency for International Development (AID). Promoted each time he moved, Dr. Adams worked in Vietnam and Cambodia in Southeast Asia, and in Nigeria, Mali, and Morocco in western Africa. In Morocco, he had risen to the position of Director of the U.S.-AID Mission to Morocco. The next step up was to the United States Embassy in the Republic of Niger.

After holding two high posts in the State Department in Washington, **Dr. Samuel Z. Westerfield** was appointed Ambassador to Liberia by President Nixon in 1969. Westerfield came originally from Chicago, graduated from Howard University, and earned a Master's degree and a Doctor's degree in economics at Harvard. For a time, he was a professor of economics in the Atlanta University System.

His start in government was as an economist in the Bureau of Labor Statistics and the Tennessee Valley Authority. In 1961, he was with the Treasury Department as a senior adviser on the economics of underdeveloped areas, especially in Africa and Latin America.

In 1963, President Kennedy put him in the State Department as Deputy Assistant Secretary for Economic Affairs. In 1964, President Johnson promoted him to Deputy Assistant Secretary for African Affairs. In 1969, President Nixon chose him to be Ambassador to Liberia.

Jerome H. Holland is an educator and an executive. When President Nixon selected him to become United States Ambassador to Sweden, he had been president of Hampton In-

Samuel Z. Westerfield   **Jerome H. Holland**

stitute for ten years, the second college of which he had been president.

Holland had been a poor boy, who had worked his way through Cornell University, earning a Bachelor's degree in 1939 and a Master's degree there in 1941, as well as starring on the football team. Nine years later, he earned a Doctor's degree at the University of Pennsylvania. While he was working toward this degree, he spent three years teaching sociology and coaching football at Lincoln University in Pennsylvania, and four years during World War II as director of employee relations in a Sun Shipbuilding Company yard, where a main part of his job was to keep down racial friction.

In 1953, he was made president of Delaware State College, a predominantly black college. After seven years there, he left to become president of Hampton Institute in Virginia. When student unrest was at its height in many universities a few years later, he was able to keep it under reasonable control at Hampton.

When Dr. Holland accepted the post of Ambassador to

Sweden, he knew that he would face a special problem there. For some years, Swedish public opinion had been strongly and loudly against United States policy in Vietnam. In addition, the Swedish government had allowed deserters from the United States Armed Forces to come into Sweden and stay there, safe from prosecution by the United States Government. Each nation was highly critical of the other, and the usual friendship between the two was at a low ebb. The Ambassador preceding Dr. Holland had come home from Sweden in 1969, and President Nixon had left the post vacant for almost a year. This delay was widely taken as a sign of unfriendliness on the part of the United States. Thus, Dr. Holland faced the task of bringing back to life the traditional friendship between Sweden and the United States and at the same time "selling" the Swedish people on United States policies which were extremely unpopular in Sweden. He was chosen as the best man to carry out this difficult piece of diplomacy, and he agreed to try.

Terence A. Todman, like Samuel C. Adams, has built a career for himself in the Foreign Service, serving in United States embassies in India, in Lebanon in the Near East, in Tunisia in northern Africa, and in Togo in western Africa. In 1969, President Nixon appointed him Ambassador to the Republic of Chad, an inland nation in northwest Africa. Chad is about half black and about half Arab. Todman, however, is no stranger to the Arab world, after his service in Lebanon and Tunisia and after some of his work in the United Nations, especially as a delegate to the Trusteeship Council.

Todman was born in 1926 on St. Thomas in the Virgin Islands. He was an officer in the Army for four years, 1945–1949, before graduating from college in Puerto Rico and earning a Master's degree in public administration at Syracuse University.

While still a young man, **Clarence Clyde Ferguson, Jr.,** a North Carolinian, moved rapidly up the ladder of promotion in the Department of State. Since 1964, he has served as civil rights adviser for the United States to the United Nations on the UN Subcommittee on Discrimination, as special coordinator on Relief to Civilian Victims of Nigeria Civil War, beginning in 1969, and as ambassador, beginning in 1970. President Nixon appointed him Ambassador to Uganda, an inland country located between Kenya and the Republic of the Congo in central Africa.

Ferguson's prior activities led to his later successes. He graduated from Ohio State University in 1949 and studied law at Harvard University. Although he passed both Massachusetts and New York bar examinations and served as a teaching fellow at the Harvard Law School in 1951–1952, he continued advanced study in law at Harvard until 1957. Meanwhile, he was a professor of law at Rutgers University from 1953 to 1963. In 1963, he became a law professor and dean of the law school at Howard University.

A FINAL WORD ON
THE STATE DEPARTMENT

The people about whom you have been reading make up only a small part of the whole group of black men and women who work for the Department of State. Those whose stories have been told here were the most notable, people who held high-ranking posts. Others, not named in this book, may also be moving up, and some of them may reach high positions. But there is just not room enough here to include them all.

Many of the ambassadors had distinguished themselves in other professions before they were asked to serve in American embassies abroad. Among them were college presidents, professors, journalists, lawyers, and so forth. Others built professional careers within the State Department, moving up step by step with each assignment until they reached the post of ambassador.

Ambassadors and ministers must have their appointments confirmed by the Senate. You have had a chance to see that Presidents who pioneered in appointing blacks to serve as ministers and ambassadors began cautiously, nominating them to capitals of black nations such as Liberia. This strategy gradually got the Senate accustomed to confirming them without much fuss. The result was that by 1958, Clifton Wharton was confirmed as Minister to Rumania, and again in 1961 as Ambassador to Norway. Also in 1961, Carl T. Rowan was confirmed as Ambassador to Finland. In 1965, just twenty years after President Truman sent the first black Minister to

Liberia, the Senate confirmed the appointment of Mrs. Patricia Roberts Harris as Ambassador to Luxembourg. In that twenty-year period, the country had grown accustomed to the appointment of black ambassadors to European countries. When President Nixon sent Jerome Holland to Sweden in 1970, the question whether he, or any ambassador, could regain Sweden's friendship and at the same time defend the United States position in Vietnam was more prominent in the news coverage than the fact that he was black. His problem in Sweden was difficult, but it had little to do with color.

14

Channels of Communication to the White House

THE people whose stories were told in the previous chapter were all in one department, the Department of State. There are eleven other departments, as well as agencies, boards, and commissions, in which members of minorities serve, including blacks. Presidents appoint these officials, and often their positions are of such importance that the Senate is asked to confirm them. Often, the term "subcabinet" is used to describe these positions, indicating a nearness to the real power of the White House. It suggests that these officials are actually able to get the ear of the President of the United States. There is no doubt that many in the black community believe that such officials are so placed that they can advise the President—men and women making known the wishes of their race, playing important roles in decision-making. This may or may not be true, depending on the President in office.

Decision-making in our Federal Government is a very complicated affair. Each President determines the levels from which he will accept information. On the basis of this information, after discussion with trusted advisers, the President makes his decisions. The entire process depends upon the personality of the President and his view of the nature of the

Presidency. He, and he alone, is responsible for decisions and for implementing them.

How much bearing black and white channels of communication have upon the White House can only be determined by the response of the President in his programs and his key appointments. In the main, black officials are given responsibilities which pertain largely or exclusively to racial problems. When this is the case, the officials are said to be in "traditional" roles. Very recently, and so far only here and there, however, a new role seems to be appearing. A black official may find himself in an area where purely racial matters are not even in the picture.

Since the 1950's, a good many officials appointed to play traditional roles have been unhappy about being consulted only as "race specialists." They have felt that in their fields of advanced study they are trained and talented persons competent to handle a wide range of problems not connected with race. Not only established custom but also a very real need for competent race specialists have kept the majority from getting out of the traditional role, whether they like it or not. Presidents have learned that the appointment of blacks to Cabinet or subcabinet positions is good politics, hopefully a deposit in the public bank likely to pay voter dividends.

President Franklin D. Roosevelt started making such appointments back in the 1930's. Prominent persons from many walks of life were given titles, and sometimes, but not always, functions to go with the titles. Seen from the standpoint of the 1970's, some of these titles and functions seem very minor, but writers in the 1930's referred to people holding such titles as "the President's Black Cabinet." President Truman expanded the pattern, passing out titles of higher rank. President Eisenhower brought a black man into the White House staff. John F. Kennedy put one on the White House Press staff; Lyndon B. Johnson put one in the Cabinet; and Richard M. Nixon put one on the White House staff.

IN THE CABINET

We begin with a man who could make decisions and develop policy, the head man in his department. He was not an under-secretary or an assistant secretary but *the* secretary, a full member of the President's Cabinet and responsible only to the President.

Robert C. Weaver

The Department of Housing and Urban Development was not authorized by Congress until the fall of 1965. In the January following, President Johnson named a man to be the first Secretary of Housing and Urban Development as well as the newest addition to his Cabinet. The man whom the President named was **Robert C. Weaver.** Weaver thus became the very first secretary of the new department and also the first black member of any President's Cabinet.

Robert Weaver earned a Ph.D. degree in economics from Harvard University. In the early days of President Roosevelt's New Deal, in 1933, Weaver came into the Department of the Interior as an assistant to the Secretary, Harold Ickes. At the age of twenty-six, he was one of the group of gifted young blacks whom Secretary Ickes and the President sponsored and used to the full.

In 1934, he was a consultant in the Housing Division of the Public Works Administration, and in 1938, special assistant to the Administrator of the Federal Housing Authority. Weaver was in on the ground-floor planning of the nation's first Federally funded housing program. He knew its birth and its weaknesses. In 1940, he shifted to labor and employment and became administrative assistant to Sidney Hillman in the Labor Division of the War Production Board. Later, he was director of the Negro Manpower Commission.

In 1944, Weaver left the Federal Government and turned to education, especially to the financing of graduate study. He took a position with the John Hay Whitney Foundation as director of Opportunity Fellowships. These were grants made to promising black students to support them while they were earning advanced degrees and preparing for college teaching. Two other foundations and the Federal Government also consulted with him in respect to fellowships.

In 1955, Weaver went back to the field of housing, starting as Deputy State Rent Commissioner in New York and becom-

Robert C. Weaver

ing Commissioner within a year. This position made him the first black member of a Governor's cabinet in New York. He next went to New York City as vice chairman of the city's Housing and Redevelopment Board, the agency which supervised urban renewal and middle-income housing programs.

At President Kennedy's request, Weaver returned to Washington in 1961, as head of the Housing and Home Finance Agency. For the next five years, he directed the Federal programs aimed at better housing and improved communities. Along the way he wrote four topflight books on labor, housing, and urban development.

In 1961, it was already clear that the country needed an executive department of housing. President Kennedy asked Congress to create one. The four-year delay before such a department was set up was due to two factors: the death of President Kennedy and the recognized fact that if the new department were set up the man who was best qualified to run it, the one man with the knowledge, experience, and ability, was a black man, Robert C. Weaver.

In 1965, the new department was created, and in January, 1966, President Johnson chose the one man to run it, Robert C. Weaver.

IN THE WHITE HOUSE

E. Frederic Morrow was the first black member of a President's White House staff. He was born in Hackensack, New Jersey, in 1909. After graduating from Bowdoin College in Maine, he earned a law degree at Rutgers. He then worked first for the National Urban League, next for the NAACP. In World War II, he held the rank of major. From 1949 to 1952, he was in the public affairs division of the Columbia Broadcasting System.

In 1952 he dropped everything to take part in General Eisenhower's Presidential campaign. He traveled over 100,000 miles going around the country making speeches. After General Eisenhower was elected, Morrow was appointed for a short time in the Department of Commerce. Later, in 1955, he was appointed Administrative Assistant to the President in the White House. He held the position for six years.

Morrow left the White House when President Eisenhower did. He first became vice president of the African-American Institute, a large, privately endowed foundation set up to improve this country's economic and cultural relations with the African states. His next move took him to the Pacific Coast, where he became the first black assistant vice president in the Bank of America, later becoming a vice president in New York City.

In 1963, Morrow published a book about his experiences entitled *Black Man in the White House*. In it, among other things, he tells about his tireless but unsuccessful efforts to make the Eisenhower Administration more active in the field of civil rights. He also expresses disappointment that, although he was consulted as a specialist on race relations, his very considerable knowledge in other areas was not recognized and drawn on.

The "Kennedy Years" began for **Andrew T. Hatcher** with a long distance phone call which reached him in Trinidad in the West Indies, May, 1960. The call came from John F. Kennedy's friend and associate, Pierre Salinger, and his first words were, "We need you to clinch the nomination." Salinger and Hatcher had worked together as newspapermen and were good

E. Frederic Morrow   **Robert J. Brown**

friends. Salinger had chosen a good opener to persuade Hatcher to join him on the Kennedy team. Hatcher did join the team immediately, and he was a vital member of it as long as President Kennedy lived.

After the election, President Kennedy's first appointment going to a black man went to Andrew Hatcher, making him Associate White House Press Secretary. His friend Salinger was named Press Secretary a little later.

Andrew Hatcher was thirty-seven at this time. In addition to his newspaper work, he had been an Air Force officer and assistant labor commissioner of the state of California. On the White House press staff, reporting the President's views, correcting press misinterpretations, advising key officials of behind-the-scenes events, preparing press releases, and making advance arrangements for presidential visits, Andrew Hatcher was an official spokesman for the White House.

Immediately after President Nixon's election of 1968, he appointed **Robert J. Brown** of High Point, North Carolina, to the White House staff as a special assistant to the President. Robert Brown followed E. Frederic Morrow of the Eisenhower days as the second executive aide.

"Bob" Brown attended Virginia Union and North Carolina A. and T. He started work as an agent in the Bureau of Narcotics, U.S. Treasury Department, and law enforcement officer with the High Point, North Carolina, police department. Energetic and fast-moving, this young man established his own public relations firm, B. and C. Associates, with important clients from nationally known business firms. His other business ventures made him the vice president of the Citizens' Housing Corporation, partner in the Harlem Freedom Associates land development firm, and president of the Friendly Leader Manufacturing Company, Inc. While he was serving on numerous civic boards in his city and state, the Governor of North Carolina appointed him to state-wide advisory positions, inclusive of two trusteeships—a college and a university.

All through his thirty-three years, Brown had demonstrated the private initiative which made American business successful. He was also an ardent supporter of the NAACP, Martin Luther King, and the YMCA of the two Carolinas. He concludes that in marches and sit-ins during the racial turmoil of the 1960's, "He paid his dues." In 1964, he was given the Distinguished Service Award as the most outstanding young man in his city by the High Point Junior Chamber of Commerce of the Southern Region, and named one of the outstanding young men of America in 1965. Brown threw his public relations firm into the Nixon campaign in 1968. He began his new career with the new President.

Among the many concerns of black people, these seven are the major ones: employment, the principal business of the Department of Labor; education, health, and welfare, the three areas which make up even the name of the Department of Health, Education and Welfare; civil rights, guarded by the Justice Department and other Federal agencies; housing, the principal business of the Department of Housing and Urban Development; equal treatment in the Armed Forces, a concern of the Defense Department; the elimination of poverty, handled by an independent agency responsible to the President; and equal opportunity, handled by independent agencies responsible to the President.

The black community is naturally vitally interested in these Federal departments and agencies which promote or protect gains in the areas of these seven major concerns.

LABOR

Beginning with labor, unemployment, and the providing of equal opportunity, the story goes back to the New Deal. At the beginning of World War II, when it seemed that industries handling Federal defense contracts were going to leave blacks out of the employment picture, A. Philip Randolph threatened a march on Washington. President Roosevelt responded with Executive Order 8808, holding that discrimination could not exist in plants where the United States Government footed the bill. In guarding equal employment opportunity, President Truman appointed a Fair Employment Commission. Dwight Eisenhower created the President's Committee on Defense Contracts Compliance, and a year later promoted the black vice chairman of that committee to the rank of Assistant Secretary of Labor. This unprecedented appointment indicated the importance of fair employment in the President's eyes. There have been, by 1970, three such assistant secretaries and one director in the Labor Department: Jesse Ernest Wilkins, George Leon-Paul Weaver, Arthur A. Fletcher, and Mrs. Elizabeth D. Koontz.

Jesse Ernest Wilkins was appointed Assistant Secretary of Labor in 1954, the first of his race to hold this position. Wilkins, born in Mississippi in 1894, served in the Armed Forces in World War I and graduated from the University of Chicago in 1921. He studied law, and then practiced law in Chicago for many years, serving both black and white clients. He was nearly sixty before he was attracted to government office.

In 1953, President Eisenhower had made him vice chairman of the Committee on Government Contracts Compliance. The purpose of this committee was to persuade manufacturers of defense products to adopt fair employment practices and thus give more jobs to black workers. Vice President Nixon presided over meetings of the committee, and the Secretary of Labor was a member. They were in a position to see how good Wilkins was at persuading defense contractors to give more jobs to black workers. The result was that in 1954 Wilkins was made Assistant Secretary of Labor. In 1958, when he was sixty-four, he retired.

George Leon-Paul Weaver graduated from Roosevelt University in Chicago and earned his law degree at Howard University. In 1941, he went to work for the CIO, and soon became assistant to the director of its Civil Rights Committee. In 1955, when the CIO and the AFL merged, he was made executive secretary of the AFL-CIO Civil Rights Committee.

Weaver's experience with civil rights inside organized labor plus his legal training made the Government want him. He represented the United States at the International Confederation of Free Trade Unions, served on various missions to the Far East and Southeast Asia, and attended annual conferences of the International Labor Organization (ILO). In 1961, President Kennedy appointed him Assistant Secretary of Labor for International Affairs. All through the Kennedy-Johnson Administrations, he continued to attend ILO conferences, heading the United States delegation.

Arthur A. Fletcher was born in Phoenix, Arizona, in 1924. He went through college at Washington University in St. Louis and played football well enough to be chosen as a small-college all-American. He went on to play professional football with the Los Angeles Rams, the Baltimore Colts, and a Canadian team. He then became an assistant coach at Washburn University in Kansas, meanwhile doing graduate work at Kansas State University and San Francisco State.

In the 1950's, after a short stay in California, he moved to southeastern Washington, near the huge Hanford Atomic Energy Facility. There he became director of a manpower development project, a specialist in employee relations, and a special assistant to the state's governor. In 1967, he was elected to the city council in Pasco, and in 1968, startled the whole state by coming very close to winning the post of lieutenant governor.

On the basis of his personality and record, he was appointed Assistant Secretary of Labor, supervising the Wage and Hour and Public Contracts Divisions, the Bureau of Labor Standards, the Women's Bureau, the Bureau of Employees Compensation, and the Wage Determination Unit. Some of these agencies supervise compensation payments to workers injured on the job, safeguard working women and children, and try to insure safe and healthful working conditions. To see that blacks get employment on constructions jobs which use Federal money, Fletcher is in a position to implement "The Philadelphia Plan," the fair share labor plan.

When Richard Nixon became President in 1969, one of his first appointments went to **Mrs. Elizabeth D. Koontz,** making her director of the Women's Bureau in the Department of Labor. Mrs. Koontz was already nationally known. In 1966, she had been chosen as the first black president of the National Education Association, an organization of teachers and professors with over 1.4 million members. The president of the NEA is known to teachers throughout the United States and in many foreign countries.

Most of Mrs. Koontz's life has been devoted to education. She graduated from Livingstone College in Salisbury, North Carolina, where she was born, and earned a Master's degree at Atlanta University. She did additional graduate work at Columbia, Indiana University, and North Carolina Central University at Durham. Mrs. Koontz has served at the state level on the Family Service Council, Council on Human Relations, and the Governor's Commission on the Status of Women. Further

Arthur A. Fletcher   Mrs. Elizabeth D. Koontz

recognition came on the national level when she served on
the President's Advisory Council on Education of the Disadvantaged.

American women have made great strides in training and
employment at the higher levels. Mrs. Koontz faces the problems of unskilled women who are either unemployed or under-
employed. Black women without developed skills form a large
part of this problem.

As Director of the Women's Bureau, Mrs. Koontz represents
the women of America at international conferences.

HEALTH, EDUCATION AND WELFARE

Lisle C. Carter, Jr., was born in New York City in 1925, but
grew up in Barbados in the British West Indies. At fifteen, he
came back to the United States to go to college, and graduated
from Dartmouth. After military service, he studied law, the

profession of both his parents. He earned his degree from St. John's University in 1950, and started a private law practice in New York City. This included serving as legal counsel for the National Urban League.

In 1961, President John F. Kennedy, looking for bright young men to make his "New Frontier" move, chose Lisle Carter to be Deputy Assistant Secretary in the Department of Health, Education and Welfare. Carter brought home the widespread existence of discrimination in Federally assisted programs by a comprehensive survey.

Beyond a doubt, **James Farmer** is the most prominent and nationally known appointee of the Nixon Administration. He was a pioneer in the civil rights crusade in the 1940's when it was dangerous to one's life, in many parts of the nation, to violate the laws and practices of segregation. A minister by training, he determined to reach a larger audience than a church could hold. Farmer was associated in 1942 with the founding of the Congress of Racial Equality (CORE) to achieve just what its name implied—racial equality, racial justice.

Farmer's fellow ministers formed The Fellowship of Reconciliation in 1947 for the purpose of attacking segregation and discrimination in American life. In the late 1940's and early 1950's, CORE and the Fellowship jointly tested these un-American practices in segregated seating patterns in eating places above the Mason-Dixon Line and in the same patterns on trains and buses, and in stations below that line. Farmer and his group faced angry mobs in the Deep South, bus-burning, and personal harassment in the early days of 1961.

When the fruits of Farmer's labor became evident—supported by Supreme Court decisions eliminating segregation in travel, and changing attitudes in the South on these matters— Farmer left CORE around 1966. (Picture is on page 206.)

In 1968, James Farmer entered politics as the Liberal and Republican candidate for Congress in the Bedford-Stuyvesant area of Brooklyn, New York. He was defeated by Congresswoman Shirley Chisholm. President Nixon appointed him Assistant Secretary for Administration in the Department of Health, Education and Welfare. At the close of 1970, Farmer decided that he could do more for his people outside of government than from the inside. He resigned. His brief two-year service will be remembered, among other things, for having secured the continuation of Head Start program in Mississippi against the wishes of that state's governing authorities. The program provides early training for disadvantaged children, and the bulk of black children need Head Start.

Charles C. Johnson, Jr., is a man equipped by training and experience to attack the big problems of environmental health which must be solved soon if mankind is to survive on earth. They are already threatening the health of people living in big cities.

Charles Johnson studied civil engineering at Purdue University, earning advanced degrees after graduating. He then spent twenty years, 1947–1967, as an officer in the Public Health Service, working mainly in the field of environmental health. He served on the Surgeon General's Task Force on Health, Housing and Urban Development, organized a national center for urban and industrial health, and advised the government of India on the management of its national water supply. As engineering consultant with a U.S. mission to Liberia, he worked out a program to control malaria, planned drainage systems, and conducted sanitary surveys of hospitals and schools.

In 1967, he left Federal employment to become Assistant Commissioner of Environmental Health in the New York City Health Department. Three years later, in 1970, he received from President Nixon the appointment of Administrator of Consumer Protection and Environmental Health Service in the Department of Health, Education and Welfare.

HOUSING

Samuel C. Jackson held two positions in the Department of Housing and Urban Development in 1970, one as important as the other. He was General Assistant Secretary, working with the Secretary and having responsibilities which extended throughout the department. He was also Assistant Secretary for Metropolitan Planning. Metropolitan planning relates to the use, or reservation, of open land space in cities, water and sewer facilities, city parks and beautification, and neighborhood facilities of other types. Jackson's office provided Federal financial aid to state and local governments to encourage comprehensive city planning.

Samuel Jackson attended college and studied law at Washburn University in Kansas. He was deputy general counsel for the Kansas Department of Welfare. In Washington, D.C., he became president and director of the American Arbitration Association Center, and served as mediator and arbitrator in disputes involving public employment, landlord-tenant conflicts, community organizations, and the Model Cities program. In 1965, he was one of the first five men appointed to the Equal Employment Opportunity Commission, serving until 1968.

Samuel J. Simmons was also in the Department of Housing and Urban Development in 1970, and even more directly concerned with equal opportunity in housing and employment than Samuel Jackson.

Simmons was born in Michigan in 1927. He graduated from Western Michigan University, and did graduate work in sociology at the University of Michigan and Wayne State. As a graduate student working with boys in a Detroit settlement house and in a prison, he displayed unusual feeling for human problems and an ability to communicate with young people. Later, with the Detroit NAACP, he studied civil rights and equal opportunity. He went to Washington in 1962 as a member of the Board of Appeals and Review in the Post Office Department.

In 1969, President Nixon appointed Simmons Assistant Secretary for Equal Opportunity in the Department of Housing and Urban Development. His work with equal opportunity in housing and employment is based on Title VIII of the Civil Rights Act of 1968, prohibiting discrimination in programs and activities receiving Federal money.

DISCRIMINATION IN THE ARMED FORCES

Prior to 1917, there was stubborn resistance to commissioning Negroes in the Army. The United States entered World War I in April, 1917. Immediately, Negro leaders and college students began to put pressure on the War Department to provide training for black officers. The NAACP supported the idea, although it recognized that the training camp would be segregated. During the summer of 1917, a segregated officer-training camp was established, as an experiment, in Des Moines, Iowa. The experiment was successful, and the camp's first class graduated on October 15, 1917. Discrimination, however, continued to exist at and below the officer level. The severity of the problem caused Presidents to name special investigators to examine unfortunate conditions and bring back reports on them. Woodrow Wilson used Emmett Scott. Franklin D. Roosevelt first used William H. Hastie and, later, Campbell C. Johnson.

Campbell C. Johnson grew up in Washington, D.C., graduated from Howard University, and earned his law degree there. For many years he taught at Howard University, and was active in a number of civic organizations.

President Roosevelt appointed Colonel Johnson, a Reserve officer, to serve as executive assistant to General Lewis B. Hershey, head of Selective Service (the military draft). He was later reappointed by President Truman.

After the military draft had been put in operation but before America entered World War II, black troops were expressing their unhappiness about segregation in the Armed Services. In 1941, the Office of War Information chose **Theodore M. Berry** of Cincinnati as a Morale Officer with the task of improving their mood or their situation.

After Harry Truman became President, he issued an order to end segregation in the Armed Forces immediately. Obedience to this order was not quick; and up to 1970, it has never been complete. The cry of discrimination, aired by the black press, continued to make headlines.

It was this racial tension which **James C. Evans** had to face during most of the many years in which he served as adviser first to the Secretary of War, then to the newly created Secretary of Defense.

Evans graduated from Massachusetts Institute of Technology and earned a Master's degree there in electrical engineering. He then taught at West Virginia State College. He was also an inventor, thereby becoming a winner of the Harmon Award in Science. He went into government work in the early years of President Roosevelt's New Deal, and by 1943 he was a full-time civilian assistant to the Secretary of War. In 1947, the

Army, Navy, and Air Force were grouped in a single Defense Department. Reappointed by President Truman and later by President Eisenhower, Evans kept his position in the new, combined department during most of the 1950's. He was mainly concerned with black manpower problems in the Armed Forces. Although the status of black troops had unquestionably improved between World War II and the 1960's, the new generation entering the Armed Forces in the 1960's knew nothing about how bad discrimination in the Armed Forces had once been and had no basis for comparison. They did not like the discrimination which still lingered on. These young troops grew up during the racial tensions of the 1960's, saw and took part in protests, supported the "Black Pride Movement" at home, and did not discard in the service the extreme freedom of speech which they had enjoyed in the days of civilian confrontations. There were even racial clashes between uniformed personnel. It was felt in high Pentagon circles that conflict between the independent spirit of these young troops and the deep-seated prejudice of some white troops would, if continued, seriously undermine the morale of the nation's fighting units.

In the summer and early fall of 1970, President Nixon gave serious thought to this emerging crisis. It is, of course, a two-sided problem, and he considered both the black and the white sides. In September, 1970, to assist in the solution of the black side, he appointed **Frank W. Render** to the highest rank in the Department of Defense ever held by a member of his race, Deputy Secretary of Defense.

Render was born in Cincinnati, received his first degree from Hampton Institute, earned a Master's from Syracuse University, and continued his education there as a fellow in urban studies. During the same time, 1967–1969, he was executive director of the Human Rights Commission of Syracuse and Onondaga County. The Syracuse Junior Chamber of Commerce voted him "Outstanding Young Man for 1969."

As Deputy Secretary of Defense, Render is specifically charged to examine race relations at every United States military base around the world and plan steps to reduce friction. One of his immediate requests is that all troops be required to take a course in race relations.

In addition to Render, two high-ranking military officers

are engaged in encouraging blacks to join the military. **Brigadier General Daniel (Chappie) James, Jr.,** highest-ranking black man in the Air Force, is one. **Brigadier General Frederick E. Davison,** the highest-ranking black man in the Army, is the other. Both are thirty-year veterans, as well as combat veterans of Vietnam. These men claim that black troops want only "A fair shake, a fair chance, and fair recognition." They believe that untold opportunities await blacks in the military. General James is a Deputy Assistant Secretary of Defense for Public Affairs, and General Davison is director of the Army's enlisted personnel division.

If you are registered for the draft and if you believe that your local draft board is treating you unfairly, you have the right to appeal to the President of the United States. He will not personally review your case. The National Selective Service Appeal Board will study it and make a ruling on it in his name. Since 1969, the chairman of that board has been **Levi A. Jackson,** a former black football star at Yale and an executive in the Ford Motor Company.

The Selective Service Appeal Board has been important to many boys and young men facing military service, and has grown even more so since attitudes toward the war in Vietnam divided so sharply.

Levi Jackson was born in Connecticut in 1926. He himself was drafted into the Army in 1945, shortly after he had started college. After receiving his discharge, he went back to Yale University, graduating in 1950. That same year, he went to work for the Ford Motor Company, and gradually moved up in labor relations and personnel work until he was Retail Personnel Manager and manager of Personnel Services in the Administrative Department of the company. Most Ford dealers own their own agencies, but they are franchised and trained by the Ford Motor Company to handle Ford sales and services. Jackson ran a program which selected and trained black people to own or operate Ford agencies. Another of his responsibilities was to study and deal with any problems which arose in connection with black people as either employees or customers of the company. In addition to his work with Ford, he took on the new post on the Selective Service Appeal Board when President Nixon chose him.

James Farmer   Ronald B. Lee

THE POST OFFICE

In 1969, when **Ronald B. Lee** was appointed Assistant Postmaster General, although he was only thirty-seven years old, he had already had a wide and varied experience. Lee was a graduate of the United States Military Academy at West Point, and had eleven years of service in the Army, including duty as a combat adviser to a Vietnamese infantry division, and as a planner and systems analyst in the Army Materiel Command in Washington, D.C.

On the civilian side, Lee had earned a Master's degree in business administration at Syracuse University. He became a professor, assistant provost, and director of the Center for Urban Affairs at Michigan State University. In 1965–1966, he was one of the first group of fifteen White House Fellows selected from more than 3,000 applicants, potential leaders to be given a year's experience at the top level of government. Lee started on the White House staff, but transferred to the Post Office Department. There he took part in designing an Office of Planning and Systems Analysis, and helped to change many of the Department's old-fashioned approaches to management.

In 1969, when Lee was appointed Assistant Postmaster General, it was to take charge of the newly created office which he had helped to design three years before. The name had been changed to the Bureau of Planning and Marketing, but otherwise it was about as they had designed it in 1966. Thus, Lee was the first head of the new bureau, as well as the first black Assistant Postmaster General.

"BLACK CAPITALISM"

The Kennedy-Johnson Administration encouraged small businesses and minority businesses to use the loan funds of the Small Business Administration. Some few qualified. President Nixon made it evident in the campaign of 1968 that he favored special consideration for struggling black businesses. In ordinary conversation, the program became "Black Capitalism." It was placed in the Department of Commerce and a man found to head it.

Abraham S. Venable graduated from Howard University and earned a Master's degree in economics there. In 1957 he took a job as assistant to the eastern regional manager of a large brewery company, and stayed three years. This was experience in big business. In 1962 he became president of a small company manufacturing cosmetics in Washington. Later that same year he became vice president of a cosmetics manufacturing firm in Philadelphia. These were experiences in small business. In 1963, he went to work for the Department of Commerce.

There, he was a conciliation specialist with the community relations service and assistant executive secretary of the Department's task force on equal opportunity in business. He was able to coordinate the Department's equal opportunity programs. In the spring of 1969, he was made deputy director of the Office of Minority Business Enterprises, and in the fall was promoted to director.

The effectiveness of such an office depends very largely on whether or not he gets support from the Secretary of Commerce and from the White House. Only time will tell how much Venable will be allowed to do.

COMMUNITY RELATIONS

How do you inform Americans about their civil rights, the most recent changes, and penalties for violations? **Benjamin A. Holman** was selected for that task. Early in life, Holman had an interest in journalism which led him, with a stopover or two, from South Carolina to the William Allen White School of Journalism at the University of Kansas. After graduating, he spent two years in military service, coming out a first lieutenant in 1954. In Chicago for graduate study at the University of Chicago, he took a job as a reporter for the *Chicago Daily News*. He soon branched out into television, first as a reporter and commentator on Station WBBM–TV and later as a reporter and editor with CBS News. Altogether, he had thirteen years of experience with news media.

In 1965, President Johnson appointed him assistant director of Media Relations with the Community Relations Service in the Justice Department. Holman left in 1968 to take a job with NBC News in Washington as reporter and producer of a specialized news program. In 1969, President Nixon brought him back into the Justice Department with a promotion when he appointed Holman director of the Community Relations Service. He directs activities intended to help communities settle racial disputes and make peaceful progress toward equal opportunity and justice for all.

Holman was not the first to serve in this job. **Roger W. Wilkins** of New York City held it during the Johnson era when Vice President Hubert Humphrey was the mentor for the young blacks in government. Wilkins is a graduate of the University of Michigan and also holds a law degree.

THE OFFICE OF ECONOMIC OPPORTUNITY

In 1964, President Johnson declared war on poverty within American life. In response, Congress enacted the Economic Opportunity Act in 1965. It created an agency directly under the President's supervision. The Economic Opportunity Program, with its emphasis upon career training and improving the lot of the poor, became available to every community which could show a workable plan and also show that the group requesting it included all social elements of the community and all income levels. Sargent Shriver was named director, and his top aide was a black man, Lisle Carter, who came over from Health, Education and Welfare. Carter remained one year before being again appointed to HEW.

A major and very important feature of the Economic Opportunity Program was the Community Action Program. Sargent Shriver chose **Theodore Moody Berry** to be its director, and President Johnson appointed him.

Born in Kentucky, Berry attended college and studied law at the University of Cincinnati and began private law practice in Cincinnati in 1931. He was in the Federal service during World War II as a Morale Officer. Back at his law practice in Cincinnati, Berry also became active in politics. He ran for the city council as an independent. In Cincinnati politics, an independent can sometimes win, but Berry's first attempt failed. He was successful in 1949, and served until 1957. Political observers in the city believed that someday he would be elected the city's first black mayor. When he ran for the office, however, the opposition, with tremendous effort, beat him. He was again elected to the city council in 1963. Meanwhile, in 1960, Berry was chosen as special Ambassador to go to the celebration of Nigeria's independence in Africa.

In 1965, soon after the Office of Economic Opportunity was getting started, President Johnson called Berry back to Washington and made him director of the new agency's Community Action Program.

OVERSEERS OF EQUALITY OF OPPORTUNITY

There has been a growing tendency in each of the executive departments to appoint officials whose job is to see that equal opportunity is extended to racial minorities. At the same time, it was realized that only some sort of central committee or agency could accomplish what was needed.

Before 1965, two or three committees had been set up for

this purpose. In Eisenhower's day, there was the President's Committee on Government Contracts, of which Jesse E. Wilkins was vice chairman.

President Kennedy created the Equal Opportunity Committee, a new committee with a new name but the same purpose. **Hobart Taylor** was President Kennedy's appointee as vice chairman of it. He also served as legal counsel to Vice President Johnson, who acted as chairman of the committee.

Hobart Taylor is from northeast Texas. He graduated from Prairie View College in Texas, earned a Master's degree at Howard University, and studied law at the University of Michigan. He then practiced law with a firm in Detroit.

In 1965, Lyndon Johnson, by this time the President, appointed Taylor to a new and higher post, as one of the five directors of the Export-Import Bank, who oversee the financing and expediting of the nation's imports and exports.

Meanwhile, in 1964, President Johnson asked Congress to pass an act which would spell out equal employment opportunity to businesses and companies receiving Federal funds. Congress finally passed such an act. The act set up an independent agency, responsible to the President, named the Equal Employment Opportunity Commission, but did not give the new commission great powers. It set up no required percentages of workers from minority groups, and carried no penalties for discrimination in hiring. It relied mainly on persuasion. Any gains in the hiring of black workers resulted more from the moral leadership of the President and the goodwill of business than from the act itself.

In 1967, **Clifford Alexander, Jr.,** was named as chairman of the new commission, by President Johnson. Clifford Alexander was born in New York City in 1933, graduated from Harvard, and studied law at Yale. When he was only twenty-six, he became assistant district attorney of New York County. Later, in order to offset pressures on young blacks in Harlem, an organization named HARYOU was set up there, to provide a better life for young people—job training, new jobs, new careers, recreation. Clifford Alexander was made executive program director of HARYOU.

When Alexander came to Washington as chairman of the Equal Employment Opportunity Commission, he ran into the same problems which Wilkins and Taylor had faced—business and industry not being moved by persuasion. After a time, he came to feel that the act was not strong enough and was failing to carry out its purpose. He argued and pleaded for a law with teeth in it.

In 1969, in the early days of the Nixon Administration, things came to a crisis. Alexander was repeatedly attacked by people such as the late Senator Dirksen, who charged that Alexander's continual demands for the hiring of more black workers were excessive and were interfering with business. Alexander, feeling that he and his commission were not getting proper backing from the President, resigned, and took a post offered to him at Harvard University.

William H. Brown, III, was appointed by President Nixon to take Alexander's place as chairman of the Equal Employment Opportunity Commission in 1969. Brown was born in Philadelphia in 1928. He graduated from Temple University and earned a law degree at the University of Pennsylvania. From 1955 to 1968, he practiced law with a Philadelphia firm, becoming a partner in 1963. During those years, Brown was actively helping the disadvantaged, especially in the areas of employment, housing, and health care. He also served on the boards of civil rights organizations, the Mercy Douglass Hospital, and so on.

Brown was made a member of the Equal Employment Opportunity Commission in 1967. Two years later, in 1969, when Alexander resigned, Brown was appointed to take his place as chairman. The commission by that time had 600 employees and an annual budget of $12 million. Its purpose continued to be the elimination of discrimination in employment, whether based on race, color, religion, national origin, or sex.

The departure of Alexander had left the commission with only one black commissioner in 1969. When **Colston A. Lewis** was appointed by President Nixon to the commission early in 1970, he brought the number of black commissioners back up to two, the other being the chairman, William Brown.

Lewis was born in Lynchburg, Virginia. He graduated from Virginia Union University and earned his law degree at Howard. In private life, Lewis practiced law in Richmond, Virginia, and was active in politics. He helped to organize the Voters

William H. Brown, III   James E. Johnson

League of Lynchburg and the Crusade for Voters in Richmond. In 1957, he ran for a seat in the Virginia House of Delegates and lost by only 500 votes.

THE CIVIL SERVICE COMMISSION

The Civil Service Commission was set up in 1883 to stop abuses in passing out Federal jobs. For a number of years before that, when a political party won an election, party bosses rewarded their helpers by giving them government jobs. Many were not qualified to do the work called for. The Civil Service originally covered only about 14,000 jobs out of a total of only about 110,000 Federal employees. By 1969, the Civil Service had become an immense personnel system, covering 3 million jobs—2.8 million within the United States and over 240,000 outside the country.

Civil Service is probably the most widely known independent agency of the government, since a large majority of civilians working for the government had to take Civil Service examinations to win their jobs, and many others took examinations without success.

As for black Americans, the Civil Service Commission historically has had a very bad record. The old formula called for the selection of an appointee from the three highest scores made on the exams. Negroes, however, have felt for years that when the highest three included a single Negro, he just did not stand a chance. They believed that if the highest three included two blacks, both would lose. Beginning in the 1960's, the Commission began to give itself a fresh look. As late as 1969, however, the three highest civil service grades—including forty-three high officials—contained no blacks. At the next grade below, there was a roster of 118 officials, but only four were black.

The Civil Service Commission serves as the chief recruiter of talent for government, and it is required by law to enforce equal opportunity practices.

It is the duty of all the commissioners to see that there is a fair and honest chance for all races. One commissioner has a special obligation to recruit blacks. That man is **James E. Johnson.** President Nixon appointed Johnson one of the three commissioners in 1969. He soon became vice chairman, another "first" for his race. Johnson came to the Civil Service Commission by the route of the Marine Corps, a position with the Prudential Insurance Company in California, and a directorship of the California State Department of Veterans Affairs. The last was an appointment by Governor Ronald Reagan.

MANAGERS OF MONEY AND ATOMIC ENERGY

The Federal Reserve System was set up in 1913 to supervise member banks and to adjust interest rates and the currency so as to keep the nation's economy as steady as possible.

The country is divided into twelve Federal Reserve Districts, each with one Federal Reserve Bank. The operation of the whole system is directed by a seven-man Federal Reserve Board. Each board member is appointed for a seven-year term.

In 1966, President Johnson appointed **Dr. Andrew Felton Brimmer** to the Federal Reserve Board. The appointment was history-making.

Brimmer was born in Louisiana in 1926. He graduated from the University of Washington in 1950. Financed by a Fulbright Fellowship, he did advanced work in economics in India. On his return, he studied at Harvard, earning his Ph.D. degree in 1957. From 1955 on, he supported himself while finishing his studies by working in the Federal Reserve Bank of New York. From 1958 to 1963, he taught economics, first at Michigan State University, then at the Wharton School of Finance in the University of Pennsylvania. During this period, he kept up research and published various economic papers. It is believed that some of his research had an influence on the United States Supreme Court's ruling on the constitutionality of the public accommodations section of the Civil Rights Act.

In 1963, Dr. Brimmer entered government as Deputy Assistant Secretary of Commerce, and before long he was promoted to Assistant Secretary. He served as an economist, and also supervised the Bureau of the Census and the Office of Business

Andrew F. Brimmer on the Reserve Board

The AEC (Nabrit second) with LBJ (fourth)

Economics. His good work in the Department of Commerce led to his being chosen for the Federal Reserve Board in 1966.

Samuel N. Nabrit is the youngest son of a prominent Atlanta family, although he was born in Macon, not Atlanta, in 1906. He graduated from Morehouse College, and earned both a Master's degree and a Ph.D. degree in biology at Brown University. He was the first Negro student to receive a Doctor's degree there. After a year of research in Belgium, he became a professor of biology at Morehouse College. After moving over to Atlanta University, he soon became head of the biology department, and in 1947 dean of the graduate school. In 1955, he left Atlanta to become the second president of Texas Southern University at Houston.

In 1956, President Eisenhower appointed him to a six-year term on the National Science Board.

In 1966, Dr. Nabrit was appointed a member of the Atomic Energy Commission, just twenty years after the commission was set up. In 1945, near the end of World War II, atomic bombs had been dropped on the Japanese cities of Hiroshima and Nagasaki. Because these bombs were so destructive, many people felt that the new force of atomic energy should be kept under civilian control, not military control. President Truman strongly favored a civilian board. In 1946, Congress passed an act establishing the civilian Atomic Energy Commission. Exactly twenty years later, President Johnson's appointment made Dr. Samuel Nabrit the first black member of the commission.

OTHER BLACK OFFICIALS

In the Kennedy-Johnson years, many other prominent black men and women were offered appointments in the Executive Branch of the Government. Some were able to accept. Others were not free to leave their regular duties for full-time government work. Some were able to take advisory positions which would bring them to Washington only for short visits now and then. Others had to decline the offered appointments entirely.

Here is a list of some of those who did enter government service during the Kennedy-Johnson years: **Mark Battle** of New Jersey, deputy administrator of the Neighborhood Youth Corps; **Arthur Chapin** of New Jersey, special assistant in the Department of Labor; **Alice Dunnigan,** women's feature writer on the *Pittsburgh Courier,* member of the Equal Employment Opportunity Commission; **Alfred Leroy Edwards,** Deputy Assistant Secretary of Agriculture; **Dr. Grace Hewell** of New York, program coordination officer of HEW; **Oliver W. Hill,** prominent Virginia civil rights lawyer, assistant to the commissioner of the Federal Housing Administration; **Howard Jenkins** of Washington, D.C., member of the National Labor Relations Board; **Ruth Jones,** collector of customs for the Virgin Islands; **Jean Lightfoot** of California, liaison officer in the Bureau of Public Affairs, State Department; **Dr. Arenia Mallory** of Mississippi, manpower development specialist; **Anne Roberts,** deputy regional administrator of the Housing and Home Finance Agency; **Alvin C. Rucker** of Missouri, labor adviser to the assistant secretary for African affairs; **Herbert Waddy,** assistant postmaster in the Post Office Department; **D'Jaris Watson** of New York, **John R. Wheeler,** prominent North Carolina banker, and

Harry Woods, executive editor of the *St. Louis Argus*, all members of the Equal Employment Opportunity Commission; and **Jerry Whittington,** personal secretary to President Lyndon Johnson.

The Nixon Administration has followed the example of the Kennedy-Johnson Administrations in the appointment of black officials. Here is a list of some of those who have been appointed in 1969 and 1970: **T. M. Alexander** of the New Communities Division of HUD; **Calvin Banks** of the Urban System of the Department of Transportation; **Howard L. Bennett,** acting deputy assistant secretary for civil rights; **John Blake,** deputy manpower administrator in the Department of Labor; **Ella Branson,** special assistant in HUD; **Ruby Burrows,** special assistant in the Metropolitan Development of HUD; **Gilbert DeLorme,** special assistant in HUD; **Alfred L. Edwards,** deputy assistant in Agriculture; **Clyde Ferguson,** special coordinator for the victims of the Nigerian War in the State Department and later Ambassador to Uganda; **Alexander Gaiter** in the civil rights area of the Department of Transportation; **Robert Grant,** special assistant in HUD; **Connie Mack Higgins,** special assistant in the Small Business Administration; **Melvin Humphrey,** deputy director in HUD; **Benjamin Hunton,** director of Civilian Job Conservation Centers in the Department of the Interior; **William B. Jones,** deputy assistant secretary in educational and cultural affairs in the State Department; **Oliver Lofton** in community relations services in the Department of Justice; **Arthur B. McCaw,** assistant in civil rights in HUD; **William Seabron,** assistant in equal employment opportunity in the Department of Agriculture; **Joseph J. Simmons,** administrator in the oil import administration; **Stanley B. Thomas,** deputy assistant secretary for youth; and **William Thompson,** judge in the District of Columbia Court of General Sessions.

15

Positions in Public Education

THE United States is still involved, as it was in the 1960's, with the serious challenge of desegregating its public schools and colleges. The most difficult problem everywhere has been encountered in the levels from the primary grades through the senior year of high school.

What brought this country to face the problem of desegregation? The Southern states had laws which required blacks and whites to attend separate schools. The Supreme Court in 1954 declared the requirement by law of separate schools is unconstitutional.

In the Northern states, as in much of the country, people practiced segregation in housing, either by refusing to sell or rent to blacks in white areas or by continually providing low-cost housing inside the already existing black neighborhoods. Schools are built where people live. In all-white neighborhoods, the schools fill up with white children. In big-city neighborhoods into which segregated housing has crowded many black families, the schools fill up with their children. The result of segregated housing is separate schools for the children of the two races. Federal courts have declared that separate schools resulting from housing patterns are also unconstitutional, and they have ordered many cities in the Northeast, North Central, and West to desegregate their schools. Thus, segregated schools were outlawed everywhere.

Some towns, cities, and counties began to integrate their schools fairly soon after the Supreme Court decision of 1954. Others delayed as long as they could and moved toward integration only after they had been thoroughly prodded. Even then, a good many did not move any farther toward integration than they could help. Sometimes all-black schools were closed, or their names were changed. Sometimes, when a few black students lived near a white school, they were transferred to it. Black children were often bused out of their neighborhoods in order to give a distant school a legally acceptable racial mixture. Sometimes a token number of black teachers were transferred to white schools, and a similar small number of white teachers to black schools. It sometimes happened that black principals and teachers lost their jobs as a result of even very incomplete integration.

In the South, white parents who opposed any and all integration established private academies for their children. In the North, whites fled faster to the suburbs, knowing that schools followed people and that the end result of "lily-white" suburbs would be all-white schools.

The story of integration has more aspects than are described here. It is sufficient to say that in the process of integrating the public schools, two strong forces came into collision. First, many white political office-seekers in towns, cities, counties, and states opposed school integration, sometimes expressing their opposition in blunt terms, sometimes wrapping it in fancy phrases. Integration of the public schools became the nation's raw, exposed nerve. At a time when calm planning should have been the approach, integration was hauled into politics, where more heat than light was generated. Meanwhile, in the 1960's, when integration of schools was taking place or about to begin, the black revolution was also taking place—a new birth of dignity and pride in being black, a more spirited demand for civil rights, and a strong unwillingness to accept anything less than equal treatment and equal opportunity.

These two sets of forces created problems for those schools which had integrated, for those which had begun to integrate, and even for those which had not yet started. The racial friction between black and white students in Washington, D.C., was mentioned earlier in the book. It can be said here that similar unpleasant situations arose in many cities and towns across the nation. Blacks in formerly all-white high schools demanded courses in black studies, more opportunity to participate in extracurricular activities, larger representation among class officers, cheerleaders, and the like, and less-prejudiced teachers. Militant extremists of both races, people who were not high school students, often fed the flames of passion. Parents of both races often lifted the confusion to higher levels.

Perhaps you are already asking: Why give us such a lengthy background before telling us about those blacks who held key positions during these tragic times? The answer is that these very problems created the opportunities, yes, the demands for qualified black people to share in decision-making at the highest town, city, and county levels of public education. That level is the local school board. And the topmost single responsibility is to serve as chairman of the school board.

From the 1940's on, it was usual to have a token black on the school board of a racially mixed community. In the 1960's, a larger number of black school board members became common because of the black-white strains among the students. And in those urban areas where racial friction was really severe, so many school boards turned to the same policy that it became almost an unwritten rule. They said, "Let us make a black man chairman. Perhaps he can help us out of this confusion." At the very least, school boards felt that a strong black personality would be admired by students of his race, might be an inspiration to them, and would be a restraining influence in times of stress.

There are two ways in which people get to serve on school boards: election and appointment. When blacks were elected in racially mixed communities, whites joined in voting for them. This book could not begin to tell you about all the blacks who serve on school boards. The South, which was late in electing blacks as state legislators, county commissioners, and city councilmen, was early in electing or appointing them to local school boards. Any tiny town is likely to have a black school board member. Southern towns and cities have approximately five hundred. Areas outside the South, which were cautious about naming blacks before 1960, have now become staunch supporters of the practice.

Some examples are interesting. Durham, North Carolina, a city of about 100,000, selected a black university professor, **Dr. Theodore S. Speigner,** to serve as chairman of its school board. A man who serves as head of the department of geography at North Carolina Central University, and who organized a program in conservation and resource-use education in use in seventy-five of the state's one hundred counties has to be considered an admirable choice.

Cincinnati, Ohio, is one of the nation's large cities north of the Mason-Dixon line. It has a black population of about 25 percent and only a rather recent history of racial liberalism. This city selected **Calvin H. Conliffe** as president of its school board. Conliffe had hardly taken his seat before the school board had tossed a hot potato into his hands—black students of Cincinnati demanding a school holiday to celebrate the birthday of civil rights leader Martin Luther King.

Conliffe is a graduate of Howard University, an engineer, and an aircraft pilot. He has held various high-level engineering and managerial positions in the Aircraft Engineering Group of the General Electric Company in Cincinnati. His newest post there is consultant in educational relations.

Conliffe first became associated with the Cincinnati Board of Education in 1963. He served two terms as a member, became vice president in 1968, and rose to president in 1970.

Back South, again. Atlanta, Georgia, has long been Georgia's major city and is one of the thirty largest in the country. Slightly more than 44 percent of its population is black. Even as late as 1960, whites in the city would never have dreamed of selecting a black administrator to head the city's school board. It was even exciting in the 1960's when Dr. Rufus Clement, president of Atlanta University, was chosen to be a *member*. In 1970, however, a black scholar was made chairman of the board of education, **Dr. Benjamin E. Mays,** former president of Morehouse College. This author, scholar, and nationally known educator, who had long been a consultant to the Federal Government and had been awarded some thirty

Benjamin E. Mays   **Calvin Conliffe**

honorary degrees, many from famous universities, was surely an able and distinguished choice as the leader and chief of Atlanta's board of eduction.

One of the highest elective positions in the field of education anywhere in the nation is that of the State Superintendent of Public Instruction in California. The State Superintendent has broad authority over the schools and colleges throughout the state. This position went to a professional black educator, **Wilson C. Riles,** when he defeated the incumbent, Max Rafferty, in the November election of 1970. Rafferty was white, a politically ambitious, extreme conservative and a controversial figure. Riles was already recognized for having developed one of the nation's best "Title 1" educational programs for disadvantaged children. In addition, he headed a blue ribbon task force in the Nixon Administration which made an exhaustive study of urban education, concluding that urban education is a major national priority. Voters intent on seeing Rafferty defeated and voters eager to elect Riles combined, regardless of color, to give Riles an overwhelming victory.

Riles is the first black man ever to win state-wide office in California. He now heads the state's total school system, with 4.5 million students and an annual budget of $2 billion. By law, he is also a member of the state's Board of Regents, a position of power and influence at the college and university level.

California's public education was badly entangled in politics during the 1960's. College and university students in Berkeley, Oakland, San Francisco, Los Angeles, Palo Alto, and smaller academic centers often adopted extreme methods of protest, including violence. Large numbers of police were brought into some campuses to enforce order. Some of the college students' protests and violence spilled over into the high schools.

Riles, however, focused his campaign on Rafferty's record. He built up a strong case that Rafferty had done a bad job as an administrator, bringing forward specific mistakes and poor

Wilson C. Riles

handling of other matters. Riles also called attention to Rafferty's continuing neglect of his high educational office while he was running, also unsuccessfully, for a seat in the United States Senate.

The election of Wilson C. Riles was considered by the press to be a clear demonstration that Californians wanted their schools taken out of politics and allowed to get on with the real business of education under competent management.

Born in Louisiana, Riles worked his way through Northern Arizona University. In his present position and facing very big problems, he has his work cut out for him. His message, however, is that a good early education is the key to the future man or woman, and that a leader who will set aside the emotional issues of education can give reasonable men and women the opportunity to analyze their problems and decide what to do.

16

Black Mayors

THERE is a strong similarity between the organization of the Federal Government and the organization of many state governments, except that state governments are smaller. Black men and women hold positions in many state governments. Some are heads of departments or directors of agencies or bureaus. Others are farther down the ladder. The work that they do is much like the work done by equivalent Federal officials whom you read about in the last two chapters.

The mayor of a city is different. He is the chief executive. The area which he governs is smaller than a state governor's or the President's, but in it, like them, he is the head man. The mayor is close to the people in his community. They can see him on TV news or read about him in the newspaper. If he fails to give them what they want or does something that they do not like, they let him know.

Until a very few years ago, the mayors of all big cities and most towns were white. This is fact. Between 1965 and 1970, however, big cracks in that pattern began to show clearly. They were biggest in the North Central states. They were large in the Northeast and in the West. Smaller ones have appeared in the South. Many factors have helped to cause them, but the most powerful single cause was the movement of people into cities, and the opposite movement out of cities into the suburbs. These two movements have changed the balance of the city vote.

Between 1965 and 1970, in the three regions outside the South, eight cities with populations ranging from roughly 70,000 to 800,000, or a little more, have chosen black mayors. Washington, D.C., has also had a black mayor since 1967, but he was appointed, not elected. If we put Washington with the eight other large cities with black mayors, the combined populations amount (in round numbers and 1960 census figures) to 2,917,000 people.

In two more of the nation's largest cities, Los Angeles and Houston, black candidates ran for mayor in that five-year period, 1965–1970. Both made good showings, though they were defeated.

Over twenty smaller cities and towns, not only in the regions outside the South but also in the South, chose black mayors. Some of the smaller towns were practically all black, and had had one black mayor after another. At least one small city in the South had a large majority of white voters but elected its first black mayor.

All these happenings were signs of the times.

Let us look at the black mayors.

BLACK MAYORS OF SMALL CITIES AND TOWNS

Highland Park, Michigan, is an industrial city almost entirely surrounded by Detroit. Its 1960 population was 38,000, of which about 38 percent were black.

In 1968, **Robert B. Blackwell** was elected to a two-year term as mayor. When this Republican ran for Congress in 1960, he got less than 10 percent of the black vote, and lost with 49 percent of the total vote. In 1965, running for the city council, he cultivated the black vote and won. Although white backlash in 1968 kept many black candidates from winning, Blackwell got more than 70 percent of the total vote, including a large slice of the white vote. This was a major achievement for this Mississippian, educated at Talladega and Howard University.

As mayor, he faced problems. Highland Park housing was rundown. Public health facilities were poor. According to the FBI, the city's crime rate was the highest in the nation for cities of its size. There had just been a police scandal. Within

Robert P. Blackwell   Douglas F. Dollarhide

six months, Blackwell had Federal funds pouring in: $1.7 million of Model Cities money and $10 million for neighborhood development. Blackwell believes Highland Park can become a model for Federal-municipal cooperation.

Ypsilanti, also in eastern Michigan but not a close-in part of metropolitan Detroit, is smaller than Highland Park. In 1960, its population was just under 21,000, of which only 4,671 were black. Within our five-year period, **John Burton** was the black mayor of Ypsilanti. Since black people made up less than a quarter of the population, he could not have won without solid white support.

Lincoln Heights, Ohio, is about 12 miles north of Cincinnati. In 1960, its population was just under 8,000, of whom all but 85 were black. The little city needs only one public school because there are two Catholic schools there. People rely on Cincinnati hospitals, TV stations, and newspapers.

In 1967, **Penn W. Zeigler** got 1,070 votes out of a total of 1,700, and became the black mayor of the city. He was a real estate broker and president of the savings and loan association he operated. He was also on the executive committee of the Ohio-Kentucky-Indiana Regional Authority, which seeks out new industry. This last position may explain why twelve large manufacturing companies have plants in Lincoln Heights. The mayor is very active in civic activities and civil rights organizations.

Woodmere Village is a Cleveland suburb with about 1,500 people, of whom about a third are black. Since 1965, when **Samuel V. Perry,** a Republican, was elected to a two-year term, it has had a black mayor. Perry was reelected in 1967 to a four-year term. In each election, he got the bulk of the black vote, and the large white majority was split for and against him about half and half.

Samuel Perry graduated from Adelbert College in Cleveland and studied law at the Cleveland Marshall School. He is a lawyer, engaged in private practice. He has special knowledge of labor problems and long experience in arbitrating the most complex labor cases. He has also been a hearing examiner for the Ohio Civil Rights Commission.

We go now from a village to a medium-sized city, Xenia, in central Ohio, south of Dayton. Xenia's city government is built on what is called the city commission–mayor–city manager plan. This means that the voters elect the city commissioners, who in turn elect one of their number mayor, and hire a city manager to run the city government as they direct.

The 1960 census credited Xenia with just over 20,000 population, but it was estimated that by 1969 some 29,000 people were living in the city. Only about 8 percent were black.

As early as 1952, a college professor, **James Thurman Henry, Sr.,** head of the Department of Earth Sciences at Central State University, ran for a place in Xenia's city commission, and became its first black member. He was reelected in 1957, 1961, 1965, and 1969. Between 1957 and 1968, his fellow commissioners twice elected him vice president and once president of the commission. In 1969, they elected him mayor. Actually, he held two offices at once, becoming mayor and continuing to be a commissioner.

It is plain that Henry enjoyed strong white support. In a community 92 percent white, Henry could never have been elected to the commission five times in a row without steady white support. His record within the commission makes it just as plain that the white commissioners had great confidence in him, too.

New Jersey had black mayors in 1970, in communities of assorted sizes from the tiny borough of Lawnside to the state's biggest city, Newark. Newark comes later, with the big cities. The others come here.

Lawnside is unusual in New Jersey, a nearly all-black community. **Hilliard T. Moore, Sr.,** has been the mayor since 1961. He grew up in New Jersey, graduated from Fayetteville State College in North Carolina, and studied further at Trenton State College, Glassboro State College, and New York University.

Chesilhurst is another small community, located in the western part of the state. Most of its residents are black, and most of them work in Philadelphia. A small plastics factory is the only local industry. In 1969, **George J. Phillips** was elected mayor of Chesilhurst. The first time he ran, in 1967, he had been defeated, but he won in 1969. He is a Republican, and his victory was especially pleasing to him because in 1969 Chesilhurst had only fifteen registered Republicans.

Princeton Township is larger than Lawnside or Chesilhurst. Late in 1970, Princeton Township elected its first black mayor, **James A. Floyd,** employee relations manager for a company in Trenton, a sizable city not far away. Floyd had been serving since 1968 on the Township Committee, the town's governing body. Race played little part in his election as mayor, because more than 90 percent of Princeton's 13,454 residents were white.

Montclair is larger still, with about 43,000 people, of whom a little over 10,000 are black. A fairly large part of the people who live in Montclair work in New York City. The city government has the commission-mayor plan. Five commissioners are elected by a city-wide vote. They elect one of their own number to be mayor.

Matthew G. Carter was elected a commissioner in 1964 and again in 1968. In 1968, the commissioners elected him mayor.

Carter, born in Danville, Virginia, studied to be a minister, but instead of becoming pastor of a church, he turned to Christian service in other areas. He was executive director of the YMCA in Petersburg and Richmond in Virginia and in Columbus, Ohio, then supervised YMCA work in a three-state area in the Southwest. In Montclair, he is in charge of community relations for Hofmann La Roche, a large chemical company. Both in being elected commissioner and in being elected mayor, Carter clearly had white support.

William S. Hart, Jr., mayor of East Orange, was born in Ohio, graduated from Delaware State College in Dover, and earned a Master's degree at Seton Hall University. He became a teacher and guidance counselor in the New Jersey school system. Politics interested him. He succeeded in winning election to the city council in East Orange and served from 1960 to 1962. In 1963, Governor Hughes appointed him director of the New Jersey State Youth Division. He was the first of his race in this position, and he held it for five years. In 1970, East Orange elected him mayor.

In Glasgow, Kentucky, **Luska J. Twyman** has been principal of the Ralph J. Bunche Grade and High School for some twenty years. He holds degrees from Kentucky State College and Indiana University. In 1961, Twyman ran for one of the twelve seats in the city council and won. He was reelected every two years thereafter. In 1968, when the mayor then in office resigned, the city council elected Twyman to take his place, as the city's first black mayor.

Both as the long-time principal of a well-run school and as a citizen active in civic affairs, Twyman had won the respect and liking of Glasgow's people. Although 93 percent of them were white, they were glad to give him their support at election time regardless of race.

The town of Kinloch in Missouri, like Lawnside in New Jersey, is practically all Negro. It is a short distance north of St. Louis, and had about 6,500 people in 1960. **Robert P. Metcalf** was elected mayor in 1969. Before that, he had been police court judge, health inspector, and deputy election commissioner.

In the South, a number of all-black or nearly all-black towns have elected black mayors. Nine out of about a dozen are mentioned briefly here. Few towns or cities with considerable numbers of whites have elected black mayors. There are a couple of interesting exceptions, however, which you will hear about a little later.

The oldest all-black town in the nation is Mound Bayou in Mississippi. It was founded shortly after the Civil War, and there is a lot of legend about how the original residents managed to secure the land. About 3,000 people live there now. The mayor of Mound Bayou in 1970 was **Earl Stancil Lucas,** a young man born in Bolivar County in 1938. Lucas graduated from Dillard University in New Orleans and afterwards studied at De Pauw University.

Like most mayors, Mayor Lucas has had to face problems, the biggest of which is the town's lack of money. The median annual income there is less than $900 per person. The small hospital in the town is always terribly overcrowded, but it takes in black patients from several counties around. Mound Bayou is too poor to pay its mayor any salary at all, but this does not much disturb Lucas because he is able to carry on his regular work in an adult literacy program.

Grambling, Louisiana, had 3,144 people in 1960, and all but five were black. This town is the home of Grambling College, which is nationally known, among other reasons, because of its graduates who have become professional football stars. When Grambling was incorporated as a town, an instructor who taught mathematics and tailoring at the college, **B. T. Woodard,** was chosen as Grambling's first mayor. He has served four four-year terms.

Alabama has three small, practically all-black towns with black mayors, and Arkansas has four.

Hobson City, Alabama, was incorporated in 1899, and the mayor in 1970, **J. R. Striplin,** was its thirteenth black mayor in succession.

Triana is a very small town not far from the George Marshall Space Flight Center. Its mayor, elected in 1964 and reelected in 1968, is **Clyde Foster,** a graduate of Alabama A. and M. College, who serves as a mathematician and computer specialist at the space center.

Roosevelt City is a nearly new all-black town near Birmingham, incorporated in 1960. CBS television made this town of 3,146 people nationally known in 1968 when it reported that the town at last had enough money to buy its first fire truck and a police patrol car.

Its mayor, **Fred C. Rogers,** a Democrat elected in 1968, is also a civil rights leader. Working through the Labor and Industry Committee of the Birmingham chapter of the NAACP, he helped eliminate discrimination in the Birmingham mills of the U.S. Steel Corporation. He has been active in all sorts of community affairs both in Birmingham, where his business is, and in Roosevelt City.

Of the four black towns in Arkansas, Dumas-Mitchelville is interesting because it had probably the oldest mayor in the nation in 1970. **Charles Kelly,** a successful farmer, then retired, became the town's first elected mayor in 1966. Kelly was born in 1879, and in 1970 was ninety-one years old.

The other three Arkansas towns are Allport, with **Johnnie E. Gay** as mayor; Menifee, with **Frank Smith** as mayor; and Reed, with **John Moses** as mayor.

We come now to one of the two exceptions mentioned a little earlier, Chapel Hill, North Carolina.

Chapel Hill is not far from Durham. The University of North Carolina is at Chapel Hill, and Duke University is at Durham.

In 1964, **Howard Lee** came to Chapel Hill to study for an M.A. degree in social work. When he got the degree, he started doing social work in Durham but continued to live in Chapel Hill.

In 1967 and 1968, black workers at Duke University claimed that they were being discriminated against and protested. White students sided with the workers, and tensions grew. Officials at Duke decided to hire a black personnel director trained in human relations as well as personnel relations, to straighten out the trouble. They hired Howard Lee.

In 1969, Lee ran for mayor in Chapel Hill, and beat a white newspaperman who had been an alderman there for twelve years. Lee got 4,567 votes against 4,167.

This result was not unexpected. Although Chapel Hill's population of about 12,500 was nine tenths white, the university community there had been a center of racial liberalism for many years. Chapel Hill had had a Negro on its city council as early as the 1940's. Some of its churches had had integrated meetings and integrated church memberships for more than twenty years. The city was one of the first Southern communities to desegregate its schools after the 1954 Supreme Court decision. These facts reflect the attitude of the university community, though not, of course, of everybody in Chapel Hill.

Lee's first comment after the election, made at a press conference, was: "How I perform could have a heavy bearing on the political future of other Negroes. If I do a good job, it will pave the way for others to present themselves for office." He thought of his position as being between two fires: "I could be slaughtered from both sides, by the white racists or by the black militants."

The second of the two exceptions took place in the little town of Fayette, Mississippi, which was about one third white. When **Charles Evers** was elected mayor of Fayette in May, 1969, his victory attracted nation-wide attention.

Charles Evers was the brother of Medgar Evers, field secretary of the NAACP in Mississippi. In 1963, Medgar Evers had been gunned down as he stepped out onto his porch in Jackson, the state capital. He rightly became a national martyr. Charles Evers immediately took his brother's place in the NAACP. He also moved to the little town of Fayette in the western part of the state, north of Natchez.

One of his purposes in coming to Fayette was to register black voters. In 1965, not one was registered to vote in Fayette, where there were about 1,200 blacks and about 600 whites. The Federal voting acts of 1964 and 1965 and Charles Evers changed that. By 1969, the number of registered black voters had gone up from zero to 460.

Howard Lee

Charles Evers

Fayette was not an easy place in which to register new voters. It was in rural Mississippi, and black people were poor and scared. The county in which it is located was listed in 1960 as the county with the lowest per-person income in the whole nation. More people were on relief than were working in Fayette. Over half of the population were living in what the Federal Government classed as poverty. A third of the town's black people had not been taught to read well enough to follow written or printed directions. Two thirds of the young men were rejected by draft boards as unfit for military service.

Evers insisted that his newly registered voters should stick with the regular Democratic Party, which in Mississippi had been kept all white. He also encouraged blacks to run for office in their towns. Within a few years, twenty-five had been elected in a four-county area.

Evers himself was on friendly terms with national Democratic Party leaders. He had been with Senator Robert Kennedy in Los Angeles the night that the Senator was shot. When Evers ran for mayor a year later, both black and white college students who had been supporters of Senator Kennedy came to Mississippi to help. Gifts of money for campaigning came from all over the country.

Evers campaigned to get white votes as well as black, assuring Fayette whites that if he won, there would be no hate, no vengeance, but fairness and greater prosperity for all.

In the election in May, 1969, Evers did win—389 votes to 261. When he took office, the small white police force resigned, and he found the town treasury empty. Even his $75-a-month salary could not be paid, but this did not disturb Evers, as he operated his own supermarket in Fayette. He hoped to solve the town's money problem.

In 1970, a year later, Fayette was on its way. Evers is bringing in new industry, which is providing jobs. He set up a manpower training school, serving four counties. He told a group celebrating the completion of his first year in office: "We see that the white man's trump cards are economics and the vote. Now we are beginning to use the same trump cards." Using those trump cards, Evers had been showing Fayette—and America—that good government and racial fairness benefited both blacks and whites.

BLACK MAYORS OF LARGE CITIES

In 1970, nine cities with combined populations (1960 census) amounting to more than 2,900,000 people had black mayors. The mayor of one, Washington, D.C., is always appointed by the President of the United States. The mayors of the other eight were elected, either directly by the people or by city councils.

Black mayors of cities with populations above 70,000 people are something new in American history. In this century, before 1965 there were none. Then suddenly, in the six years from 1965 to 1970, the number rose from zero to nine. The California city of Richmond elected the first one in 1965. The year 1967 was the year of the bumper crop, with the black mayor of Washington appointed, and the black mayors of Cleveland, Ohio, and Gary, Indiana, elected directly in citywide elections. By 1970, close to three million people, black and white, were living in cities with governments headed by nine black mayors. This never happened in the United States before.

What these black mayors had in 1970 is not what most people think of when they hear the words *black power,* but whatever people want to call it, these nine mayors had and were using black power as they worked to solve the problems of their cities and make them better places to live in.

Let us see who these men are, how they reached office, and how they have met the difficulties all big cities face today.

The city of Richmond has a fine harbor across the Bay from San Francisco. During World War II, its shipyards built ships, and it multiplied its population. In 1950, it had 99,545 people, many of them wartime workers who were still there but not permanent. As they left, the population dropped down sharply. But Richmond has large oil refineries, makes heavy machinery and precision instruments, processes food, and manufactures chemicals. In 1960, the population was 71,854, and it was growing.

George Livingston ran for mayor in 1965, and was elected. This made him Richmond's second black mayor. (George Carroll was chosen by the City Council for one year, starting in

1963.) Livingston has been regularly reelected since 1965. The last time he won a new term, he faced twelve other candidates, ten of them white, in the primary, and he won that with 6,400 votes. In the general election, he won with 8,400 votes. That term will not end until 1971.

The Federal Government regards the District of Columbia and the city of Washington as its property, and manages both. The people of Washington cannot elect their own mayor. The mayor and other city officials work for the Federal Government, and are chosen by it. They get their positions by appointment, not by election.

In 1967, President Johnson appointed **Walter E. Washington** mayor of the city and a commissioner of the District of Columbia. In 1969, President Nixon, having just come into office, appointed Mayor Walter E. Washington to a new term, running into 1973.

Walter Washington, born in Georgia, graduated from college and earned a law degree at Howard University. He also had four years of graduate study in public administration at American University.

From 1941 to 1966, Walter Washington worked for the National Housing Authority, moving up until he became executive director. This agency built and maintained some 9,000 housing units in the District of Columbia, accommodating 50,000 residents.

In 1966, he left Washington, D.C., to become chairman of the New York Housing Authority, which administered 143,000 housing units, with 500,000 residents and 11,000 employees.

While Walter Washington had been working in the capital city, he had been a member of the Model Cities and Metropolitan Advisory Committee and of the Insurance Panel of the National Advisory Commission on Civil Disorders, and he was vice president of the Capital Area's Health and Welfare Council.

As you can see, when Walter Washington became mayor in 1967, he was equipped by education and experience to deal with some of the city's most stubborn problems. In addition, it was high time that the city should have a black mayor.

Cramped within the boundaries of the District of Columbia, the city of Washington has no room in which to grow. It has actually lost population since 1950, although it appears to have held its own since 1960. Washington's metropolitan area,

Walter E. Washington

which includes the suburban cities in Virginia and Maryland, shot up from 2,000,000 in 1960 to a probable 2,875,000 in 1970, but this growth was all in the suburbs.

Within the city itself, the proportion of black people to the city's total has steadily increased. It was roughly three eighths in 1950, and over half (54 percent) in 1960. When the 1970 census figures have been analyzed, they are expected to show that from two thirds to three quarters of all the people in Washington in 1970 were black. Certainly a black mayor is fitting and proper in a city so largely black.

Walter Washington's job as mayor is in some respects more difficult than that of an elected mayor. Because of his position between the Federal Government and the people of Washington, he is less free than most elected mayors to plan and carry out his own programs. Before he can do anything for his people, he has to persuade the Federal officials first.

Another reason why his job is difficult is that when he became mayor in 1967 he inherited a city in very poor shape. All big cities had been having problems, but some of Washington's were especially acute.

Traffic congestion was horrible. A new rapid transit system, intended to relieve congestion, was being built, but was not far enough along to help. Many residential buildings had not been kept up and were decaying. Others were being torn down to make room for more Federal office buildings.

Schools had been desegregated, but educators, teachers, students, and neighborhood groups complained that the schools were not effective in educating either black or white students.

Both schools and public libraries were continually being damaged by vandals, and sometimes uniformed police had to be stationed in high schools because of student shootings, knifings, and other violence. Crime rates kept climbing, with record numbers of unsolved murders. The city had not escaped racial rioting, looting, and burning of buildings.

Meanwhile, taxable property kept diminishing, and costs of running the city kept going up. Poverty and unemployment strained every welfare budget.

Walter E. Washington has been doing his best, and will continue to do so. He is a good man, and well trained.

He has another value. Diplomats from foreign nations come to Washington. The city is also a great tourist attraction, visited by thousands of Americans from all parts of the country and by foreign tourists. A good many of them come to Washington already convinced that all white Americans are racists and that all black Americans are kept from getting anywhere. The presence of a black chief executive in charge of the capital city is both an answer to critics of American society and government and a comforting testimony that black people are making progress toward full equality.

Richard G. Hatcher also became the black mayor of a large city in 1967. He was elected, not appointed. The city was Gary, the second largest city in Indiana, in the northern part on the shore of Lake Michigan.

Gary was originally built by the country's biggest steel company and named for the company's chairman of the board, Judge Elbert H. Gary. Steel is still the city's main industry. In

Richard G. Hatcher

1960, Gary had 178,320 people, and by 1967, the population was up by perhaps another 10,000. Also by then, the population had become almost but not quite three fifths black.

Both Gary and Lake County, in which the city is located, had long had a powerful Democratic machine, and they normally produced large Democratic majorities.

Richard G. Hatcher ran for mayor as a Democrat, beat the mayor still in office and another candidate in the Democratic primary, and won the general election, but the Democratic machine opposed him throughout, bitterly and sometimes viciously. Political experts believed that he could not overcome the machine's opposition, but he did. He won largely with the black vote. Some whites supported him though some never stopped fighting him.

Richard Hatcher went through Indiana University with a small athletic scholarship, a church grant, some help from his twelve brothers and sisters, and a job as a waiter. He then studied law at Valparaiso University, supporting himself by working an eight-hour shift in a hospital. He got his law degree in 1959, when he was twenty-six.

Early in 1960, he was appointed deputy prosecuting attorney in the Lake County Criminal Court, and served there until he ran for the Gary city council in 1963. He won that post, and was also elected council president, the first freshman member in the city's history to head the council.

In the council, he fought without success for an open occupancy law. After several setbacks, he did manage to get the city's public housing units integrated. After a few years, he found he needed more power than the council gave him to put through the reforms he wanted. He ran for mayor.

As part of his primary campaign, he published a 32-page reform program, entitled "Program for Progress." It laid out detailed plans for major attacks on the city's problems in housing, education, recreation, municipal employment, law enforcement, civil rights, city financing, air and water pollution, and poverty.

As you already know, Hatcher was elected mayor. As mayor, he had his problems. Some white groups just didn't like having a black mayor. His program looked expensive. Nobody wanted higher taxes. Disgruntled whites tried to push a section of Gary called Glen Park, with 40,000 people, to secede from the city, and redoubled their efforts when Hatcher proposed to locate an integrated housing project there.

Other problems made the mayor's road hard: a garbage collectors' strike, a school boycott, sniper fire, vandalism, an increase in purse snatching, mugging, and other street crimes, and the old established evils of gambling, dope, and prostitution.

On the credit side, Gary did not have a riot, as so many big cities did. Also, among all the criticisms heaped on Hatcher, nobody ever said that he has not been running an honest government. In the past, a number of Gary officials landed in jail, and others might have if they had been turned in.

Again on the positive side, Hatcher was able to get $30 million in Federal and foundation funds, more than the city ever got before, and he has been using the money for job training, urban renewal, and low-income and middle-income housing, as well as for taking part in the Model Cities program. With United States Steel and Ford Foundation money, he streamlined the city government. After black complaints of police brutality, he began retraining and enlarging the police force. He may never make Gary perfect, but in 1970, it appeared that he was making it a better place to live in.

Carl B. Stokes, Mayor of Cleveland

Cleveland is a much bigger city than Gary, and has many industries, though, like Gary, its principal industry has been steel and steel products. Cleveland's problems in the 1960's were probably worse than Gary's and were certainly on a bigger scale.

In 1950, Cleveland had reached its peak population, 914,808. By 1960, the population of the city had dropped to 876,050, though the population of its metropolitan area had increased 22.6 percent in the same period. These figures indicated a wholesale move to the suburbs. Between 1960 and 1970, the loss of population within the city was even bigger and quicker. Early 1970 census figures gave the city only 739,000, and Cleveland, which had been the eighth largest city in the nation, had dropped to eleventh.

Once before, Cleveland had been in serious trouble—in the late 1890's. In 1901, Cleveland had elected Tom Johnson as a

Carl B. Stokes presides

reform mayor. Before he left office in 1909, he had made Cleveland what many people called the "best-governed city in America," and he had started a new period of prosperity there.

In the 1960's, the spirit of united effort and the prosperity which Tom Johnson had inspired were nearly dead. Clevelanders needed a new leader to unite them in a common effort to make Cleveland once more a good place to live in and a place with a future. The leader whom Cleveland voters chose in 1967 was **Carl B. Stokes,** the city's first black mayor.

Carl and Louis Stokes were brought up by their widowed mother. They were very poor. Mrs. Stokes worked as a maid to support them. For a time they were on relief. Both boys helped out by delivering newspapers and working in neighborhood stores. Finally, Carl dropped out of high school to work in a foundry.

When Carl was eighteen, he went into the Army and was stationed in Germany. When he came back to Cleveland, he returned to high school and graduated, and then paid his way through the University of Minnesota by working weekends as a dining car waiter. He then put himself through the Cleveland Marshall Law School.

In 1962, when Carl Stokes was thirty-six, he was elected to the Ohio Legislature, the first black Democratic member, and held his seat until he resigned in 1967. In the House, he led an unsuccessful campaign to persuade the Legislature to redraw Ohio's Congressional districts. Within a few years, the United States Supreme Court's one-man, one-vote decision forced Ohio to redistrict, just in time for Carl's brother, Louis, to be elected to Congress in 1968.

In 1965, Carl Stokes ran for mayor, in spite of the fact that the local Democratic Party leaders were backing the reelection of the mayor then in office, Ralph Locher. Naturally, they did not support Stokes, but he made a pretty strong campaign on his own. He made the primary election into a real cliffhanger, finally losing by about 2,000 votes.

In 1967, Carl Stokes ran again, this time backed by both of Cleveland's powerful newspapers, and with funds and support from the city's white business community. His Republican opponent was Seth Taft, grandson of William Howard Taft, United States President from 1909 to 1913.

After a hard-fought campaign, Stokes received an estimated 20 percent of the white vote, and nearly all of the black vote, perhaps 96 percent. Seven years after the last census, and with Cleveland's population changing rapidly, it is impossible to say just what part of Cleveland's population was black in 1967, but a guess of 40 percent will not be far off. Twenty percent of the white vote and almost all of the black vote gave Carl Stokes enough, though just barely enough. He won by fewer than 1,700 votes. The grandson of a slave had beaten the grandson of a President. When Stokes took office, he said, "This vindicates my faith in people. . . . This is the American dream."

Many people would not have wanted the job that Carl Stokes was taking on his shoulders. Cleveland's problems were big and numerous. To Carl Stokes, they were challenges, and he tackled them boldly.

There was not enough low-rent housing, and what there was was rundown. Some areas were so dilapidated that urban renewal was needed. The sewage system was out of date and inadequate. The crime rate went up every year. The police force was too small, badly paid, and badly equipped. Blacks accused the police of brutality, and were probably right.

Cleveland had for many years lured immigrants from Europe to work in its steel plants. More than sixty ethnic groups descended from those immigrants kept their separate identities in the city, distrusted one another and the blacks, and refused to cooperate. These groups had not voted for Stokes.

In the black sections of the city, Hough and Glenville, unemployment was up, and family incomes were down. People in these sections lived a hard life. There had been a riot in 1966.

Meanwhile, air and water pollution in the city was bad. People joked that the Cuyahoga River, which winds through the biggest industrial area, was so full of waste that it was a fire hazard. Lake Erie, which borders the north side of the city, was not much cleaner.

Fixing all these things was going to take money. The movement of middle-income groups to the suburbs had greatly lowered the number of taxpayers in the city. The poor, who had taken the places of some of those who had moved out, owned no property to be taxed, and had little income. The amount of tax money that could be collected was not likely to pay for everything that had to be done.

These were some of the chronic problems that Carl Stokes faced.

First, Stokes set up his government. Of ten department heads, five were black, and five were white. Black people criticized him for not appointing enough blacks. White people criticized him for appointing too many blacks.

Second, he laid out a program which he called "Cleveland NOW!" Although he was sure of being mayor for only two years, the program was to take ten years to complete. Its aim was to start the city moving again and improve it. The cost, over the ten-year period, might run to $1.5 billion. The cost for the first eighteen months was to be $177 million. Parts of the $177 million were to be spent to speed up urban renewal, to expand opportunities for jobs and small businesses, to pay for new housing and for the repair of sound older housing, to increase facilities for recreation, and to improve health and welfare assistance.

Stokes demanded that businesses and business leaders should give money to help get things started. Companies and individuals in Cleveland and some outside foundations put up $4.3 million. The Department of Housing and Urban Development in Washington, which had refused to pay out money to the mayor before Stokes, made large grants to Stokes's administration. For long-term improvements, such as cleaning up the polluted waters of the Cuyahoga River, bond issues of more than $100 million were floated.

The program was in motion.

By the time Stokes's two-year term was nearing its end, however, much of the big program was still in its early stages and was not yet showing results. In addition, his administration was marred by racial violence. The tensions that followed the murder of Dr. Martin Luther King in April, 1968, passed by with no serious trouble in Cleveland. In July, however, an organized group of black nationalists and militant snipers had a shoot-out with the police, which killed three police and four militants, wounded fourteen, and touched off looting and arson.

By ordering white police out of the riot-torn area and urging black leaders to keep their people off the streets, Stokes stopped the violence, but lost the support of many of the white police.

On the other hand, Cleveland's white business community appears to have developed even greater confidence in Carl Stokes. In 1969, when Stokes ran for reelection, he hoped to become the chosen mayor of all elements of Cleveland's people. Although he won, his hope of city-wide support did not come true. The same forces which had elected him in 1967 gave him their votes again, more than enough to defeat the Republican, Ralph Perk. He still lacked the trust of many of the white police. He failed again to win support from the ethnic groups descended from European immigrants. His victory, however, gave him at least two more years in which to put Cleveland on its feet.

Early in his second term, Stokes made an appointment which appeared likely to end his difficulties with the white police. Benjamin O. Davis, Jr., the highest-ranking black officer in the Armed Forces, was retiring from the Air Force with the rank of lieutenant general. Although General Davis could have secured a much higher salary from a private corporation, Carl Stokes persuaded him to become Cleveland's Director of Safety.

In April, 1970, Davis took command of Cleveland's 2,200 police and 1,200 firemen. His mission was to finish reorganizing the police force and to establish mutual confidence between the police and the people. The experiment was not successful, and General Davis left for Federal service.

Cleveland was a great city for many years. It was a sick city when Carl Stokes became its first black mayor in 1967. No elected black mayor before him had faced such a great challenge. Can he cure the city's ills? Is he too much handicapped by white bias? Will growing black disaffection overtake him? Will white or black militant extremists embarrass that city? The answers to these questions mean a lot to people who love Cleveland. They mean even more to people who see his success or failure as the key to the success or failure of future black leaders in government.

For the next black mayor, we travel back to California and to the city of Compton, which is not far from Los Angeles. In 1960, Compton had just a shade less than 72,000 people, and it was growing. By 1969, the population had probably climbed to about 78,000. A good many black families had been moving there. Although the city's policy was integration and peaceful change, white families had been moving out. By 1969, it was estimated that almost two thirds of the people were black.

In June, 1969, the city elected its first black mayor, **Douglas F. Dollarhide.** The election was practically unaffected by race. In both the primary and run-off elections, Dollarhide's only opponents were two blacks. In the same election, black voters elected a white treasurer and city councilman, who defeated black candidates. (His picture is back on page 227.)

In contrast, a week before, the mayor of Los Angeles, Sam Yorty, had beaten an excellent black candidate, Thomas Bradley, by playing on white fears of black domination and black militancy, in what newspapers from the *New York Times* on west called a dirty campaign.

Compton has a Federal grant for redevelopment of a run-down neighborhood under the Model Cities Program, a plan to lease housing for the poor, and plans for a new industrial park on the edge of the city. The industrial park should help the city's growth and strengthen its tax base. There is some tension, however, between Compton's people and its police force, which is four fifths white.

Wichita is the largest city in Kansas. It had 254,700 people in 1960, and may have reached 300,000 by 1970. About 12 percent of them were black.

The city commissioners run the government of Wichita. They elect one of their own number mayor. Sometimes they pass the office around in rotation.

In 1967, a black lawyer, **A. Price Woodard,** was elected a city commissioner. In 1970, Woodard's turn to be mayor came around by rotation. Without bothering to mark ballots or count votes, the other commissioners declared him elected with no dissenting vote. So Wichita's one black commissioner became mayor.

Although Wichita has not had any specific segregation laws, it has not had open housing either. Less than 1 percent of Wichita's black people have been able to find places to live outside the ghetto in the northeast section of the city. Not laws but real estate practices have made Wichita's schools as thoroughly segregated as any in the country.

It was not until late in the 1960's that Wichita's people came to realize that they were going to have to do something about their schools so as to meet the requirements of Federal law. The only quick answer which occurred to them was to bus the children, and busing was not popular with blacks, whites, or children of either race. In 1970, they were feeling the strains that go with desegregation.

When A. Price Woodard took office as mayor in 1970, his comment on the school problem was: "I have faith in the white community. We are too prone to complain." Many black people in Wichita did not share his faith.

In Michigan, two rather large cities had black mayors—Flint and Saginaw.

Flint is a satellite of Detroit, primarily involved in the manufacture of automobiles, automobile parts, and accessories. It is best known nationally as the home base of Chevrolet cars and trucks. In 1960, it had 196,900 people.

Saginaw had its first growth as a lumber town. As the trees were cut down, it developed diversified business and industry, only a small part of which is automotive. In 1960, Saginaw had 98,265 people. Between 16,000 and 17,000 were black.

Both Flint and Saginaw have the city council–city manager form of government. Under this plan, although the mayor has some functions and gets considerable honor, he has neither the power nor the responsibilities which come to a mayor elected by the people to take over the city and run it.

In Flint, the black mayor was **Floyd McCree.**

In Saginaw, the black mayor was **Henry G. Marsh.**

Kenneth Gibson, Mayor of Newark

In 1970, the city of Newark, New Jersey, followed Cleveland's example and elected a black mayor. He was **Kenneth Gibson,** Newark's city engineer before he was elected mayor. Although Newark was considerably smaller than Cleveland, it was New Jersey's largest city, and big enough to make it the second largest city with an elected black mayor.

Newark is both a rich city and a very poor one. There is a wide gap between rich and poor there. It is a seaport with a large harbor. Large national corporations are located there. Across the gap between rich and poor, unemployment was running high, about 9 percent, and roughly double that for

Kenneth Gibson

nonwhites. Poverty was widespread, with family incomes under $3,000 for 13 percent of the people. The city and state were spending too little on education, hospitals, and medical care. The death rate of nonwhite babies was not matched by any other major city's. Housing was rundown and inadequate. The fact that Newark had a major riot in 1967 is not surprising.

Most of the time for at least fifty years, the city has suffered from boss rule and corruption in government. From 1950 to 1960, the city's population dropped about 33,000, to 405,200. Early figures from the 1970 census indicate that the city lost another 25,000 in the 1960's.

In 1970, a grand jury which had been looking into the activities of city officials and their alleged connection with organized crime indicted Mayor Hugh Addonizio and a group of others, including some city officials, for extortion (shakedowns of contractors, especially) and other crimes. No trials were held, however, until after the election for mayor. Being under indictment did not discourage Mayor Addonizio enough to keep him from running for reelection.

It was time for the black people of Newark to try to get an honest government. There were more black people in Newark than white, but fewer blacks were registered to vote.

The election brought out three black candidates, including Kenneth Gibson, and three white candidates, including Mayor Addonizio. In the election on May 12, Gibson was ahead with 37,666 votes and Addonizio second with 17,925. Although Gibson had more than twice the number of votes Addonizio received, neither had over 50 percent of the total vote. A runoff election was needed.

Don't think that the lead Gibson ran up in the first election made him a sure winner in the second. In the first election, the three white candidates had split 48,333 votes. The black candidates had only about 40,000 between them. Gibson had some catching up to do.

He got help. Money was raised from all over the country. Groups came in from Chicago, especially from the Southern Christian Leadership Conference. People as different as Dr. Ralph David Abernathy, head of SCLC, the writer LeRoi Jones, and Dustin Hoffman came to Newark and campaigned with Gibson. They built an alliance of blacks, poor people of any color, and civic-minded whites. At least 5 percent of the white vote was won over.

Over 90,000 votes were cast in the late-June runoff election, and Gibson had a solid majority.

It is hard to say whether Addonizio's troubles with the law cost him many votes. Not long after the second election, Addonizio was brought to trial, convicted of extortion, and sentenced to prison.

It hardly matters whether Gibson's victory was a result of white weakness or black strength or both. It was an important victory in New Jersey's largest city. Although Newark was too sick for any instant cure to make it well overnight, it looks as if Newark people can look forward to better days under Kenneth Gibson's government.

17

A Touch of Grassroots Representation

THE GOVERNOR

THE governor is the highest executive officer of a state. He is elected by the voters of the state. Normally, he appoints persons to departments, agencies, commissions, and boards in the state government. Black faces are seen in governors' cabinets and on boards and commissions. Here are some of the men and women who were put in high places during the 1960's by the appointments of governors:

Arthur Murphy, a former deputy U.S. attorney for the district of Maryland, was senior staff executive for Community Relations and the Administration of Justice in Maryland.

Julian Steele, Commissioner of the Department of Community Affairs for the Commonwealth of Massachusetts, was the department's chief executive officer.

Samuel Cornelius was Nebraska's State Director of Technical Assistance, and **Emmett Dennis** was State Director of the Motor Vehicles Department.

Stanley Van Ness, graduate of the Rutgers University law school, was Public Defender of the State of New Jersey. He supervised a staff of attorneys who provide legal services to the accused poor.

Horace Bryant served in the same State House as Commissioner of the Department of Banking and Insurance.

Mrs. Ersa Poston, former director of the New York State Office of Economic Opportunity, was appointed by Governor Nelson A. Rockefeller as president of the New York State Civil Service Commission. The appointment was a demonstration of the Governor's new thrust in recognizing qualified women.

William O. Walker, prominent newspaperman, publisher and editor of the *Cleveland Call and Post,* held the high cabinet post of Director of Industrial Relations in Ohio's state government. He was appointed by Governor James A. Rhodes in 1962 and reappointed in 1967. (His picture is on page 254.)

Frederick C. Williamson was Director of Community Affairs in the Rhode Island state government.

Southern states have moved in the same direction with such appointments, but usually at lower levels. The Governor of Tennessee, however, appointed **H. T. Lockard** as an administrative assistant.

COUNTY, CITY, AND TOWN GOVERNMENT

Forty-nine of the fifty states are divided into smaller governmental units known as counties, and the lone exception—Louisiana—has corresponding units called parishes. The number of counties varies widely from state to state. Delaware has only three counties, whereas Texas has two hundred fifty-four. In the New England states, counties either never developed much governmental power, or later allowed it to decay.

The chief governing body of the county goes under different names in different states: county commissioners, supervisors, board of revenue, fiscal court, or board of chosen freeholders. The normal way of winning a post at this top level of county government is by public election. Normally most of the other major county officers are also elected, not appointed: sheriff, public prosecutor, coroner, treasurer, auditor, recorder of deeds, assessors, clerk of county court, and county surveyor.

The town or city is the unit of local government closest to the majority of citizens. It handles most local needs. The highest elected official in a town or city is the mayor. Serving along with the mayor, there is a group which may be called the city council, or the board of aldermen or the city commission. The function of such a board is partly legislative and partly executive. The group passes city laws, usually called ordinances. Individual members or small committees help to supervise departments of city government. Like the mayor, members of such a group are elected. The procedure by which councilmen or aldermen are elected is usually determined by the specific requirements of the city's charter.

In a fairly large city, a good many municipal officials are appointed by the mayor. These appointees form the mayor's cabinet of advisers. Although many Negroes have been put in office in this way by mayors across the nation, and although they have held positions which are important to the black community, space will not permit a listing of every name. The emphasis has to be on black representation at the top levels of state, county, and city or town government.

Blacks have been elected to city offices in major cities since very early in this century. It happened in Cleveland, Ohio, as early as 1909. They had other municipal victories here and there, prior to 1920. In the New Deal years—1933–1945—increased numbers were successful in running for local offices. It was during the 1940's, however, that numerous blacks won election to city councils, boards of aldermen, and boards of education in cities of the North, East, and West, and some were elected county commissioners.

It is often harder for a Negro to win election to a county or municipal office than it is to get elected to a state legislature or even to Congress. Candidates for a seat in a state legislature, or a seat in Congress, run in a single specific district, frequently one covering only a small area. Candidates for a county office usually have to win in a county-wide election. In many parts of the country, especially in the South, candidates for a place in a city council or on a board of aldermen must win in a city-wide election.

In a city or county where white voters make up more than half of the total number of voters, a candidate usually needs white support in order to win.

These are not easy handicaps to overcome. A candidate must make himself known and acceptable to the whole community, by his professional record, by his education, and by his civic activities—the church, often the YMCA or the Boy Scouts, civil rights organizations, labor organizations, fraternal organizations such as the Elks, and so on.

There may be more glory in being elected to the State Senate or to Congress, but do not make the mistake of thinking that the men and women who choose to serve at the local level are of lesser stature. Often they are as well qualified as mayors, state legislators, or Congressmen. Many are lawyers, physicians, dentists, morticians, bankers, insurance executives, real estate dealers, clergymen, or educators.

It would be interesting to see how every city councilman or alderman overcame his handicaps and won election, but there is not room in this book for so many stories. We can, however, make room for one such story, the story of **C. W. Seay** of Lynchburg, Virginia. It illustrates some features which a good many candidates for city councils experience: (1) He had to run in a city-wide election with ten candidates taking part, of whom only the top four or five could win. (2) He was the first of his race elected to the city council in his city. (3) His position as a respected educator enabled him to win white support in a city 75 percent white.

William O. Walker

C. W. Seay

Here is Mr. Seay's story:

The city of Lynchburg, Virginia, elected its first Negro councilman in 1970, and by no narrow margin. Running city-wide where black voters do not constitute as much as 25 percent of the registered voters, he showed that a qualified candidate could command large support from both races. Esteemed and admired by the white and black communities as the outstanding principal of Dunbar High School for three decades, and in 1970 an assistant professor at Lynchburg College, Seay ran second on a ten-candidate ticket with 6,507 votes. His service on the city's Housing and Redevelopment Commission was also an asset.

With a B.A. degree from Fisk University and an M.A. degree from Columbia University, C. W. Seay had evidenced leadership far beyond the limits of his city. He served as president of two state-wide organizations: the Virginia State Secondary School Principals Association and the Virginia State Teachers Association. A crowning recognition came in his election as president of a national organization, the Association of Colleges and Secondary Schools.

In the majority of the cities and towns in the Northeast and North Central regions and in some states in the West, a candidate for the city council or board of aldermen runs in a single ward, and only the voters in that ward can vote for or against him. In large cities where segregated housing has led to the formation of racially separate neighborhoods, some wards have large white majorities, and other wards have very large black majorities. In a strongly black ward, no matter how many candidates enter the race, it is a foregone conclusion that a black will be elected.

It is very difficult to predict how voters in an area will react to black candidates, or even to increased black participation in politics. It is even hard to pinpoint which factors enter into and affect voter opinion. Local factors often appear to play a major role. Some of these are: the education and income level of typical voter groups, fear of "black domination" when other racial or ethnic groups are in the minority, the threat of job competition between white and black low-income groups, and possible backlash following rioting or violence on the part of either race.

Another important feature is the customary pattern of voting in a particular community. Do Catholics vote only for Catholics? Do whites vote only for whites, and so on? Or have voters formed a habit of looking for the best candidate and supporting him regardless of race or religion? In this book, we have seen the pattern of racial voting many times and, in some instances and some places, the pattern of interracial voting. These patterns make a difference.

IN NORTHEASTERN CITIES AND TOWNS

Connecticut and Massachusetts

Connecticut had black councilmen, commissioners, or aldermen in seven cities: New Haven, with four; Bridgeport, with three; Hartford, with two; Stamford, with two; and Bloomfield, Danbury, and Meriden with one each. New Haven also had two constables, and **Mrs. Ella Scantlebury** as city treasurer. Waterbury had one constable.

In Connecticut and in other New England states, the word *town* has a special meaning in addition to its regular sense. While the New England states were still British colonies, they were cut up into geographical units called *towns*. A town was smaller than a county, but otherwise it could have any size and shape. A town usually had a village or small city near its center, but in the early days most of its area was just farms and woods.

Towns in New England handled most of the local government which was handled by counties in other parts of the country. These towns are still there and still handling local government. Elected officials in a town of this type are called *selectmen*. A selectman's duties are somewhat like those of an alderman, but not exactly.

About 1970, Connecticut had selectmen serving in three towns: one in the New Haven area, one in the Bridgeport area, and one in the Bloomfield area.

In Massachusetts, black city councilmen were serving in two cities, one large and one of medium size: **Thomas Aikens** in Boston and **Paul Mason** in Springfield.

Delaware

In Delaware, the city of Wilmington is the hub of black participation in politics, although Dover, the capital city, is becoming important in that direction. Wilmington had five city councilmen, including **Mrs. Hattie Phelan.**

Maryland

As late as 1967, when the Baltimore area was sending seven assemblymen and two Senators to the State Legislature, only four Negroes, including **Mrs. Victorine Adams,** were serving on the Baltimore City Council.

Annapolis had two blacks on its city council, and Cambridge had one. The all-black town of Glenarden had six.

Maryland is noted for its all-Negro residential beaches. The residents are largely middle-class professionals who work in Washington, D.C., or Baltimore but maintain summer homes along Chesapeake Bay, in incorporated beach areas. **Theodore Brown** was president of Venice Beach, and **Mrs. Bessie H. Johnson** was mayor of Highland Beach. Both beaches had commissioners.

New Jersey

It was something of a breakthrough when Newark elected three blacks to its city council: **Reverend Horace Sharper, Irvine Turner,** and **Calvin West.** Asbury Park, Atlantic City, Camden, East Orange, Englewood, Jersey City, Long Branch, Montclair, Morristown, New Brunswick, New Shrewsbury, Orange, Passaic, Paterson, Plainfield, Princeton, Rahway, Red Bank, Roselle, Somerset, Teaneck, Trenton, and Union each had one. Asbury Park also had a police chief, **Thomas Smith.** The small town of Lawnside had the largest number of black city councilmen, six, and also a tax collector, **Mrs. Mary A. Nelson.** East Orange had five councilmen.

An elected freeholder is the same thing as a county commissioner. **Reverend John Henry Hester** of Atlantic City was an elected freeholder in Atlantic County. **Mrs. Wynona Littman** of

Montclair and **John Watson** of Trenton held similar positions in Essex County and Mercer County, respectively. **Dr. C. Harris,** who lives in Morristown, was a county coroner. Many district school boards had black members.

New York

Except for the mayor and perhaps the president of the city council, New York City's highest municipal official is probably the President of the Borough of Manhattan. In 1970, **Percy Sutton** held that office.

Two members of New York City's city council and two members of the council in Buffalo were black. Mount Vernon and Springfield each had one black member.

In the State of New York, there are about 500 incorporated villages. The elected official in a village having a role similar to that of a city councilman is a *village trustee*. Hempstead, Nyack, Hillburn, and Spring Valley have black village trustees.

At the county level, New York State has officials called *county legislators*. A county legislator is much like a county commissioner in other states, but not quite the same. Monroe County, which includes the city of Rochester, had two county legislators: **Ronald J. Good** and **William D. Smith.** In the Buffalo metropolitan area, two counties governed together, Erie and Niagara, also had two: **Robert Bowles** and **Roger I. Blackwell.**

In the city of White Plains, **William Sudderth** was fire commissioner.

Pennsylvania

At the end of the 1960's, Philadelphia, the state's largest city, had three black members in its city council. Pittsburgh, with less than half as much population, had five. Harrisburg, Homestead, Norristown, and Rankin each had one member.

Rhode Island

In the late 1960's, Providence, the state's capital and also its largest city, had one member in its city council, **Phillip Addison.**

IN NORTH CENTRAL CITIES AND TOWNS

Illinois and Indiana

In the late 1960's, Chicago had ten black members in its city council. This was double the number the city had had in 1958. Men with long tenure on the city council were **Kenneth Campbell,** a major in World War II, and **Ralph Metcalfe,** the famous Olympic Games star who was elected a Congressman in 1970.

Among the smaller places in Illinois, Urbana had two members on its city council, and Champaign and East St. Louis each had one member. The town of Brooklyn, situated right beside East St. Louis, had black local officials along with its mayor. The town of Robbins could point to not only a mayor but four city trustees and a city clerk.

In Indiana, in addition to Mayor Hatcher, the city of Gary had four city councilmen; and in the same area, there were a county coroner and a trustee of Center Township. East Chicago had two city councilmen, and Indianapolis and Fort Wayne each had one.

Kansas

The city of Wichita had one black city commissioner in addition to its mayor. There was also a county commissioner serving in the Kansas City area.

Kentucky

Kentucky, often thought of as a border state of the South, has one of the country's best records in its election of black city councilmen or aldermen. In the late 1960's and 1970, sixteen Kentucky cities and towns elected nineteen. Louisville, Hopkinsville, and Nicholasville each elected two. Burkeville, La-Grange, Munfordville, Horse Cave, Glasgow, Danville, Shelbyville, Paducah, Georgetown, Greenville, Lebanon, Lexington, and Russellville each elected one. In Louisville, **Neville M. Tucker** held the important position of police court judge, and another Negro was head of the Sanitation Department.

Michigan and Wisconsin

Although much of Michigan's black vote is concentrated in the metropolitan area of Detroit, a surprising number of city councilmen have been elected in cities at a distance from Detroit. For example, Detroit had four city councilmen, but Benton Harbor had three. Albion had two; Kalamazoo, Lansing, and Saginaw each had one. More or less in Detroit's orbit, Inkster and Ecorse each had two; Highland Park, Ypsilanti, Mt. Clemens, and Dowagiac each had one.

Michigan voters also elected a large number of black county supervisors. In 1969 or 1970, four were serving in Detroit, four in Flint, four in Saginaw, and two in Grand Rapids. One was located in each of these eight cities: Battle Creek, Ypsilanti, Lansing, Baldwin, Idlewild, Kalamazoo, Muskegon Heights, and Niles.

In Wisconsin, Milwaukee's black vote had elected two members of the city council, **Mrs. Vel Phillips** and **Orville Pitts**. There were also two county supervisors there, **Calvin Moody** and **Clinton Ross**. Racine had one member of the city council, **Lloyd Jackson.**

Minnesota

Six Minnesota cities have elected school board members: Bloomington, Maplewood, Minneapolis, North St. Paul, St. Louis Park, and St. Paul. Bloomington, however, was the only one to elect a black city councilman, and it elected only one, **Ray Pleasant.**

Missouri and Nebraska

The people in two Missouri towns, Kinloch and Howardville, are just about all black, and so, of course, are their municipal officials. Kinloch had a city council of ten, with **Mrs. L. B. Tallie** as tax collector and **Robert Smith** as municipal judge. Howardville had four city councilmen, with **Mrs. Laura Howard** as treasurer and **J. B. Rowe** as police judge. Meanwhile, the big city of St. Louis had seven black city councilmen. Kansas City had two, and also the coroner.

Omaha, the large city of Nebraska, had elected black members on its school board.

Ohio

Ohio began electing black city and county officials years before the New Deal. Cleveland Negroes pioneered. As early as 1909, Republican **Thomas W. Fleming** was elected to the city council in Cleveland, and he served on it until 1929. Two more Republicans, **Dr. J. E. Gregg** and **Dr. Leroy Bundy,** joined Dr. Fleming in the mid-1920's, and **Lawrence O. Payne** was elected in 1929.

In the 1930's, Cleveland elected four more Negroes to its city council. Two, **Septimus Craig** and **Thomas Davis,** were the first Democrats, and **John E. Hubbard** and **Harold G. Gassaway** made two more Republicans. The 1940's brought three more Republicans into the city council: **Augustus Parker, W. O. Walker,** and **Charles V. Carr.** The 1950's saw five new black members added to the city council: **Theodore Williams, John W. Kellog, Norman McGhee, Leo Jackson,** and **Mrs. Jean Murrell Capers,** an attorney and the first black woman to serve on the council.

As Cleveland had outstripped Ohio's other cities and towns in the early years, it continued to outstrip them in the 1960's. In 1970, in the thirty-three-member city council, fourteen members, including **Mrs. Carrie Cain,** were black.

Although Mrs. Capers, mentioned a few lines above, was the first black woman to serve on the city council in Cleveland, she was not the first black woman elected to a city council in the state. That honor went to **Mrs. Esther Archer** in the late 1940's, when she was elected to the city council in Canton.

Cincinnati, until recently a very conservative city, did not have a black councilman until 1931, when **Frank A. B. Hall** was elected. **Jesse Locker** was elected in 1941 and served six terms. **Theodore Berry** was first elected in 1948, reelected a number of times, and named vice mayor in 1957.

In the 1960's and in 1970, a number of Ohio cities and towns elected black members to their city councils. In 1970, Akron, Bellefontaine, Cincinnati, and Toledo each had two councilmen. Alliance, Columbus, Dayton, Mansfield, Newark, Springfield, Yellow Springs, Youngstown, and Winterville each had one. The black town of Lincoln Heights had seven. In addition, **Calvin Conliffe** was elected president of Cincinnati's school board, and **Mrs. Mildred Madison** was serving on the State Board of Education.

At the county level, **James Ford, Sr.,** was a county commissioner in Green County; **Dr. James Scott** was coroner at Portsmouth; and **Theodore Wilburn, Jr.,** was police chief of Scioto County.

Oklahoma

Two Oklahoma cities had black city councilmen. Muskogee had two, and Oklahoma City had one. Tulsa had none, although it had elected one black member to the State Legislature. The people of two Oklahoma towns, Boley and Taft, are practically all black, and so, of course, are the officials, including the mayors. Boley had five councilmen; Taft had two.

IN WESTERN CITIES AND TOWNS

Arizona

In Phoenix, two blacks were elected to the school board; and in Maricopa, one.

California

In 1970, Los Angeles had three black city councilmen: **Thomas Bradley, Gilbert W. Lindsay,** and **Billy G. Mills.** Nearby Compton also had three councilmen, in addition to its mayor. Richmond, on San Francisco Bay, had two councilmen, in addition to its mayor. Berkeley had three councilmen. The largest number in any California city, five, were elected in East Palo Alto, an indication of the growing black vote there. The following cities each had one: Bakersfield, El Centro, Gardena, Milpitas, Modesto, Oakland, Sacramento, San Bernardino, San Diego, Seaside, and Tulare.

Colorado, Hawaii, and Nevada

Two cities in Colorado each had one black city councilman in 1970: Denver with **Elvin Caldwell,** and Colorado Springs with **Floyd W. Pettie.** Honolulu, the capital of Hawaii, also had one, **Charles M. Campbell.** In Nevada, **Aaron Williams** was a member of the city council in North Las Vegas.

New Mexico

Although New Mexico had only a tiny black population, with a correspondingly small vote, two cities each had a black city councilman in 1970: Carlsbad with **Ray P. Hardwick,** and Las Cruces with **Albert N. Johnson.**

Washington

In 1970, Seattle had **Sam Smith** serving on its city council.

IN SOUTHERN CITIES AND TOWNS

In the states of the Old South, the election of black local officials increased at a rapid rate in the last half of the 1960's. When victories in local elections win posts which call for decision-making, they mark real progress for the race.

Alabama

In 1970, Alabama cities and towns had 38 councilmen in office. When you realize, however, that there are 7 practically all-black towns in the state, and that 33 of the 38 councilmen held office in those 7 towns, it will be clear that candidates in racially mixed towns and cities were not finding it easy to get elected. Only 5 had succeeded.

Birmingham, the state's largest city, had one, **Arthur Shores,** an eminent lawyer who had been associated for twenty years with the Alabama Negro's struggle to win the ballot and other civil rights. In addition, Bessemer, Homewood, Jacksonville, and Uniontown each had one.

The distribution of the 33 councilmen in the 7 all-black towns was as follows: Hobson City had 8; Triana, 5; Fairfield, 6; Ridgefield, 3; Roosevelt City, 4; Tuskegee Institute, 4; and Brighton, 3.

At the county level, Green County had **John Hewlett** as sheriff, and **Vassie Knott, Harry C. Means,** and **Levi Morrow, Sr.,** as county commissioners. Lowndes County had **Reverend Thomas Gilmore** as sheriff. Tuskegee Institute had its own sheriff, **L. D. Amerson.**

There were also nineteen justices of the peace in the state, as well as eight constables and marshals, including two in Birmingham.

Arkansas

The people of two Arkansas communities are all black and so are their officials. Dumas-Mitchelville had two councilmen in 1970, and Menifee had one. Racially mixed Arkansas towns each having one black councilman were: Earle, Helena, West Helena, and Wilmot.

Florida

In 1970, Jacksonville, which has a substantial black vote, had four black members in its city council. Two were women, **Mrs. Sallie B. Mathis** and **Mrs. Mary L. Singleton.**

Miami had two city commissioners, one of whom, **Mrs. Athalie Range,** had already served several terms and was elected vice mayor of the city in 1970. The town of Welaka had two councilmen. The following towns and cities each had one councilman: Bartow, Belle Glade, Dania, Daytona Beach, Deerfield Beach, Del Ray Beach, Eustis, Fort Pierce, Gainesville, Inverness, Lakeland, Lawtey, Melbourne, and St. Petersburg. The councilwoman in St. Petersburg was **Mrs. Bette D. Wimbish,** an attorney. Florida has one practically all-black town, Eatonville, which had five councilmen, as well as its mayor.

Earl J. Ward was a county commissioner in Dade County, the county in which Miami is located.

Georgia

The city of Atlanta has a board of aldermen, not a city council. At the end of the 1960's, five of the aldermen were black. In 1969, **Maynard Jackson** scored a notable triumph for his race when he defeated a white opponent who had been an alderman for eighteen years and won the post of vice mayor in a city-wide election. Jackson had graduated from Morehouse College and had earned a law degree with honors at North Carolina College in Durham.

Augusta had four city council members. The towns of Hiram, Greenville, Palmetto, Riceboro, and Sylvania each had one. Two county commissioners were located at Sparta.

Louisiana

Baton Rouge, the state capital, had one black city councilman. The city of Crowley, about a tenth the size of Baton Rouge, had two. The city of Lake Charles and three small towns, Ferriday, Edgard, and Maringouin, each had one. Three all-black towns had decided to have aldermen, not councilmen. Grambling had six; Grand Coteau, four; and East Hodge, four.

Louisiana towns also had nine black constables, seven justices of the peace, eleven police jurors, and four town marshals. Even the smallest towns in the state elect these officers.

Mississippi

In Mississippi toward the end of the 1960's, about the only places where a number of black aldermen or city councilmen could be found were the all-black towns. Mound Bayou had seven aldermen, and Winstonville had five, in addition to their mayors. Jonestown had three, and Bolton and Edwards each had two. Racially mixed towns had none, or at most one. Arcola, Bude, Friars Point, Hollandale, and Shelby each had one. The only racially mixed town which put a number of black aldermen into office was Fayette, about a third white. There, five aldermen were elected along with Mayor Charles Evers.

Also in office in the state were four county supervisors,

seventeen election commissioners, ten justices of the peace, and six constables. **Osborne Bell** was coroner in Holly Springs, where Rust College is located.

With Mississippi's growing voter registration, it is expected that a considerably larger number of blacks will win local office in the 1970's.

North Carolina

A large number of racially mixed cities in which whites are in the majority and in which candidates for the city council must run in city-wide elections have elected one or more black councilmen. Durham, East Spencer, Lumberton, and Winston-Salem each had two. Twenty-four additional cities, covering the whole state from the Atlantic Coast to the Smoky Mountains near the Tennessee line, each had one. In Gastonia, **Thebaud Jefferson** was mayor pro-tem as well as a councilman, and **Felton J. Capel** had the same double role in Southern Pines.

The state has two practically all-black towns: Greenevers, with three councilmen, and Princeville with five.

At the county level, **Asa T. Spaulding** was a county commissioner in Durham County; **Dr. J. S. Colson** had a similar position in Granville County; and **John Faison** was a county commissioner in Northampton County.

South Carolina

There was special significance in the election of **St. Julian Devine** to the city council in Charleston, of **Dr. E. L. McPherson** to the council in Greenville, of **Lawrence A. Dunmore** to the council in Georgetown, of **Franklin R. DeWitt** to the council in Conway, of **Joseph M. Wright** to the council in Beaufort, of **William J. Heath** to the council in Winnsboro, and of **John L. McCoy** to the council in Great Falls. The victories of these men in city-wide elections in seven racially mixed towns and cities, ranging in population from about 4,000 to almost 100,000, marked the emergence of a spirit of interracial cooperation in the politics of the state. In addition, the following smaller towns and cities each elected one black councilman: Frogmore,

Jenkinsville, Lobesco, Loris, Lynchburg, Mayesville, Sellers, Society Hill, and Timmonsville. The all-black town of Atlantic Beach had four councilmen, and Lincolnville, another black town, had three. The towns of Hopkins and Seabrook each had a black magistrate, similar to a justice of the peace.

Tennessee

Of the ten city councilmen in the state, Nashville had four, Memphis had three, and Gallatin, Knoxville, and Murfreesboro each had one. One of Nashville's four was **Z. Alexander Looby,** a nationally known civil rights lawyer.

Texas

By 1970, three large Texas cities, Dallas, San Antonio, and Fort Worth, each had one black councilman; but Houston still had none. Among the state's smaller cities, Bryan, Hearne, Huntsville, Malakoff, Port Arthur, Waco, and Wichita Falls each had one.

Virginia

By 1970, black city councilmen were serving in twenty cities and towns in the state. Portsmouth in the Tidewater area and the smaller towns of Port Royal and Chesapeake each had two. Seventeen other cities and towns, including Norfolk, Richmond, Petersburg, and Lynchburg, each had one.

Index of Officeholders

Index of Officeholders

Page numbers in italic type refer to pictures.

A 1
B 2
C 3
D 4
E 5
F 6
G 7
H 8
I 9
J 0